M000004902

Becky Dennis

Brain Wreck

A Memoir

*A patient's unrelenting journey to save her mind
and restore her spirit*

"It's not what happens to you,
but how you react to it that matters."

- Epictetus

Brain Wreck. Copyright © 2012 by Rebecca Dennis. All rights reserved. No part of this book may be reproduced in any form or by any electronic means, including information retrieval storage and retrieval systems, without permission in writing from the author, except by a reviewer who may quote brief passages in a review.

Printed in the United States of America. For information, see www.bdbrainwreck.com. Published by Majamo Publishing, LLC.

The Library of Congress has catalogued an edition as follows:

Dennis, Rebecca

  Brain Wreck / Rebecca Dennis - 1st ed.

  p. cm.

ISBN 978-0-9884961-0-1

  1. Dennis, Becky - Medical (Diagnosis and neurology). 2. Humor (Relationships).
  3. Self-Help (Motivational & inspirational). 4. Body, Mind & Spirit (Healing).

Cover design by Tanja Lavone.

To my grandmothers, Pauline Tyson and Isabelle Dunlap,
whose silent courage in facing the trials in their lives
taught me perseverance

And in memory of Marian Arnold,
Chad Palmer and James Wakefield

Author's Note

Some names have been changed in this memoir. Some of the events may be out of sequence. Interviews with family members, doctors, friends and colleagues helped me fill in the blanks where my memory lapsed. So if I sound crazy, they made me out to be that way. I'm sure of it.

Brain Wreck

*It's **all** in my head, but I'm **not** crazy*

Contents

Chapter 1: Recharging the Batteries

August 2007

"Stop the car!" I shouted, scaring my hubby into a screeching halt. I threw my door open, my photography instincts on fire.

"What?!?" Gary asked.

"Uh ..." I didn't have time for an explanation.

My fingers fumbled to adjust the zoom lens. *It's just like a nightmare when my legs won't run when I need them the most.*

"Well, what?"

"Hang on ..." I fidgeted with the camera.

The lens snapped in place. *I'm not sure I should be doing this, but what the heck? Gotta get the photo.* Gary looked beyond me into the trees that lined the road. My heart pounded.

"You're not ... "

"Ohhhh, but I am."

"Becky ..." His voice switched gears to a parent cautioning a teen. I bailed from the car.

"Leave the passenger door wide open, and the car in drive!" I uttered his direction.

I moved my feet swiftly through the grass, avoiding sticks and pine cones to prevent sound. My pace slowed as the momma bear picked up my scent. Her head lifted. Her rounded ears perked up. Her eyes locked in a gaze with me. Her two unsuspecting cubs buried their noses in the grass, hunting insects.

My heart beat like a drum-roll. I poised my camera, ready for the shot. *Now is not the time to avert my eyes from her, but I really need to know how far I am from the car in case of a chase.* I stole a quick glance back to gauge the distance between me, the brown bears, and the car. Roughly 50 feet. Although I couldn't see him, I knew the exact expression on Gary's face: pissed off. Biting his nails.

I surveyed my only buffers. Tall trees without any reachable limbs.

Oh well. I want the pictures, dang it. Cautiously, I snapped several shots, pausing to check the mom's reaction. She stood in the ready position, all four paws planted in my direction. Dark eyes stared back at me. Daunting claws. *What in the world am I doing?* Yet in one-foot increments, I moved closer, determined to get photos revealing their coarse fur and wet brown snouts. I inhaled deeply, attempting to slow my pulse, taking in the scent of the pines towering around us. *I swear that mama bear can see my heart pounding through my golf shirt.*

Their thick coats draped like oversized pajamas. *They actually look cuddly.* Being so enthralled by the moment, I forgot that this stocky creature could sprint up to 30 miles per hour or shred something like ... me ... in a matter of seconds.

The mom nosed her cubs, encouraging them to inch along. She maintained eye contact with me. My body tensed. My teeth clenched. One of the cubs playfully pawed at a new toy, invisible to me. *This cub looks just like our cats when they discover a bug. Oblivious to the world around them.*

I thought about Gary, probably wanting to shout at me. Or shoot me. I feared that any attempt at communicating with me might startle the bears. Yet they meandered, seemingly content. Looking for food after the recent Tahoe fires drove them from the mountains to the lake area. I rapid-fired the remainder of the roll. All three bears looked my way. My sanity surfaced. A surge of adrenaline shot me into a sprint back to the car. *Gary always says I'm crazy. Maybe I am!*

I imagined the bears behind me, yet I grinned all the way, pleased with my shots.

The passenger door welcomed me.

Gary didn't.

I plunged into the car.

"I love you!" I greeted Gary, careful to meet his piercing eyes.

Play the love card in exchange for forgiveness. It's gotta work.

I stole one last glance behind me as I slammed the door shut. The bears waddled through the grass, looking for food. They lost interest in me.

Silence.

Oops.

The car moped down the road. *Wonder how long I should wait before speaking again?*

Gary cleared his throat, and like a child who expected punishment, I braced for a lecture. Only extreme situations provoked a speech from Gary. Like missing an easy putt. Leaving the bathroom door half shut in the dark. Showing up less than five minutes early for anything. Washing my pants with his clothes and discovering Kleenex clinging to every dark article of clothing. Or putting myself at risk. Nothing else seemed to rattle him.

"I'll never get your death wish with that damn camera," he managed to say.

Still enraptured by the thrill of shooting the bears, I decided keeping my mouth shut was appropriate. I wasn't sorry.

A deep breath. More silence.

We pulled slowly into a parking spot, Gary evidently considering his next statement. I covered my mouth to hide my grin, staring out the passenger window.

His door opening broke the silence. I wasn't sure if I should follow his lead.

"You already *know* what I have to say," he said, trying to get a read through my sunglasses.

"Yep."

Peck on his cheek. Sheepish grin. Followed by another "I love you."

Forgiven.

I imagined our honeymoon in Whistler, Canada, six years prior. My turn at the wheel resulted in pulling over several times to shoot the stunning landscape. He awoke one time to find me across the highway on foot, gaping at a natural 40-foot waterfall. I remembered him saying, "You disregard all danger when it comes to your photo-taking mania."

Shame overcame me at that moment until I realized that he really meant he loved me and didn't want to lose me to something trivial like a picture. Maybe it also had something to do with crossing the highway on a blind curve. Hmmm...

"Wanna play Edgewood or are you staying in the car?" His voice struggled to convey mercy.

"What do you think?" I asked.

"Are you gonna play golf or take pictures?"

"Do I have to choose between the two?"

"Why do you answer every question with a question?"

"Why _do_ you think I do that?"

"Wifette, you make me crazy sometimes." *Likewise, but I know better than to say anything in this moment.*

Our golf clubs probably cheered at the opportunity to play a world-class course. Edgewood's resort-style club house backed up to Lake Tahoe, lined by the Sierras. While I took in the view, Gary's eyes darted back and forth from the tee boxes to the luscious greens. His eyes calculated the distance. I snickered at how he was already playing the game in his mind. As a 20-plus-year PGA member, he relished the opportunity to play the course that hosted celebrities like Mickey Mantle, John Elway and Michael Jordan.

Gary presented his PGA membership card at the pro shop. Usually, this meant golf on the house. But at this ritzy establishment, it translated into allowing us the opportunity to play without needing a tee time. The green fees easily registered two car payments.

"Still wanna play?" Gary asked.

His eyes pleaded for a favorable response while his front teeth bore down on the right side of his bottom lip. His face resembled a hopeful little boy who just asked his dad if he could keep the newfound puppy.

"Let's savor every shot ...," I answered.

"You're the best. I don't care what everyone else says about you."

"Whatever. Five minutes ago you were mad at me."

"I don't remember that."

"Yeah, right."

They ushered us to the first tee box as a twosome. Being fast players, we felt lucky. An expensive kind of lucky. The long fairways invited Gary to swing his driver. Balls soared. Geese honked overhead.

Squirrels scampered across the greens. The sun lounged between trees. I kept a lookout for more bears. Gary noticed.

Golf tempted both bonding and friction between us. Praising his birdies: good. Missing the near-holes-in-one: bad. Listening to one of his golf tips and executing on it: good. Taking photos instead of being ready for my next shot: bad. Being quiet during his swings: good. Forgetting to put my phone on mute: really bad, especially when ringing mid-swing.

Gary moseyed up to hole number six like a John Wayne impersonator. The par four stretched 442 yards for him and 352 for me.

"Watch this, Beckster. See that farthest trap?"

"Yep."

"Keep your eye on it. My ball is gonna land just shy of it."

"Let's see it."

Gary's head swung in a studious rhythm from ball to fairway to ball. His back side wiggled as if revving up for the drive. He always denies the wiggle. I find it cute. Makes me want to play golf more with him to admire the finer things in life.

The ball exploded into the air, screaming from his power. He held his photo-finish swing, as if posing on tour, then let the club slide through his fingertips. The ball rolled to a stop where he had called it. He tipped his hat at his invisible crowd – his trademark. I smiled at his love for the game.

"So howdja like that, Dollface?"

"You play your best when you show off."

"I know. You always tell me that."

"You should do it more often. Pretend you always have a crowd."

"You playing this hole or laying out?"

"Camera calling ..."

"So your back hurts ..."

Busted. I can never hide anything from him. Knows me too well. Dang four-wheeler accident. I have the desire to play every hole, but just not the back strength. My half-smile acknowledged his statement, compromising my heart. I can't stand to be around whiners, so I choose to sacrifice my true feelings, thinking I'm sparing others the frustrating truth of my ongoing ailments from the accident so many years ago.

To avoid answering him, I grabbed my camera. In the absence of bears, I attempted a more artistic view of pinecones, mountains, bark and geese. They didn't match the bears. I lost interest.

The west side of the course bordered the lake, distracting us briefly from our game. Speed boats zipped at seemingly record speeds. Para-sailers Fred-Flintstoned the sky with their legs. My Ping clubs dared me to take one more swing to get my money's worth. With a massage in my future, I banged out the last few holes. My scorecard revealed smiley faces and frowny faces instead of numbers.

"I'm on vacation!" I shouted, like an excited teenager anticipating the beginning of summer break.

"You've been on vacation for two months now," Gary replied. "That's old. Get a new line."

"Whatever, Hubby. I won't be able to say that soon."

"Yep. In seven days you're a slave to corporate America again," he said, now animated, rubbing it in that my enviable two-month stint between jobs sped by as quickly as the last quarter of a tank of gas. "But, wait. Maybe that should be corporate *Asia*."

"Funny. You suck."

And we giggled, a common outlet for our unorthodox banter.

Heading southbound on U.S. 50, we lowered the windows, breathing in the wooded area, cut grass and fish from the ocean-like lake.

The sun rhythmically flickered like a strobe light through the quickly passing shade of the trees. Gary's hand inched toward me, lacing his fingers through mine as he playfully wrinkled his nose at me.

I swallowed hard, quickly wiping away the salty drip down my cheek. I silently acknowledged how my profession drove a wedge between us, making trips like this necessary. I ached for more from our marriage. I'd forgotten how to allow myself to be intimate. My tears exposed me. I wasn't *really* the callous career crackerjack that my job demanded. I longed for a conversation without mention of business.

Somewhere along the way I'd become aspirational for more. But to prove what? I really wasn't sure.

As I pictured our evening, I fantasized about having the courage to make myself vulnerable enough to crumble into Gary's arms. To express a need to connect on a deeper level, to sustain us throughout travel separations. To tell him I could be strong among corporate stresses, tough decisions and pains that lingered from the past. But I didn't know how to express that I didn't <u>want</u> to have to be so strong. I wanted to tell him that the safest place in the world to me was spooning during the middle of the night, our limbs finding each other and wrapping like ivy.

I debated telling him how his patience was an enviable trait, one that he clearly needed to be married to me. Why was it that being away from home was required to find our groove? I promised myself tonight I'd find the words, and remove my protective cape that I always wore.

Countless conifers danced in the breeze. Sun beamed down between mountains like someone switched a light on and off. Jimmy Buffet strummed his six-string, unfortunately not loud enough to drown out our discordant voices.

"Some people claim that there's a woman to blame," we sang. Gary pointed at me, nearly driving off the road to read my reaction.

"But I know," I countered. "It's all your fault."

The scenery warmed me as I tried to distract myself from the few remaining days between jobs. Although almost giddy about my new senior vice president role at an India-based company, my spirit's recharge level was still depleted.

Guilt plagued me from the previous 11 years of 80-hour work weeks and lost weekends. Tahoe promised us a marriage makeover with its abundant golf courses and lake-side restaurants. With mountains on every side of us, I felt like we were in a bowl, a million miles from Dallas and its flat, traffic-infested streets and bushes trying to be trees.

Back at the hotel, we got in our indecisive mode of: "What do *you* want to do?" "I don't know, what do *you* want to do?" A restaurant by the water finally appealed to us, luring us back out of the room. Candles flickered. Laughs spilled over from nearby tables. The wind chilled the air just enough to give me goose bumps. The smoke from the sizzling fajitas made my stomach growl and the tequila shots broke down years of emotional bricks that prevented us from sharing our thoughts.

"Thanks for saving your last week for us."

Wow! Gary being sentimental? Don't screw this up with a joke, Becky. Just allow it. Let yourself say the things you thought and felt this afternoon. Don't hide.

"I miss you already, Gary. You know the travel is going to be every week for nearly the first year with the new job, right?"

"You've told me ..."

Brief silence. Our eyes diverted briefly to other tables. Groups of businessmen cackled, their eyes staring at inappropriate parts of their waitress.

"... I don't have to like it, but I'm proud of you. You've worked hard for this promotion. Just don't make it so stressful on yourself."

"I know you worry about me, and I appreciate the gesture behind it."

It was partially true. I wanted him to understand me. To "get" the demands of my career. But when travel separated us, he clammed up. He talked as if I were across town without any inconveniences. His dialogue maintained a normalcy of chit-chat before dinner, not of me being hundreds of miles away. I found this annoying. I wanted more. Needed more.

Another pause. Gary focused hard, holding his breath without realizing it. *It's like we're in the same place. He's afraid to show his feelings. Why do we do this?*

"I know you can handle yourself wherever you go, but I feel helpless not being there to protect you. You're one tough lady on the outside, but I know you're scared."

He was dead on. My eyes teared up. The waiter recognized the tender moment, thankfully choosing not to interrupt us. I held my breath, begging the tears to stay in, not wanting to ruin our last evening together. But Gary's extended hand forced the drops.

"You know, I cried my eyes out last night because I'm already homesick."

"I know, Girlfriend. You can't hide anything from me. You're scared, aren't ya?"

"What do you mean?" I tried to sound innocent. My pulse swelled a notch higher.

"Unfamiliar territory. New culture. Taking more vaccinations to prepare for your travels than you've taken in your whole life. Missing your cats instead of me."

"That's not true."

"I don't know about that."

"Well, you're right," I said, trying to be courageous about his mention of fear. Trying to accept this moment as him being a strong, caring husband. Not me feeling fragile. Like a beginner at chess, I didn't know what move to make next.

"About missing the cats more than me?"

"No. You're right about me being scared." *It's out there now.*

"Here's the deal. I'm always right. When will you learn that?"

We both forced smiles. To anyone who didn't know him well, he sounded egocentric. I knew the facade he secretly reveled in. I knew he was at his brink for intimacy. A simple request for "more chips, please" would break our attempts for emotional connection.

With his arm still stretched across the table for my hand, I slid my hand into his. His eyes flashed to nearby tables, hoping they didn't notice. I excused him for caring what they thought.

"File it," he said, a common saying from him.

"How do you do that?"

The atmosphere shifted. We both grasped a hidden commitment to stay in the moment, but it was gone. Even though I yearned for it, I didn't know how to maintain it.

"Just write your worries on a piece of paper. Acknowledge them, then file them. Pull them out when you need them, but there's no need to have the list out at all times."

He's in 'fixing it' mode now. That's what guys do when they're helpless. But I really want to release this. I need to release this, whatever it is.

This filing system worked for him on the course. He "filed" his worries before tournaments to maintain focus on playing each hole. Didn't work for me. The wind blew the papers right back out of my filing cabinet, exposing them. I leaned back, folded my arms and took a sip of the tequila, souring my tongue and torching my windpipe.

"This SVP role *sounds* glamorous, but it doesn't *feel* like it. I want to feel adventurous, excited about the new people and places. But inside I'm a coward."

"You're the strongest person I've ever known."

"You're always my biggest fan, Hubby."

"And don't you forget it."

"Thanks." I cried some more.

Make this go away. This is our last night. I wanted it to be special. Not me being a wimp. I looked away, scared of making myself this vulnerable even though it's what I had hoped for. Trapped tears doubled my vision. I blinked hard, forcing them down my cheeks. I strained a smile back in his direction.

"Just know that wherever you are, all I want is for you to be happy," he said.

"I know."

"You can give presentations to large crowds. Debate with a CEO. Coach sales teams on the right strategy. But when I see you, you're Becky. My wife. Stubborn as hell. Funnier than any comedian. Annoying with your constant singing. But the best mom and wife I could ever hope for."

I accidentally snorted at the stubborn and annoying comments. They were too true.

"Thanks for being so good to me. For being so patient ..."

I hope he knows I'm sincere. That this isn't just lip service.

"... For putting up with my demanding career. This time will be different ..."

I sound like a drug addict asking for yet another chance. My thumb rubbed back and forth across his thumb. I felt every groove of his thumbprint.

"... I'll maintain a balance from the beginning of this new job."

I mean it. I really mean it. For Gary, for our son Cole. Heck, for me!

"You just do what you need to do. I'll be fine."

My heart swelled in pride of knowing that somehow we always managed to filter through the dry spells where we struggled to let each other in.

Even after arriving back at the hotel, I set my sarcasm aside long enough to maintain this awkward comfort. We snuggled tightly like when we first met. I felt loved. Secure. I wanted to figure out how to be like this all the time. I knew he did, too, but couldn't say it out loud.

After he fell into a deep slumber, I lay there thinking about where I was in life, contemplating the changes I was about to undergo. *A promotion. My closest office in New York. A foreign-based company. Lots of travel. More pressure for quarterly results. Yet the balancing act of being a wife, mom, sister, daughter and friend. And oh yeah, what about me?* I wanted to let go of turbulent events before I met Gary and embrace the future that promised so much. My thoughts swarmed like an active beehive, going all directions.

In times of uncertainty like this I used to be able to pray about it. I'm still a Christian, but I'm so turned off by hypocrites who "play church." Church used to be my only constant, but I gave up religion after the incident in college. I was so devoted to the church before. Why did God allow that to happen to me? My career was going to be a youth director with the church. Now, I don't feel like I really trust God. And I feel guilty for that. Unresolved. Like He owes me an explanation. But who am I to ask for that?

I feel like I'm trying to choose between who I was, who I was forced to be, who I want to be and who I currently am.

I listened to the thunder rattle the skies and the rain play rhythms on the car tops, feeling alive. *I feel like there's something bigger and better out there. I still believe in God, but I'm hurt. I'm afraid to trust Him again.*

I silently acknowledged the opportunity to have this little hiatus between jobs. Getting to play golf every day, whether it was sunny, foggy or rainy. Getting to see friends in several parts of the country. Reuniting with my husband. Investing in therapy to work a bit on myself.

I have to figure out this work/life balance thing.

With each rumble of Gary's snoring, I made decisions: *Two cell phones. One for personal: always on. One for work: on when necessary, but not 24x7. Two laptops: one for work, and one for personal to remove the temptation of constantly checking work email.* I was thankful my new employer didn't have a Dallas office. When I wasn't traveling, I'd be at home. Literally.

When we woke the next morning, life seemed a bit easier.

Chapter 2: Removing "Y'all" from My Vocabulary

September 2007

After three weeks with the company, I journeyed to Mumbai, India, for my first visit. Being so busy leading up to it, I really had no preconceived ideas about what to expect. So when I awoke the first morning at 7 a.m., after getting in during the wee hours, I eagerly pulled the curtains to get the sunlit version of what I had missed the previous night.

I had dreaded the trip. Sad to leave my cat, Henry, whose failing kidneys meant that his death was imminent. Henry felt like a friend to me. He understood me. And he soothed me through so many hurdles for the last 15 years. To keep him comfortable, Gary and I administered "go-go juice," large bags of subcutaneous fluids weekly to hydrate him. Then every other day. Then daily. I feared he'd die while I was away.

My window offered two contrasting views. Immaculately manicured Grand Hyatt gardens with magnolia-looking trees and hibiscus-like flowers framing lush waterfalls. This visual made a pleasant treat, especially if I squinted just right with my head pressed against the window. Rows of shacks covered in blue tarps held down by worn-out tires or pieces of brick was the more visible view. Most residents wore torn clothes without shoes. Colorful laundry hung across makeshift lines.

On my way to the office, I sat in the back of my assigned driver's car with Deborah, my boss. During our hour-long commute, random paved roads stuck out as a luxury. Mumbai's 16 million residents seemed to live by the same alarm clock, all leaving home at the same time. Puzzled by the absence of road signs, I wondered how my driver navigated to different locations without a GPS. Congested traffic fought for the front row at traffic lights, leaving me amazed at how commuters avoided wrecks among the chaos. In Mumbai, lanes weren't even suggestions of boundaries. Traffic erupted like an ant pile just kicked by a kid. Lights meant jockeying for position. Putting an arm out the window meant losing a limb to a passing rickshaw, motorcycle or car.

"I want you to be brutally honest today, Beck," Deborah said.

Our driver slowed for a family of four on a "donor cycle" that cut him off. The woman sat sideways with her legs dangling in her brightly colored skirt with two kids tucked between her and her husband. Their faces conveyed no concern about traffic accidents.

"I will. I've got a couple of slides on suggested improvements," I replied.

Thin dogs trotted through the congestion, digging through piles of trash and debris, ignoring the large buses that came within inches of them.

"But you can't afford to be too nice about it. Tell them how the consultants think our tools lack sophistication," Deborah said, oblivious to the world outside our car since this wasn't her first trip.

A random guy swept the road as cars whizzed by him, unaware of the buzz of traffic surrounding him. *Why sweep a dirt road? This is possibly the most futile job in the world.*

"Yes. I plan to cover our lack of sophistication."

"Are you going to mention the comment on how our proposals lack a professional polish?"

"Yeah, but I don't want to offend anyone. I'm not here all the time, so I want to balance my feedback."

"Beck, our role here is to teach. They can't be trained if you don't give them the honest-to-God truth."

My stomach churned. Aaron Neville's "Tell It Like It Is" rang in my ears. Our styles were quite different. I enjoyed being subtle, which wasn't in her vocabulary.

I bit at my lip, trying to decide how to phrase my feedback. In a perfect stream of traffic, a rickshaw driver, impatient from waiting to turn left through the thick stream of traffic, held up his hand and began inching across, stopping the flow of cars and buses altogether. *This is bizarre. Do they have an unspoken rule that when someone is tired of waiting, he just gestures to the rest of the free-flowing world to hang on while this guy crosses the road, creating temporary gridlock? Yet in a pattern of traffic where everyone was going the same way, they honked incessantly, trying to speed each other up. An American behind the wheel here would be a catastrophe.*

The office itself resembled corporate America. Security badges demanded access to sensitive areas. Conference rooms hosted continuous meetings. Cafeterias featured marginal meals, but with things I couldn't pronounce or identify. Security guards yawned, lacking excitement. Malnourished dogs scooted between buildings, scrounging for food. Wait. That was definitely different.

All employees dressed professionally, but only the most senior dressed in stuffy business suits.

I greeted colleagues, including Shilpa, Arijit, Ramesh, Pradeep and Neeraj. Picturing my gringo face, I never imagined these names easily flowing off the tip of my tongue. For the first time, I felt global. Just a year before, my passport, full of Mexican stamps, revealed my typical border-hopping Texan status.

After a few hours, I adjusted to the harsh realization that Indians don't hesitate to question a speaker. I felt thankful for witnessing this before presenting. Americans might consider peppering someone with endless questions or presenting an opposing view in front of an audience as impolite or condescending. In India, attendees commonly interrupted and questioned the content of a presentation. Some gladly offered examples that rebutted or delegitimized your material. My skin thickened with experience, so this distinctive cultural trait didn't intimidate me. I actually welcomed the challenge, knowing that my background allowed me to answer their questions with ease.

February 6, 2008
10:00 a.m.

On my return trip to India just a few months later, Neeraj, our CEO, kicked off the morning meeting with a pitch concerning the state of our business. Neeraj stood a few inches taller than most Indians. Business suits looked natural on him, a sign of a comfortable executive. When making a point, he stared ahead, so serious you might think he was delivering the news to a patient that they had cancer. He shook his long thin fingers to emphasize his rationale for decisions. Despite being personable, colleagues relinquished their viewpoint to let Neeraj speak if his lips even slightly parted.

In detail, Neeraj covered the company's sales performance, the health of our accounts, where we were in the last quarter for financials, and what our key initiatives would be for the next fiscal year. Then, in typical fashion, the Q&A portion lingered on beyond what the agenda suggested for our time allotment.

Following the CEO on the agenda wasn't that common for me, but I felt confident since the content of my presentation was so second nature. I glanced around at the familiar faces in the audience. I rehearsed names in my head, fearful of mispronouncing them. Anxiety crept up as I dreaded my bigger fear: not being able to understand them when they asked questions. *Take a deep breath. They like you. They even gave you your own Indian nickname.* I laughed to myself, remembering the name they gave me at the bar the previous night. Bhavani, meaning creative and imaginative.

I glanced around the room at all of my dark-haired, brown-eyed colleagues, listening to their thick accents, some in English, some in Hindi, all with British undertones. I momentarily debated about how to begin my presentation, and then announced with utmost sincerity in my voice, "For those of y'all who don't know me, allow me to introduce myself..."

Refraining from saying the word "y'all" proved the most difficult part of working for an India-based company. Never in my life had I realized how often this word rolled off my tongue until I tried eliminating it. Some thought it was cute. Others found it as annoying as hearing their favorite rock song botched as elevator music. After a few months, I finally quit trying to eliminate it from my vocabulary. A diehard Texan, I honestly couldn't figure out a word to replace it. The collective "you" sounded like I was picking on someone in particular. And "youse guys," I mean come on. No self-respecting Texan would ever attempt that.

I paused after getting everyone's attention and continued, "I'm Becky Dennis, senior vice president ..."

Another pause for effect.

" ... Most people are surprised when I tell them, but I'm not actually from India. I'm from Texas."

Laughter erupted. My eyes dashed a look at Neeraj. *Thank God he's laughing.* Deborah rolled her eyes. *Oops.* Our COO looked confused. *Oh well.* And my colleague, Peter, appeared to beg me with his eyes to just do a stand-up act and leave the boring crap for the next speaker. Peter, one of my peers, had quickly befriended me when I was able to match his wittiness on our first trip. We'd been buddies ever since our first sarcastic exchange.

For the next hour, I discussed the company's perceived position in the market and what was required for us to improve our brand. Typical of a less than $1 billion company, our company's problems involved a weak brand, limited service offering and lack of geographic diversity. I provided my observations of our sales process, not nearly as blunt as Deborah. I relayed the direct feedback from consultants who wanted to see us succeed, but didn't find our services sophisticated enough to keep up the pace that our competition demanded. We lacked a compelling message. Considering the multi-million dollar scope of our deals, we acted like vacuum cleaner salespeople instead of business and technology leaders.

Essentially, I called the baby ugly. The negatives I shared outweighed the positives. I feared how they perceived the message. Being in a minority position, this seemed awkward at best, especially when one of the items of feedback was that our teams weren't diverse enough. I noticed that only five of the company's top 75 people were women and I was one of them. Less than 20 of us originated outside India.

"What she means is that we need more than just Indian faces sitting at the table across from potential clients," Deborah piped in. "We need white folks present as well."

I took a deep breath as Deborah's words rang in my ears. She could be painfully honest and not just get away with it, but be comfortable enough saying it in the first place. I noted this ability she had and wondered when I'd be able to do this without flinching.

Chapter 3: Hang a Vacancy Sign on Me

February 6, 2008
1:00 p.m.

As soon as my session wrapped, Neeraj requested a senior marketing leadership meeting with Deborah, Anurag and me. *Cool! Show your stuff, Beck.* Anurag, passionate for marketing and driven to teach himself anything - including violin, led our India-based marketing team. He converted amateur team members into creative star performers. His soft tones, fitting for his thin frame, challenged my hearing until he defended an idea he felt strongly about. It seemed so out of character that it seemed cute, not defensive. We quickly bonded, swapping marketing strategies and personal stories.

Entering a conference room just bigger than a theater ticket booth, my heart rhythm pulsated quicker. *I'm such a corporate geek.*

My high energy buzzed from prior meetings. *The four of us are gonna be an idea machine!* We stretched back in our comfy seats, expressing a transparent trust in each other, abandoning formality. Colorful cloud-like prints sparkled on each wall, providing an extra source of energy. I restrained a smile, looking to Deborah and Anurag to see if I was the only one adrenalized by this assembly.

Neeraj's visionary leadership challenged me in new ways. He sought out his employees' opinions to balance out his thoughts, not accepting his own as gospel just because he was CEO. He didn't ask drive-by questions.

About 30 minutes into the meeting, Neeraj rang his assistant, requesting lunch for us. It was now about 1:30 p.m. We debated strategies for building a brand in an intensely competitive industry. Stimulating debates like this excited me, stretching my everyday thinking. I didn't know where it was leading, but I was glad to be part of the discussion.

Our food arrived. Neeraj interrupted, frowning at the selections. Plates of white rice, *paan*, green cream-filled sandwiches and taupe-colored goulash stared back at us.

"Please take this away. Let's get some pizza, please. This does not look appetizing to me," Neeraj told his assistant.

Even with the food's unappetizing appearance, my belly begged for food. *Wonder if they'd mind if I just grabbed the rice.*

I considered the snacks in my briefcase. *Tuna salad, anyone? Peanut butter and crackers?* I imagined Deborah's embarrassment if I left and then returned with one of the goodies in my briefcase. *Think I'll wait for the pizza.*

I forgot my hunger, eager to make the most of this exciting journey. *I've traveled all this way again. Let's get to business.*

"If our company were a car, what would it be?" Neeraj asked us, like a demanding graduate school professor.

You've got a fast car. And I've got a plan to get us outta here. I smirked at how Tracy Chapman's lyrics belted out at the mention of the word "car." I thought about Gary. I refrained from singing to my colleagues.

He probably wants us to think of his company as a Corvette. Fast. Sexy. In high demand.

Deborah's eyes shot me a cue. She was trying to position me as the next chief marketing officer (CMO), so she took every opportunity to get me more comfortable with stating my opinion to the senior executives. My parents raised me to always defer to the senior person in the room. The business world rearranged and challenged my upbringing. Speaking before my boss seemed inappropriate, but previous bosses attempted the same.

"Beck? Why don't you take the first stab? We're here to help change the company's business model. Please share your thoughts," Deborah prompted me.

"A Ford Escort," I stated. *Crap. What if this offends Neeraj?*

"Good. Why?"

"Well, because it's reliable in getting you from Point A to Point B. It's not expensive. It's not sexy. And although a lot of people drive it, they don't brag about it because it seems more of a utility than an investment."

"Very good, Becky. Thank you for your honesty."

Pleased, I leaned back, eager to learn from Deborah and Anurag's responses.

At 2:11 p.m., a wave of fatigue struck me. I squinted my eyes, trying to focus on the conversation, but words didn't register. My peers seemed invigorated, but I fought to be coherent, as if I'd overindulged at an all-inclusive Mexican resort.

Wait, wait. We were talking about the company being a car...

My concentration wavered. *Hang on. This is intriguing.*

I bowed my head in disappointment and confusion. I pictured Tom of *Tom and Jerry* jiggling his head after a bad landing. *Just shake this off and I'll be fine. I want to contribute to the new marketing strategy. I can do this!*

The exhaustion overtook me. Our conversation faded into the distance, leaving me incapable of listening despite my interest. Their words became muddled, incoherent to my ears. *I'm locked in a dream, present in the image of the scene but not in control.*

" ... then our strategy would be ..." Neeraj's voice faded in temporarily, then out again.

Throbbing pressured my head like it might ignite. *Try, Becky, try! It's not every day you get to be in India with your CEO. Make the most of it. You like this. Just try.*

"And what do you think about our competition?" Neeraj asked.

Is that ... directed at ... me?

" ... "

Nothing registered. I stared at my colleagues. A "for rent" sign popped up in my brain. *I'm done. Finished. Tonight I don't let anyone talk me into a late dinner, staying up late or drinking. Tonight I get a good night's rest so I'm not so fatigued.*

The dialogue continued.

I didn't.

Twenty minutes later, the pizza arrived.

"Want a slice?" Neeraj asked.

A slice. A slice. Slice. Huh? I couldn't get the words to come out of my mouth. My eyes hoped he'd see the vacancy that occupied me. Perhaps only a few seconds passed while my colleagues wondered if my lack of responsiveness reflected indecisiveness on my part.

What is wrong with me? Why aren't the words coming out?

Finally, I uttered, "Yes ... thank ... you."

No one reacted to my sluggishness. *How can they not see this? Am I going crazy?*

Neeraj chatted excitedly about the car metaphor as an organizational theme. Deborah and Anurag sat on the edges of their seats, equally jazzed about the analogy's promise for retooling and turbocharging our company as a muscle sports car. Neeraj directed another question at me. I stared in his direction, puzzled. I felt detached. White noise. Stunned. His lips moved, obviously talking, but my head prevented comprehension. *What's happening to me?* My lips tingled.

Dizziness and disorientation overwhelmed me. Thoughts formed, but words floated away, like clouds on a windy day. I attempted to respond to Neeraj's last question, but his question vanished, as if never asked.

I nodded toward Deborah and Anurag, imploring them to answer for me, confident we were all on the same page. Without hesitation, Deborah picked up where I left off, probably just thinking that I preferred her to respond so it was from the CMO, not a senior vice president.

Should I tell them what's going on? Am I crazy or is something really wrong? I dismissed my experience, thinking through the last few days. *I must not have allowed myself to acclimate. I should have come a day early to adjust. The time zone change has caught up with me.* I didn't dare show weakness about global travel. *Don't alarm them. Probably just tired.*

Our meeting abruptly ended at 2:55 p.m. when Neeraj needed to meet a client. *What a relief. I'll get some fresh air.*

I stood to follow Deborah and Anurag out. They disappeared. I remained standing, wondering how to move my legs to form steps.

What in the world? Come on, Beck. Just walk.

They continued down the hallway without me.

Just take steps.

I felt foolish, wondering how just two hours prior I pulled off a well articulated presentation to a room full of executives while pacing the stage.

Becky, just walk.

That annoying Santa Claus song popped in my head: *Put one foot in front of the other. And soon you'll be walking out that doooooor.*

Clumsily, my right foot thudded hard against the floor. When I attempted the left foot, I tried stopping it before it hit the ground with a hard thump. No luck.

Okay, Beck. Two steps. You're walking. I don't know what's wrong with you, but you've got several more meetings, so get your act together.

A white noise distracted me. I felt like a firearm had just exploded in my ear drums. A loud silence transfixed me.

Am I controlling the steps under me? Seems foreign. I can't tell if I'm really moving.

Finally, I managed to reach the office's front door. I focused on each step like a small child just learning to take her first steps.

Once outside, I took a deep breath. My anxiety level skyrocketed with each passing second. An endless stream of rickshaws scurried by, honking at each other, jockeying for a gap to pass. Workers on foot traipsed by, determination in their eyes. My eyes blinked hard, as if they might not open again. My balance wavered as if I'd consumed too many drinks. The outdoors offered no energy boost, so I turned around and coached myself to the next meeting.

Right foot. Now left foot. Right. Left ...

Why won't the door open? I pulled harder. I pushed. The door wouldn't budge.

I pictured the Far Side cartoon of the kid pushing with all his might on the door for the School for the Gifted. The door's sign read "Pull."

"You need to swipe your badge, miss," the security guard yelled from her station.

Oh. Duh. In.

Right foot. Now left foot. I am utterly exhausted. Just get done with the next pitch and then go back to the hotel to lie down.

Seven minutes later, I finally reached the boardroom where I was scheduled to present to the travel business unit. The journey lasted no more than 30 yards, but it felt like the length of a football field.

Ten of my colleagues sat around the table, chatting in separate conversations. None of them noticed my entry except Peter. *Good. This buys me time to get rid of this bizarre series of events. I don't know what in the world is wrong with me. I've never been so tired in my life.*

My right arm and hand began tingling. They felt like I'd slept on my side, slowing the blood circulation. My fear escalated.

I looked to Peter, wanting to explain everything. Words required too much effort. I opted for short sentences.

I forced words, "Not feeling so ..."

Spot. Shot. Hot.

"... hot. Buy me a ... minute?"

"You look like shit."

And feel like it, too.

"What? No comeback?"

My eyes blinked back at him in exchange for a simple "no." Peter's eyes narrowed with concern. He looked puzzled, probably wondering why I provided no explanation.

With that, I stood, mustering up the right foot/left foot routine.

I staggered to a stall, closed the door and sat on the toilet, fully dressed. I leaned my shoulder and head against the cool wall to hold me up. Fear held my eyes open.

What is wrong with me? This is bizarre. I'm going to sound like a complete idiot if I tell them all the strange things happening to me. I must have overdone it last night and just didn't realize it. But I felt great this morning. Doesn't make sense. How would I explain this freakish string of events?

I resolved to give my last pitch before leaving the office, and returned to the conference room. *If I leave this early, I'll have to explain this peculiar episode. This is embarrassing. How do I explain this? Must be extreme fatigue.*

At 3:22 p.m., I implored my brain to find the energy to make my presentation and field questions. However, the room brightened as if the roof suddenly disappeared and allowed direct sunlight. I squinted from the blinding, invisible rays. The windowless room, about the size of a one-car garage, blurred and seemed to stretch to twice its size. My colleagues looked like they were far away. I felt dwarfed, a visitor in *Alice in Wonderland.*

Feeling like I might collapse at any moment, I looked to Peter.

"You need to go. Use my driver to take you back to the hotel."

Thank God. I didn't argue, despite my wanting to finish the day's agenda.

In my late 20s, heart palpitations landed me in a cardiologist's office. For years, I required a daily medication to regulate my heart rhythm. But not anymore. Occasional episodes meant I kept medications on hand. I convinced myself that it was related.

If I can just get back to the hotel, I'll take my heart medication and rest until this passes. Yet my heart didn't race.

I fumbled my belongings. Each attempt to pick up my purse failed. My right hand no longer gripped anything. Peter and Anurag helped me into the car. They carried my purse and briefcase, along with a bottle of water. They studied my face while easing me into the backseat. Now my thoughts began to blur as much as my words.

Thanks, Peter and Anurag. I appreciate your help. I'll be fine once ...

I felt foolish. *Why am I struggling?*

Nothingness.

My colleagues seem ... f... f... fine. Same long days. Same ... same ... late. Same time zone cha ... llenges.

The car sped away. I leaned my head back, resting it on the back of the seat.

The tingling shock crawled up my right arm. My left arm and hand felt numb.

Something is gravely....

My breathing labored. I couldn't swallow. My head felt like it didn't have enough room. The pressure grew. I felt like someone had shaken me like a snow globe, the contents of my head now drifting, trying to settle back into place.

Pass out. What will happen? Gary ... Middle of the night for him. Not sure ... I'll make it.

My energy drained like the final sands in an hourglass.

Oh...my...gosh. I'm going...to die.

I looked around me, but saw only colors and light.

Am I going to...? Health history ... How do I dial a phone? ... Can't lift arms.

Knowing Deborah was unavailable, I decided to call Peter. I pleaded with my left arm to allow my hand to explore my purse for my phone. *Found! Need to dial.* I stared at the phone, wondering how to reach Peter. Another wave of fatigue forced my eyes shut. *Concentrate ... breathe.*

My body wavered helplessly with the car's subtle curves. I forced my eyes open, feeling an urgency to report my medical state. *Maybe I should just tell the driver. Uh ... he doesn't speak English. No use.*

I tried again to figure out the phone. *It's a phone, Becky. You use this many times. Just dial the phone. ... But how?* My thumb played with the scroll. *Too many options!* A list of recent calls appeared. *Peter!*

As if lifting a 50-pound weight, I struggled to raise the phone to my ear. Then I dropped it. I tried again, but my hands could not maintain a grasp. After several attempts, I took a different tact, propping it up on my briefcase and turning on the speaker phone. Hearing the dial tone soothed me, like hearing distant thunder after a long dry spell.

Peter answered on the second ring. As I tried to speak, Peter quickly abandoned his typical playfulness, realizing the severity of the situation. For a moment, I wanted to laugh because I'd never heard his serious tone before. But I didn't. I didn't know how to and even if I did, I didn't have the energy.

"Peter ..."

"What? What is it? Are you okay?"

"Some ... thing ... is ... ver ... y ... wrong."

"Take your time and tell me all you can."

His voice echoed in my head. He sounded alarmed, yet strove for soothing patience.

"My ... right ... side ... is ... numb," I muttered, my tongue feeling heavy as if it was tired from lifting weights.   With the same sluggish pace, I told him my heart history and a couple of the major symptoms. I felt time slipping away, certain death was imminent. I tried conserving what little energy I had in case I needed to answer questions.

Forget getting help and symptoms. Gotta call Gary. Tell him I love him. Last time. Tell family.

"Becky, give the phone to the driver. I'm going to find someone who can communicate with him to tell him what's going on," Peter said.

I wasn't sure I could extend my arm to the front seat. I took a deep breath, closing my eyes and imagining how I might get the phone all the way up there. A whole two feet away.

Chapter 4: The Last Goodbye

February 6, 2008
3:40 p.m.

The car bumped along, swinging a red Ganesh from the rearview mirror like a hypnotist's watch. I concentrated on reaching around to the front seat while maintaining a grip on the phone. The driver's eyes glanced back at me in the mirror. He looked confused, probably wondering why *he* was getting a call on *my* phone. He snatched the phone.

Gary to hold me.

Choppy English rattled in my ears. Then nothingness. A muffled voice faded back. Then louder. I struggled to open my eyes, locked in a stupor. My thoughts dissolved before I could make them out. I moved in and out of consciousness.

The driver spoke rapid-fire Hindi like a machine gun to the person on the other end. He slammed on the brakes. My body lunged forward. My head bumped the back of his seat. I lay there sideways, unable to upright myself.

Gonna die alone.

Distant sounds. I couldn't concentrate.

Cole ... wanted to see him grow ...

Nothingness. Labored breathing. My tongue locked. My vision blurred like I'd been swimming in chlorine with my eyes open for hours.

Angela ... Mom ... Dad ...

The driver inched the car forward, finding a small hole in traffic to turn around. His eyes darted in the rearview mirror, filled with concern that frightened me even more. He set the phone back on my briefcase.

"Back to office," he said in his best English.

With enormous effort, I bent my head down to listen to the phone, trying to comprehend Peter's response.

Kitties ... never return home. Won't understand.

"The driver is coming back to pick up Mita. She'll escort you to the hospital to translate with the medical staff."

I hummed the word "okay" back, unable to talk anymore.

3:52 p.m.
I have to call Gar. Love him ... one last time.
My shoulders drooped. White noise.
God ... need ... energy to do this.

It was nearly 4:15 a.m. back at home. Gary answered with the typical startled voice one expected to hear at that hour. "What? What's wrong?" he blurted.

I summoned all the energy I had to hold the phone up. I took a breath, unable to get much air. I wasn't sure where to start. I tried to relay what was happening using as few words as possible. I felt a sense of urgency to be ahead of the next wave of nothingness.

"You're gonna be all right," Gary tried to reassure me, but I detected his panic.

Just a year before I'd had an ovarian cancer scare. Gary's steady voice of optimism got me through until post-op news. A grapefruit-sized hardened cyst. Even though they took the ovary, Gary's positive outlook downplayed the news. I relied on his stance.

I replayed Gary's tone when he said the word "all right." It didn't match the previous year's spirit.

"I've ... never been so ... tired ..."

"Save your strength, Girlfriend. They'll take good care of you in the hospital."

A reverent silence took over the line. Half a globe away, words escaped me, even if it was our last time to ever talk.

Words don't do juice ... shove ... entice ...

I breathed one more shallow breath to get as much air as I could suck in. Each word I uttered drained me.

"I love ... you, Gary. ... Tell family ... ... I love them."

"Don't you talk like that. You're gonna be fine."

His voice cracked.

I wanted to cry, but couldn't figure out how.

Home. Want family.

I tried picturing Cole older, wondering if I'd ever see him that way. *Good kid. Love him. Shrinky dinks. Christmas. What career? Kids?*

Nothingness. I wasn't sure if I was still on the line with Gary.

"Becky?"

Gary. Retirement. ... Mountains. ... Passwords.

"Can't hold ... phone ... or talk."

Wait ... try to hang on.

"I wish I were there with you right now. I'm so sorry you're going through this alone. Have someone call me from the hospital."

Not gonna make it. Dying. Have to hang up.

"Love ... you. Bye."

Nothingness.

My head rested against the window. My eyes closed on their own. I swayed like a sideways rocking chair as the car zipped back to the office.

At 4:06 p.m., the car reached the office. Mita stood outside, waiting like a pit crew mechanic. The look in her eyes confirmed the worst: I was in bad shape.

Always smiling, with peaceful eyes and a petite frame, Mita was the Webster's definition of gentle kindness and optimism. But in this instant, her face was strained with deep concern. She reached for my left hand, frigid and flopped on the seat as if it belonged to a lifeless doll. She patted it, but then quickly pulled back, perhaps worried that I might be contagious.

I tried to tell her some of the same info I'd shared with Peter, but I couldn't.

Henry ... back before ... dies.

Her face twisted a little when she said, "Becky, you should just rest now. You don't need to strain yourself. We will take care of you."

My head dropped back. Nothingness.

Our car pulled into the hospital's circular drive, where a medical team awaited outside. The hospital, taking up what looked like an entire city block, appeared modern, almost new.

Good hands.

"Can you walk?" one of the medical team members asked. His small frame seemed a perfect fit for a jockey.

I shook my head, heavy like a water-filled balloon.

I hunched over. Not enough energy to get in the wheelchair by myself.

Walk! Dignity.

I stumbled into the chair, embracing their assistance.

They wheeled me at Olympic speed. The ride disoriented me further, so I squeezed my eyes shut, trying to avoid nausea. Their voices ricocheted down the wide hall, echoing Hindi between the walls. My head drooped. My energy compressed rapidly, as if my head was an inflatable toy, a child squashing the remaining air out of it.

The medical team stopped at the check-in desk. Mita pointed at me, expressing herself in articulate short phrases. My lights went out. Back to nothingness.

"Becky?"

I couldn't respond.

Voices surrounded me. I heard, but couldn't listen. Some were English. Some were in Hindi. Didn't seem to matter.

Some time later, I opened my eyes. I wasn't sure if minutes or hours had passed. I appeared to be the only patient in the ER. I squinted, making out the mini-rooms cordoned off with the barest of necessities: a bed, curtain and electrical outlets.

A cardiologist appeared as they rolled in equipment unfamiliar to me. I wanted to ask questions, but remained muted. My eyes opened and closed like a baby fighting a nap. The technician pulled off my jacket and unbuttoned my blouse, lifting me like a doll to loosen the remainder of my clothing. A large red and yellow clasp pulled back her long, dark hair. She took off my shoes and socks without emotion, as if she wanted to switch outfits on her Barbie.

Uncontrollable waves of chills overwhelmed me. My body shivered like it was caught in a plane's turbulence. Unable to talk, I requested a blanket by crossing my arms and pulling up imaginary covers while making eye contact.

Her face saddened as she said, "You're scared. You're not cold. You are trembling."

I know damn well ... I'm cold! Scared, but ... body freezing! ... Blanket!

I silently implored her to give me a blanket as I continued to shake. I struggled, knowing my thoughts but not being able to articulate them. I wished someone would play 20 questions with me to see if they got my correct meaning.

The tech rolled in what looked like a primitive shocking device. I watched nervously as she plugged the machine in and then wrapped large clamps around my wrists as if they were going to shock the symptoms out of me.

What the hell?

I felt drugged. In slow motion. My eyes lifted in the form of a question, although no words came out. She recognized the expression, then patted my leg as she announced, "EKG."

Having had minor heart problems, I was more familiar with EKGs than I wanted to be at an early age. EKGs had white round stickers with color-coded wires. This machine didn't resemble anything I'd ever seen.

I napped. Or passed out. I'm not sure which.

When I came to, the technician was standing over me.

"How are you feeling?" she asked.

"Ummm ..."

I'm talking! Kinda ...

Like E.T. learning his first words, I forced sounds out of my mouth that resembled words. *Gonna have to answer questions. Have to shell ... sell ... tell them what's going on.*

I looked down. Blankets covered me. *I told them I was cold! They must have believed me.*

"Can you talk?"

"I ... think ... so."

"Let me get the doctor. Are you okay for me to leave?"

"I'm ..."

Fizzy ... Ritzy ... Diddly?

"... ditzy."

She smiled.

"Dizzy? We might be able to give you something for that. Anything else?"

"Right ... hearted."

"Light headed?"

Yeah. I nodded.

Other technicians surrounded me as they heard us talk. They analyzed me as if I'd just landed from another planet.

"Schtill cold," I said.

Medical staff treated my statements like a Starbucks barista line-up: I uttered words and they yelled them to a colleague, demanding a reaction. More blankets appeared.

The cardiologist returned with a shuffle appropriate for a nursing home resident. He and the technician spoke in elevated tones, as if building up to a heated argument. This was typical of the Indian culture. I felt comforted from their exchange, despite my inability to understand their words, knowing they felt strongly about my care and treatment.

I studied the doctor's flawless skin. Any woman would love to have skin like his. Despite my knowing I was in a critical state, his demeanor remained calm. A stark contrast.

Please. Answers. ... What is wrong with me? His squared glasses added a few years to his age, although I couldn't imagine him a day older than I. His trim figure suggested, "I work out every morning and practice what I preach." When he spoke, his mustache appeared to crawl like a caterpillar. A big, dark, hairy caterpillar. In my confused state, all I saw was a lump on his lip. Not his pleasant eyes. Not his salt and pepper hair. Just a mustache. Similar to Gary's. Potentially a source of comfort.

"Ms. Dennis, you've had quite an afternoon," Dr. Calm said.

You could call it that. Now tell me what the hell is wrong with me.

"Do you feel like you have heart palpitations now?" he asked.

"No."

But I never did.

"I see."

His lips twitched. The caterpillar crawled. I forced my eyes to look at his, but the caterpillar stole my attention.

"And are you having any difficulty catching your breath?"

I breathed in, checking, uncertain what I really felt.

"Not now."

But earlier. Couldn't swallow. Not a deep breath. Words failed me. Too much effort.

"I understand you have experienced numbness and tingling?"

"Yesth."

He squeezed my left arm like a grip flexor for a hand exercise. *Ouch!* His tranquil voice reminded me of a preacher soothing a distraught parishioner.

"Can you feel this?"

"Yesth."

But please stop. You can't imagine how strange my hands feel in this moment. You should have squeezed them instead of my arm. I'm getting some feeling back on the left.

"I see."

Just seeing some improvements reduced my fear, like someone flipping on a light in a dark, unfamiliar hallway. *I'm not sure what just happened, but thank God I can at least feel my left side now. No more questions. Just give me some answers, please.* My right arm still felt the sensation of ants crawling on it, making me want to rub or scratch.

"Ms. Dennis, we are going to run a series of tests on you. I see you are cold. Try not to be scared. We'll get more blankets for you ..."

Tests. Blankets. More blankets? I've got enough to make an igloo warm.

" ... I need to know if you are allergic to any medications. We may not administer anything, but if we do decide a medication is appropriate, we'll need to know that."

Blank stare. *He's looking at me like he's waiting on an answer. What all did he just say?*

He walked away.

Wait. What all did you say? Did you diagnose me?

For what seemed an hour, I lay there alone. Could have been 10 minutes. Don't know. I practiced opening and closing my left hand, hoping I wouldn't lose the ability to operate it again. I stared at my other hand, willing it to be like its sister hand. Nothing. My hand snubbed me, unwilling to participate.

My lips and right side of my face tingled with intensity. *This must be visible to everyone else.* I practiced speaking, feeling a bit awkward as I glanced at the white curtain, my only audience. My tempo slowed for words with more than one syllable, requiring me to concentrate as if delivering a speech on a difficult topic. I hoped it wasn't a temporary respite.

"I can move my left hand," I said to myself.

My cell phone rested on a table next to me, just out of reach. *Gary. Needs to know I'm alive.*

A few colleagues ducked their heads into my curtained area. Their presence filled the immeasurable void of being half a globe from my family. I looked to them as lifetime friends, though I'd only been at the company six months. *I'm so grateful to be among a gentle-natured group of colleagues. Empathetic to my situation. Non-judgmental.*

A couple of them approached my bedside. *Thank God I have blankets covering me. I don't even know if I'm wearing anything.*

"Becky, you've really worried us," Mita said.

Her words continued, but I couldn't concentrate on them.

"You ... "

"And then ..."

"But we'll ... "

She squeezed my arm, as if realizing I couldn't pay attention.

"You're going to be all right," she finally said, patting me and then turning to my other two colleagues, who stood there, mute. *It's okay,* I wanted to say. *You don't have to say anything. Your being here speaks volumes.*

I nodded, saving my energy for the doctor's next appearance. The medical team hustled in and out, frowning at the obstruction my colleagues created. The head nurse raised her hand to her stomach, turning up her palm to usher them out. *Oh no. Alone again.*

The nurse looked back at me and then yanked the curtain while following them out, creating a boundary between us as flimsy as an open screen door. She began speaking in a soft tone. I assumed it was about my medical condition.

What is this? The opposite of HIPPA[1]? Do they think I can't hear them just because they pulled a cocoon ... cuticle ... curtain to separate us?

Just above a whisper, I overheard Dr. Calm and the nurse speaking to my colleagues – only some of which I could understand.

Talk to <u>me</u>! Tell <u>me</u> what's happening. Am I going to die?

Another wave of fatigue melted me into a buttery nap.

---

[1] The U.S. law strictly safeguarding the privacy of a patient's medical information and condition.

6:29 p.m.

Deborah arrived, looking like a frazzled parent unable to find her child. She took my hand in hers. I expected a waterfall of tears to consume my face. But nothing. *What is wrong with me? Why can't I express myself?* The blankets, evidently removed to run other tests on me, slumped over a medical table. I felt exposed.

"Everyone's worried sick about you. My goodness. What happened to you? You did so well this morning in your presentation. I can't imagine what happened since our last meeting. Peter said you looked horrible when you left."

She gets more words out in one breath than anyone I know. It's an art.

I nodded, mumbling something unintelligible.

"It's ok. Just know you have lots of Becky fans rooting for you. You're going to be all right."

She studied my physical state for a moment. Being quite modest, I considered the propriety of a professional colleague seeing me partially clothed. However, I didn't have enough energy to care.

After several minutes, I cleared my throat, wanting to break the silence.

"Did ... the doc ... tor ... tell you," I started.

"No. Not really anything yet. He told us they ran multiple EKGs. But he hasn't said anything that explains what happened."

Deborah was restless, as if struggling between letting me rest and wanting to figure things out on her own. She had the energy of a young child. Always on.

"So Beck, what happened? If you can't talk, that's okay."

I took a breath, able to inhale more air than before.

"I dunno. I ... started feeling really ... "

Teed. Factoid. Faggot.

" ... fatigued... during our meeting with Neeraj ... and things just ..."

39

Dedicated. Placated. Skewed. Rrrred Escalatored.

" ... escalated."

Words flowed easier now, but they still required concentration. I felt like there was a time lapse between my thoughts and words.

"Is there something wrong with your heart? Peter said you mentioned having a history of heart problems. I was not aware of that."

She looked at all the wiring still hooked up to me.

"Heart ..."

Pollution? Pollination? Population?

"... palp ... itations. SVT. ... Doesn't seem related."

Did I get the terminology right? Everything seems muddled.

"So what do you think this is?"

She pressed on with curiosity, holding my hand like I was a small child. She comforted me as I tried to wrestle with the strange series of events of the previous five hours.

"Don't know."

Lying there, I wanted to relay all the strange symptoms that plagued me, but maintaining my thoughts was as difficult as getting toothpaste back in its tube. I couldn't fathom what was wrong. Although my ability to talk slowly returned, I lay there dazed, my head pulsating as if it was swimming in an ocean of blood. Before I could elaborate, my mind shifted, unaware of what we discussed.

"Are you okay?"

She seemed to want to fill in the gaps of my vague explanation. *Tell her how difficult it is to complete a thought. Too much ... energy. Tired. .... Rest. Could take ... turn for the worse.*

"I don't know."

I felt emotionally constipated. A lump in my throat signaled a hard-earned cry that failed to result in tears. Unable to release.

At 6:47 p.m., Dr. Calm stepped into the curtained area and asked to speak with Deborah. The medical team acted as if the curtain might be a soundproof wall.

"Your colleague has a borderline EKG, which means it's not completely normal, but not exactly indicative of a serious problem, either. I think your colleague is both fatigued and stressed. Have her come back to the hospital in four days for us to recheck her. She'll need clearance before she can fly again."

Even though most of my feelings were subdued - too difficult to identify, too muted to feel - a surge of anger gripped me. I imagined my body bursting into the Incredible Hulk.

What?! Stress and fatigue? Has this guy completely lost his mind? How in the world can stress force someone to lose the ability to walk and talk? To go numb? For vision to blur? To not be able to swallow? For my lips and face to tingle? For my body temperature to change? How in the world are they just going to send me back to the hotel? What if I die by myself during the night?

But with no energy, I just lay there, dumbfounded by his unwillingness to check for other possibilities. As much as I didn't want to stay in the hospital, I was frightened to go back to my hotel room in case the swarm of symptoms returned all at once.

Deborah came back in the room with a major shift in her demeanor.

"He's releasing you tonight to go back to the hotel."

She scrolled through her Blackberry as she talked to me, apparently convinced this was no longer life or death.

"They want you back in four days to repeat all the tests."

This is crazy. Why am I being released when something is very wrong?

And with that, the hospital staff wheeled me out to the parking lot an hour later and whisked me into a van with Deborah and Gopi. A Mumbai local, gentle yet authoritative, Gopi was the glue of the office, the man who made everything happen. His sense of urgency, combined with his precision, made him the perfect office quarterback or cricket captain. With 22,000 employees in our company, Gopi filtered requests important enough for the top executives. I felt lucky when he responded to me. Our relationship was an important one to nurture.

On our way to the Hyatt, I sat there, dazed, unable to comment on the conversation. I listened as Deborah arranged for the Hyatt to move her into my room so she could monitor me for the next few days. *Generous of her, but I need my privacy. If I need sleep, I don't want to feel obligated to talk. And if I'm hot, I want to be able to just bare all.*

Moving to her room is not setting ... stepping ... seminary ... simple ... suddenary ... needary.

"Not necessary," I said, exhausted from trying so many combinations.

Everyone in the van froze, as if I were E.F. Hutton.

"... I'll manage."

Deborah held her phone away for a moment, considering what I'd just said before proceeding with the hotel staff.

"Beck, I'm concerned about you. I really think someone needs to be with you the next few days until we know if this is fatigue or your heart or something else much worse."

"I'm not comfortable with that."

"What if I'm next door or across the hall?"

"Fine."

I returned to my vegetative state, thinking I'd call my own doctor. Once I could carry on a conversation again.

Chapter 5: Trusting My Heart Again

February 2000

My former company's leadership selected Pinehurst as the venue for our company's annual customer event. Word spread internally like a sex scandal. Quickly, I found out that Pinehurst apparently was one of the country's primo golf courses. Drool streamed from my coworkers' faces when they talked about the famous Course Number Two. Their practice swings intensified as the date crept closer.

I could have cared less about the venue. As the event organizer, my only interest was in making sure the event came off without a major snag. Beating a little white ball with a stick and then trying to find it among several acres never excited me. If I ran across golf on TV, I felt sorry for the poor schmucks whose lives were so dull they'd spend time watching someone they didn't know hit a little pockmarked ball and then walk to it.

My colleagues pleaded for me to take lessons, trying to convince me I'd be hooked as soon as I hit one long drive. After hearing this at least a dozen times, I surrendered without admitting to anyone that I was signing up for lessons. If I failed miserably, no one would know. Reluctantly I bought a series of private lessons and cheap clubs.

Within a couple of days, Gary, a local PGA golf pro, contacted me about scheduling our first lesson. *Poor guy. One swing and he'll probably tell me to take up knitting.*

Our phone banter felt like I'd known Gary for years. Embarrassed, I answered his simple questions: no, I had never been on a course and, no, I definitely didn't watch golf in my spare time.

As expected, finding time for the first lesson proved difficult. My schedule resembled one of a teenager who juggles club sports, guitar lessons, and oh yeah, school. We gave each other grief over our busy lives and finally settled on April Fool's Day for that first lesson. That date turned out to be appropriate.

"Address the ball," Gary instructed.

I leaned over, "Hello, cute little ball."

Quick glance up. *He loves it, but he'll never admit it.*

He shook his head, trying to conceal a smile.

"Am I getting the hold right?" I asked.

"It's a *grip*, dang ya."

"Oh, yeah. Grip."

Silent snicker.

"We gonna go out on the golf field today or just stick to the range?"

Deep breath. He started to correct me again, but resisted. *Who knew that malapropisms could be so fun?*

On our last lesson, he escorted me around the course. Several holes sat unoccupied due to the backlog from slow-playing foursomes. The sun hosted a bright, warm day in the late spring. Squirrels darted in front of the cart like misdirected pinballs. The occasional "fore!" in the distance didn't faze Gary, yet forced me to duck each time. I breathed in the fresh cut grass scent, a reminder of the full day of yard work planned for when I returned home.

An hour passed. Gary nervously peeled off the outside of a busted golf ball, revealing a heap of rubber band wound tightly around a hard ball at the core. Another 30 minutes passed. *I don't want to leave, but I don't want to take advantage of his time.*

"Maybe this should be my last hole," I said.

"What're you doing when you leave?"

He studied his cuticles for a moment, as if he were hungry for something to bite.

"Ugh. Yard work. Hate it, but it's gotta get done."

"Oh."

He discovered one nail that required a fast nibble.

"Well, if you're working in the yard, you're gonna need a beer."

"That's a given," I confessed. "Where there's yard work, there's beer."

He paused, contemplating his next statement.

"You know the Dallas Stars are playing," he stated.

He nibbled again. *Maybe he's nervous that the Stars might have tough competition today.*

"Yep. I guess I'll come in from the yard to check the score every now and then," I answered, confused where this was going.

"What I'm trying to say is that maybe we should go watch the Stars and have a beer together."

He glanced nervously to see if his proposal finally registered with me.

"Oh!" *Am I a ditz or did he just beat around many bushes?*

Pause. *Screw yard work.*

"Sounds great."

TGI Friday's welcomed us in among the green and black jerseys that dominated the bar. Ignoring the hockey game, Gary and I shouted stories over the raucous fans for the next hour. Finally, a large cheer erupted. The Stars won, securing another playoff game.

"I know you said you have yard work to do, but I'd like to talk a little longer if you're okay with it," Gary said.

"Sure. Let's head to my place."

Oops. Hope that doesn't sound too forward. Mom would definitely disapprove.

"If that's okay," he said.

"I just invited you, didn't I?"

"I'll follow you."

"We can sit by the pool."

The unruly automatic pool cleaner sprayed us several times, filling the air with chlorine and sending us ducking for cover. The course of our conversation flowed like a dance we'd practiced for years. Hours passed like seconds. I stacked stories in line to be told next. My heart dared to climb out of its sling.

I feel like I've always known him. Why is it that I'm choosing some of my most embarrassing moments to share on a first date? I guess this is a date. Is this a date?

I accidentally sang out loud, "They keep things loose they keep it alive. Everybody's dancin' in the moonlight."

"Isn't it 'they keep it tight'?"

"Whatever. I never know the words. I just like to sing."

"I see that."

What am I doing? Singing?? Am I crazy? That's as dumb as when I drove through the McDonald's drive-through backward in high school. Or when I tried killing a roach with mace, but choked everyone in the dorm room.

With each beer, my stomach grumbled and expanded like a balloon ready to pop.

"Dinner?" he asked.

"Like I need anything else."

"So that's a yes?"

"Sure. Why not?"

At dinner my mind unlocked bizarre memories. Gary made me feel comfortable enough to share them.

"Have you played many sports?" he asked.

"Hmmm ... T-ball when I was in first grade."

"Is that the last time you played?"

"An organized sport? Just about."

"Were you good at it?"

"I had a ponytail, and it was an act of God to get the ponytail through the hole in the back of my cap. When the announcer asked everyone to bow their head for the prayer before the game, I either kept my hat on and held my head in shame or I had to go find my mom to help get the ponytail back through. That's all I remember."

"I see."

He took a swig of his beer.

"So do you watch much sports?" he asked.

Gotta be a trick question.

"Let me put it this way ..." I started.

Gary closed one eye and squinted as he stared down the neck of his beer bottle, checking for a last sip.

"When I was a kid, we always watched football after church."

"Okay."

"And when the team huddled to plan their play, I thought they were praying."

Gary laughed.

"And then I'd get so confused when they'd tackle each other after praying."

He laughed harder.

"I'd think, 'they got nothing out of that prayer. They need to try again.' And then they would."

"So I think you just answered my question."

Our laughs shook us. Customers at neighboring tables stared. We didn't care. My face hurt from laughing so hard.

I got lost in thought while Gary checked scores on the TV above me. *Opens doors for me. Check. Light hearted. Check. Adorable eyes. Check. Attractive. Great sense of humor. Good listener. Respectful. Complimentary. Confident. Intelligent. Check, check, check.*

I tried not to get ahead of myself, but with each check mark, my heart forgave the males before him who hardened my heart.

"Shall we?" Gary asked after paying the tab. *Paid in cash. Another good sign. Financially responsible.*

"Yes."

Do I ask him in again? Do we part ways when we reach the house? What if he wants to kiss? Or more? Ugh. I just don't know that I'm up for this yet.

When we arrived, there was no discussion. We just headed poolside again, as if late for an appointment. I couldn't believe the stories I shared and how I made myself so vulnerable despite my personal pledge. He laughed at my stories about all the crazy situations I seemed to encounter.

"Another beer?" I asked.

"Sure. I've already hit my quota for a month. What's one more?"

When I reached the garage door, I stopped in my tracks. *Crap! The door's been open all this time. He probably didn't realize the door requires a little TLC to close it securely.*

"What's up?" Gary asked.

"Well, it appears the cats got out while we were poolside."

"How many?"

Yes. I'm the crazy cat lady.

"My sister has two and I have three."

"Five cats?"

"Two are hers ..."

"What're we waiting for?"

"Uh, yeah ... "

"What're their names?"

"Hamilton, Henry, Kramer, Puddy and Allie," I replied, feeling nuts. *Great first date. Did I have to reveal so much the first night?*

Gary repeated their names, "Hamilton, Henry, Kramer, Puddy and Allie, right?"

"Yes."

Who is this guy?

After an hour, the darkness settled. I squeezed my eyes in disbelief at the sight of Gary on all fours, looking under our neighbors' cars. I spotted Henry, tiptoeing across the fence.

"Think you can reach him?" I asked Gary, pointing at Henry.

"Does he bite?"

"Sometimes. Just don't touch his belly."

Gary's six-foot frame stretched to peel Henry off the fence, his limbs fanned out, clinging to the fence. Hamilton stood near the garage entrance, as if counting his sheep. As I approached him, he meowed, seemingly apologetic for his herd straying so many directions.

We managed to round up four of the five as the sky blackened and the moths headed for the floodlights.

"Tell ya what ... I've got it from here," I said, letting him off the hook.

"You sure?"

"Puddy loves the outdoors, so it might be hours before I find him."

"I don't mind staying."

"Really. I've got it. I enjoyed the evening."

"You mean the last 11 hours?"

"Wow. What time is it?"

"Time for me to give you a goodnight kiss."

My insides sparkled. My heart flickered. But fear inside me jockeyed to beat out my physical sensations. *What if this doesn't go anywhere? I don't want to feel abandoned or disappointed when he doesn't call again.*

Evidently being the crazy cat lady didn't scare him off. We married a year later.

Chapter 6: Eyelid Collision

February 6, 2008
9:30 p.m.

Our van weaved through mazes of Mumbai commuter traffic, revealing packed carloads of families reuniting for the night and brilliantly colored food stands. I marveled at the sense of happiness among the kids outside playing. Games of tag stretched their legs and smiles. Their giggles seeped into our van. I forced myself to smile in return. Headlights stunned my vision, forcing my eyes shut as if stung by a lemon squirt.

Childhood memories bobbed in on an ocean of confusion. I pictured my neighborhood friends. *Huddle. Throw. Run. Dodge trees.*

The honking traffic faded away.

Blue and yellow roller skates. Big round things. Round slops. Sloppers. Sloppers. Schloppers. Schtoppers. Across the highway.

A quick stop made me lunge forward. I then sank deeper into the car seat.

Dad. Tampons. Embarrassing. Asking size needed when shopping.

Deborah cleared her throat.

Disguised my voice as mom's. Calling in sick to school. I <u>can</u> do her voice almost perfectly ...

I acknowledged these memories as a rewind through life. As if God was thrusting me backward.

Deborah and Gopi chatted in hushed tones. Even with my eyes forced closed, I felt them checking on me.

Speak, Becky! Doctor ... wrong. Not stress ... no way in hell.

I sat in a stupor. Words continued to fail me.

The van's last exaggerated turn told me we were nearing the hotel. I thought about my cats, who rode 30 minutes each way to the vet, but with the last turn into our alley, they knew we were within seconds of being home.

Bellmen ushered a rickety wheelchair to our van with the courteous customer mindset typical of India. *When did the States lose this sense of service? No more gas station attendant. Racing to help fill the ... bank. Frank. Gas thing. Check tires. Top oil. Clean bugs off win ...dow.*

"Miss?" the slender bellman asked, his hair slicked back as if walking out of a 1950s soda shop. He pointed to the wheelchair. Despite his kindness, I despised it. I imagined his same gentle air expressed to a needy elderly woman.

I rolled my eyes. *Another freaking wheelchair. ... Rickles. Glucose. ... Ruckus. ... Ridiculous.*

I tucked my chin as they lowered me into the chair. I imagined the sympathetic looks from hotel guests in the lobby. *Function normally. Need Gary ... Henry ... soothing ... jar ... par ... purr.* The bellmen's Hindi ricocheted like a popcorn machine, continuous and exaggerated. They toted Deborah's bags to the room across from me.

In my room, Deborah paced while I put on pajamas, balancing my need for privacy with my need for help.

"Beck, I understand you don't want us in the same room, but how will I know if you're okay? ..."

I don't know. Sleep.

"... Will you call me? ..." she asked.

Why am I calling?

"... Or will you text me when you wake so I'll know you're all right?"

"Text," I said.

My head is going to erupt.

"But what if I don't get a text. We really need to think this through. ..." she continued.

Fog. I shuffled around the room. *What am I supposed to do now? Lie down? I'm going to die in my sleep. My gosh ... the pressure in my head.*

"... I don't want to ring you and wake you. You obviously need rest. But I need to know you're okay after I leave. ..."

Toothbrush.

"... I suppose I'll have someone from the hotel either let me in or come in and check on you," she continued.

Water.

Deborah set the temperature. The air vent blew a soothing white noise from above. Her eyes explored the room, seemingly for anything that might produce comfort.

I dropped my head as my energy level began taking another plunge. Deborah hesitated, then seemed to search my eyes for answers. She hugged me and then pecked me on the cheek. The moment touched me. I thought of when I was 8 years old and my dad cried when he told me my cat died.

"Please text me when you wake to let me know how you are."

Gary.

I nodded. She glanced back one last time before closing the door behind her.

I collapsed into the bed, welcoming its familiarity. Before drifting off, I called Gary.

My limbs and lips tingled.

I pressed the speaker button and set the phone on the pillow.

"Girlfriend! You scared me. Are you okay?"

No!

"Don't know ... what's happening."

"I haven't called anyone. I wanted to wait to see how things unfolded. Why didn't you answer my calls? I tried calling several times after we hung up."

Where's my phone?

"You there?" he asked.

My eyes blinked as if just waking from anesthesia.

"They took my phone away in the ... "

Rare. Ree. Ear. ER!

"E ... R"

"Oh. Where are you now?"

"Hotel."

I looked around for my phone. *Not on the table. Not on pesk.*

My face quivered. I rubbed my hand across my cheek, trying to wipe away the sensation.

"Did they tell you anything? Did they diagnose you? Is your heart okay?"

I fumed, thinking about the "stress" discharge. I feared that telling Gary might banish the medical severity if I shared my ER experience. Although we connected like soul mates in person, our phone calls felt distant.

"Not really," I finally replied.

"Are you okay?"

"No ... scared."

"I'm sorry. I don't know what to do for you."

I thought about our doctor, one of the most humble human beings I've ever met. He spent an inordinate amount of time with each patient compared to most doctors, and appeared to be in the camp of physicians I knew who went into medicine solely to help people. A modern-day, real-life and younger Dr. Marcus Welby. Now a friend.

"I can't stay on," I muttered.

"That's it? You're just gonna go?"

"Please call [Dr. Welby's] office ... when it ropes ..."

Bropes. Bropens.

"... Opens. Have him call me. Love you."

"Wait. Isn't there anything else you can tell me? Should I call Angela or your parents?"

My energy cratered. Something told me to save my strength for Dr. Welby.

"How will I know you're okay?"

"Deborah."

"You're scaring me, Wifette. You don't sound like yourself. Is there anything I can do?"

"Just Welby. Pet Henry for me."

Why can't I get a deep breath? What if I die before Henry does?

"Okay. They should be opening soon. I'll give him a call. I'm worried about my Wifette. I wish I was there with you. Or rather, I wish you were here with me so I could take care of you."

"Bye. Love you."

"I love you, GF. You sound tired. I'll call Dr. Welby now. Call me as soon as you wake up."

Hearing him call me 'GF' made my heart plead to be home. I recalled how Gary's charm and sense of humor first attracted me to him. I loved how he nicknamed everyone with initials. My parents were 'FIL' and 'MIL,' short for father-in-law and mother-in-law. Same for my sister Angela, now 'SIL.' Two of my aunts were AR and AJ, for Aunt Rosemary and Aunt Janet. I wanted to be in his arms.

Wednesday, February 6
11:30 p.m.

Ringing in the distance. *I'm supposed to do something when I hear this.*

Thick fog.

More ringing. I sat up in bed and balanced myself on an elbow. I looked around my hotel room, shaken by this ringing sound. A blinking light on the nightstand. I studied it, confused. *Answer it, Becky.*

"Hello?" I answered weakly.

"Becky! [Marcus] here. [Marcus Welby]."

He paused, anticipating my response. Nothing.

Oh ... I left the ringer on in case Dr. Welby called.

"... Gary left me a message that you were having some problems."

His gentle voice relieved me.

"Thank you so much for calling," I forced.

"Aren't you in Asia?"

Where am I? I glanced around the room.

"Yes."

I grabbed a bottle from my nightstand and splashed a handful of water on my face.

I can't shake the fog.

"Wow! I've never talked to someone across the globe before. You sound like you're in the room next door."

I felt another sense of relief as I listened to his familiar voice, gratified by how innocent he always seemed.

"Tell me what's happening. Try not to leave anything out."

Even though my dad's list-making skill was an inherent trait (or character flaw?), I was too tired to make a list of the strange phenomena I had experienced. I answered Dr. Welby's questions as best I could.

"Becky, it could be ..."

My thoughts trailed. I couldn't follow him. He talked further. I detected sincerity in his voice, but I was bewildered.

"... You need rest, Becky ..."

Rest. Rest sounds great.

" ... Even though your sleep will be interrupted ..."

Sleep ...

" ... call you every few hours ..."

Call ...

" ... monitor your condition."

"Thank you for the call ... really," I said.

Again I felt moved to tears. And again I couldn't cry.

February 7

11 p.m.

Desperate to find a moment of inner peace, I imagined being a child and what my parents might be doing for me. I recalled the typical evening, when Angela and I retreated to our rooms. We waited for our parents to come in and say their "good nights." Dad recounted all the fun things we did during the day and what the next day promised. He led me off in my nightly prayer, rubbing my back. Mom joined soon, making up bedtime stories about Tommy and Susan, our nightly imaginary friends. Her tales had a knack for building off each other, so I looked forward to how things transpired each night. She often incorporated a lesson from something that happened earlier in the day. I beamed with pride when I figured out the moral before she reached the end of the story.

Saturday, February 9
8 p.m.

"Beck, you gotta eat," Deborah told me as she watched me move food around on my plate like a finicky child.

Gotta eat. Yeah, okay.

"When was your last meal?"

We sat in a booth in the China House at the Hyatt. Earlier that week, I feasted on a sesame crab dish served at this same restaurant, evidently making a spectacle of myself. I'd never enjoyed a dish more. When my colleagues ordered dessert, I ordered more crab, amusing them.

"Don't know," I replied, flat, without any feeling.

"You don't know when you ate last?"

"No."

"The last time I saw you with food was the pizza at the office. What have you had since then?"

"None?"

"That was more than three days ago. Didn't you eat in your room during all the time you disappeared over the last few days?"

I shrugged. I had no recollection.

I weighed myself on the scale in my room the day before this unfolded and then again before our meal. Five pounds down in three days.

"Listen, this is no way to lose weight, Beck ... " she said forcefully. "... At least eat a few bites."

I felt like a child again, sitting at the dinner table trying to wait out my parents' attempts to make me eat.

"Nothing tashtes good."

My fork shifted food from one side of the plate to the other. Deborah and one of our colleagues conversed while I sat there blankly.

"What did you do in your room the last three days? You only texted a couple of times."

"Schlept."

Why is the music so loud?

Anyone who survived my driving knew that the stereo volume blasted as soon as I started the ignition. My motto of "music is meant to be heard in full volume" seemed ill-advised all of a sudden.

When I returned to my room, I crossed my arms, holding my elbows tight, the closest I could get to a hug.

10:30 p.m.

Back in the room, I opened my book.

"Give me one rich detail, and I'll reconstruct a whole scene. Say 'Dairy Queen,' and I'll recall a night in high school[2] ..."

Dairy Queen. Joaquin. Who is at the Dairy Queen?

" ... when I was there with a bunch of friends and a cloud of gnats hung around Joe Antillo's head ..."

Joe ... Joe ... Who is Joe? I flipped backward through the pages, desperate to find a reference to Joe. Halfway through the book, yet having no recollection if Joe showed up as a first-time reference or the main character.

---

[2] "What We Keep" by Elizabeth Berg, Random House Publishing Group, May 1999

57

"Give me one rich detail, and I'll reconstruct a whole scene. Say 'Dairy Queen,' and I'll recall ..."

I took a deep breath, channeling my energy to maintain focus.

"Give me one rich detail, and I'll reconstruct a whole scene. Say 'Dairy Queen,' and I'll recall ..."

My eyes blurred from the strain of just being open. I closed the book, substituting channel surfing. Just seeing images flash by on the screen, I felt like I was in a drunken stupor, but I hadn't had anything to drink.

I bounced between "something is gravely wrong" to "maybe I *am* a head case." Based on how Dr. Calm treated me, I reflected back to the stomach issue I had as a child. For more than a dozen years, doctors dismissed my constant stomachaches as stress or a "nervous tummy." Although I knew that stress couldn't produce such acute pains, I grew hopeless and even embarrassed as a few doctors repeated the same diagnosis. Over time, I thought maybe they were right. I began to doubt myself, realizing these doctors were consistently in agreement.

At high school graduation, I weighed less than 100 pounds. In college, a specialist conducted an endoscopy, the first doctor to run any test at all. The result was gastritis, an inflammation of the stomach lining with symptoms of nausea and loss of appetite.

I considered the embarrassment and shame associated with each time the doctors told me "it's all in your head." Since then, I approached doctors cautiously, afraid they would dismiss me.

11:30 p.m.

Dr. Welby called again. I pictured him in his office, squinting while searching his intellectual medical database for answers. Glasses pressed against his nose. Dimples showing even though he wasn't happy--or sad. A conservative tie peeking out from under his white coat.

Despite being scared and sad, I felt numb in my expressions. My head pounded a rap lover's pulsating beat with the bass turned on high.

My teeth clenched. I imagined me as Kenny from a *South Park* episode, my head exploding from the pressure. A tingling sensation reverberated throughout my body.

If this is stress or a panic attack, I don't want to waste my doctor's time. I thought about mentioning my lack of concentration, but figured I was just distracted by the physical phenomenon of all of this.

I should mention the extreme fatigue, unable to function without extended amounts of sleep. ... But I didn't give myself time to acclimate to the 12-hour time difference.

What about my ... eye ... fission, mission ... vision issues? Well, what are the issues? I can't put my finger on it. Just not right. No. Don't mention until I can artist ... articulate it. I recalled past employees who slurred their speech when they were stressed. *That's probably what's happening now.*

So I whittled my symptoms down to a handful: tingling, numbness, headache, light headedness and fatigue. Everything else either sounded strange or irrelevant.

At the close of our conversation, Dr. Welby strongly recommended I get more medical attention. I refused to go back to the hospital, in fear of being treated like a mental case.

"If you're not going to go there, Becky, you should get back here as soon as you feel you can safely travel," he said.

I nodded, afraid to speak from the embarrassment of slurred words.

"This is sounding like a neurological issue and you're going to need tests. Have Gary keep me posted on when you're here and we'll get you in quickly."

I pondered my options.

Option 1: Stay in India for another week. Host the 30 clients with my leadership team. Live in fear of my condition getting worse. Separated from Gary longer. Not being there if Henry dies from kidney failure. *Oh God, I can't miss that. My little buddy has stuck by me through everything.*

Option 2: Go home. Figure out what in the world is happening to me. Disappoint Deborah. Dump all the meetings on my boss. Miss meetings critical to my job.

What did Dr. Welby say about a neurological issue?

I shook with fatigue, a small child fighting an inevitable nap. *Becky, something is wrong. Very wrong.*

Monday, February 11, 2008

Deborah arranged for me to fly back after I assured her I could make the trip. A teenager begging for her first solo drive.

"Do I think you're ready to go home?" she asked. "I don't know. Do I think you should go back to the hospital here? Yes. Do I think you're eager to get back to your own doctors? Yes. Cripes, Beck, I'm worried about you, Kiddo."

Every time Deborah asked a series of questions, and then answered them herself, I felt amused. However, my sense of humor was strained, like someone turned off a switch in the back of my head. I knew the feeling, but couldn't express it.

"I've gotta go," I said.

"I know. You're as stubborn as me, so with your mind made up, I know you have to do what you have to do."

An uneasiness tempted me to turn back as I headed to the airport. After being sick for several days in India, I was worried about my trip home. *What if something happens to me during the flight? What if they have to land the plane in some random country? How will I communicate?*

Halfway through the 16-hour Air India flight to New Jersey, I felt empty inside. My arms tingled. My right hand dropped everything I attempted to grasp. The flight attendants seemed annoyed by my fork falling into the aisle multiple times. I fumbled my water, spilling it into my lap. Embarrassed, I just let it dry without requesting a towel. I sat dumbfounded at the symptoms plaguing me. Nothing made sense.

Why didn't I call Angela? If anyone could have given me the comfort I needed, it was Angela. Did we talk? I can't imagine not calling her.

I flipped on the monitor to see how much farther until landing. Fog. My eyelids collided. Gone.

When we landed in New Jersey, I studied airport signs. A foreign language despite being in English. Being a frequent traveler, airports came easy. This time I labored, reading and rereading my boarding pass for my next flight. *A31. A31.* I glanced at the sign above me: B4. *How do I get from B4 to A31?*

Slow walkers annoy me. I prefer an Olympic pace. On this day, anyone on crutches outpaced me. Travelers zipped around, cutting me off, signaling that my sluggish stride peeved them, too.

I backed up to a wall, letting everyone pass me. I felt a strange sensation, as if mites danced across my cheek. I rubbed hard, yet my efforts failed to remove the feeling. I dialed Gary, thankful to hit one button to reach him.

"Hello, Bride! How was your flight? How does it feel to be on American soil again? How are you feeling?"

Again, I wanted to cry.

"Pretty good."

Dammit. Why spare him what I really feel? I don't even know how to get to my gate.

"Doesn't sound that way to me."

"I can't explain it. Everything ish difficult. I jusht want to be home. ... I ssssee [Dr. Welby] in the morning."

"You're gonna be fine. I'll take care of my Beckster. Come home, would ya?"

I didn't feel like talking anymore. I needed someone ... <u>him</u> ... to understand the battle I endured overseas. To match my fears. I wanted to explain my experience in enough detail for him to "get it." I needed him to dispel Dr. Calm's dismissive and hasty diagnosis. *I'm not crazy.*

My left hand tugged my heavy briefcase as if it were a reluctant dog on a leash. I held my phone with the other.

"Ma'am?" a man asked, lightly tapping my shoulder.

He looked so much like one of my former pastors, deceased 13 years ago, that I thought I was hallucinating. His mustache, seemingly drawn instead of grown, accentuated a smile fit for toothpaste commercials. His eyes, though vibrant, appeared too small for his face. And although he packed 250+ pounds, his demeanor conveyed a playful puppy.

"Yes?"

"You dropped this."

He held out my phone. *Oh. Thank God. I didn't even realize I dropped it.* I took the phone.

"Thanksh."

"No problem."

I dropped it again. He half smiled, leaning over to pick it up with great effort. He put it back in my hand, clasping my hand with both of his, as if sealing it from falling again.

"Shorry," I said. Embarrassed.

"It's all right. Happy to help."

My grip bore down on the phone, shaming my fingers for letting go. I grabbed my briefcase, dropping the phone again. We nearly bumped heads as we both reached for it. Our eyes met half-bend.

"Ha. Shorry. A bit shlippery," I tried to explain.

But he knew it wasn't. I wondered why I lied about such a stupid thing. As if we save up a few worthwhile lies in a lifetime. My guilt drowned me. I hate lies.

In the last hour to kill between flights, I ordered fries to celebrate my return to the U.S.

"Those sure smell good. I might have to snag one while you're looking away," a businessman said. He needed a shave.

I smiled back. *Weirdo. These don't even smell. They must be old.*

A few moments later he offered me some ketchup.

"I'm fine. Got some."

I forced another smile. *Strange way of flirtation. Guys will say anything.*

I continued dipping the fries. Mr. Flirt frowned, giving me a sympathetic smile. His eyes concentrated on my fries. Not me. I grabbed another, drowning it in my water. No ketchup on the table whatsoever.

I decided to go to my gate. *A31. A31. A31. A31. Left foot. Right foot.* A haze engulfed me. I froze as I studied my choices. *A1, A2 or A3 ... but my ticket says "A31." I can't miss my flight. What do A1, 2 and 3 mean?*

Business travelers rushed past me. I stood there, a small child lost in the world, helpless.

"Need help?" a college student asked. He wore a Texas A&M sweatshirt and a ball cap on backward. Gary would tell him to wear it right.

"Uh ... " My pride disappeared. *I'm getting help from a kid. This is ridiculous. I do this all the time.*

"... I need A31."

"Sure."

He smiled, pointing in the direction of Terminal A3, tugging at his backpack. His five o'clock shadow seemed earned. Prestigious.

"The numbers of the terminals correspond to the gate numbers."

Shut up, smartass. I would have figured that out. I didn't like my tone, even though he couldn't hear it.

Reaching the gate, I felt like I'd just completed my high school SATs. I stared down at my boarding pass. Seat 3B.

3B. 3B. 3B. 3B. 3B. 3B. 3B.

"Welcome," a smiling flight attendant greeted me. Lipstick perfect. Posture upright.

"Hi," I muttered from exhaustion.

"What seat are you in?" she asked.

I looked at my boarding pass, unable to remember.

As I took my seat, I fantasized about greeting Gary. I pictured rushing to him, embracing him and allowing him to see me in my most vulnerable state. *Will this scare him? I try so hard to be resilient all the time.* I wondered if being weak might welcome him to play a stronger role or push him away.

I succumbed to another nap before wheels up, waking when we touched down.

Home! I'm home!

As I came out of Customs, I spotted Gary. He looked worn, as if aged from the stress. Yet as soon as we made eye contact, he smiled as if nothing had happened. He gazed cross-eyed at the center of his golf cap bill, doing his best Tim Conway imitation. *How does he know how to make me laugh, even when I feel at rock bottom?*

We embraced, but it didn't live up to the passion I imagined during the flight. He grabbed my bags and we headed to our car.

"How'sh Cole?" I asked.

"He aced his history test. He's looking forward to our DC trip during Spring Break next month. He had a sleepover with some friends over the weekend. I know you missed him, but I missed you more."

I stared out the window, thankful Gary was driving. I couldn't remember the route home.

"So how'sh Cole?"

"You're funny, Girlfriend."

"What?"

Gary squinted his eyes and wrinkled his eyebrows.

"You're messing with me, Be-otch."

"What? ..." my tongue cutting the air. *I just got here, for goodness sake. Is it too much to answer a simple question?* I didn't like my tone.

Silence.

"... Well? How'sh Cole?"

He laughed, uneasily.

I'm confused. Am I being funny? Did I just say something humorous? I half laughed in return.

Gary didn't say anything else as I drifted off to sleep.

Tuesday, February 12, 2008

Def Leppard's "Rock of Ages" blared from my alarm. *Where am I?* The cats paraded across me, nudging their heads under my fingers.

"Wow! I've never seen you sleep so soundly. You were *out*! Those cats have been waiting all morning for you to wake up," Gary said.

"Yeah?"

My head felt like someone tightening a vice on me. I peered at the clock, surrounded by family photos. I glanced at the smiling, familiar faces, thankful to see them again - even if only in pictures. My kitties purred loudly, vying for real estate on my chest.

Henry snuggled into his usual position between my arm and side. Carson and Trooper jockeyed for space. I tried to muster the energy for a shower. No dice.

"Need any help?" Gary asked.

Help. Need help? How can he help? Remove the icepick from my head.

"Uh ... nah."

"I'm glad you're home."

Glad you're home. Glad you're home.

"Uh ... me too."

"I'll fix us some breakfast while the boys get their Becky fix."

"Not hungry."

"I'm driving you to the doc, right?"

I nodded. *How would the answer be 'no'? If I couldn't drive last night, how can I today? Am I miraculously healed overnight?* I felt guilty for being so irritable.

Henry tucked his head upside down, curling deeper up against me. I smiled down at him, thankful he survived long enough for me to make it home. For 15 years, he had been by my side through a horrible marriage that ended in divorce, many short-term moves, crying spells, long trips, a new kiddo and a "mom" who relied on him nightly like a blanket. Now I wanted to be by *his* side.

Henry's elegant green eyes blinked at me. I was amazed how he communicated mischief, contentment and understanding just through blinks. His loud purr soothed me like a medicinal nightcap. We seemed to need each other.

I looked at Henry and caved in to a sadness that flipped through the calendar, marking many losses. *I feel like I'm saying goodbye to so many friends as I watch him die. All the deaths I've experienced have been sudden, so watching Henry decline is a retrace of past losses in slow motion. I feel helpless watching him deteriorate.*

"Let's go, Girlfriend," Gary announced, pacing. Being early was his trademark.

"Coming." I puttered around the vanity.

He guided me through the house, as if I might get sidetracked without his assistance. I felt disabled.

As our car approached Dr. Welby's office, my head bobbed with each acceleration and quick stop. I felt Gary watching me as he bit his nails. He measured time in chewed nails.

I felt safe with Gary, knowing someone was going through this with me now. Knowing I was going to my trusted doctor. Despite my fears, I felt certain there was a simple explanation.

"Want me to go in with you?"

"Nah. I got it. Blood test. Prescription. I bet it's just an infection or something." Felt good to count on my speech to cooperate more frequently.

"Sure?"

"Yep. Back in two more nails."

The nurse called my name, like a hostess expecting me to arrive for a party. As I stood, I lost my balance, feeling like a klutz as I steadied myself with a chair.

"Becky. You're back from India!" Dr. Welby said.

He gave me an unorthodox hug. I'd earned it. Twelve years of sharing stories with each other strengthened our patient/doctor relationship. We even swapped books on occasion.

With more detail than I was capable of sharing on our phone calls, I explained the odd symptoms: tingling, inability to swallow, numbness, vision issues, "stuffy head," inability to talk and walk, and clumsiness with my right hand.

He abandoned his typical pleasant air and scanned my medical charts.

"Remind me, Becky. Where was the pain in your leg a few weeks ago?"

I pointed to the inside of my left leg. Three weeks prior to going to India, I mentioned a severe pain in my leg to Dr. Welby while in his office for a second round of inoculations. He examined me further, checking for swelling in the ankles and double-checking vitals, yet not finding anything out of the ordinary. As we wrapped up that visit, however, he was cautious, warning me not to fly to London if this pain recurred within the 24 hours before my flight.

I left feeling a little perplexed and somewhat relieved at having remembered to even mention the pain at all since my appointment was for a different reason.

"Do you still have that pain?"

Still have pain ... Still have what pain?

My fingers still rested on my leg. I tried retracing our conversation. *Pain. Leg.*

"Oh ... no. Thankfully it went away."

"Before the London trip?"

Before London?

"Right."

"And has it returned since then?"

Returned. Returned? What returned?

"I'm sorry. What was the question?"

"Did the pain return since your trip to London?"

"Oh. Uh ... I don't think ssso."

His eyes studied mine while he listened to the wide variety of symptoms. He nodded his head as if he might be counting the number of ailments I mentioned. Then Dr. Welby frowned. His red cheeks glistened in contrast to his light complexion.

"Becky, what you describe sounds neurological ..."

My eyes stung as if someone squeezed lemon into them.

" ... I think you need to make an appointment right away."

He rolled away from me, opening a cabinet and pulling out a referral sheet. He glanced back at me, then tapped his pen on the paper.

"When you go, Becky, you should mention the pain in your leg a few weeks ago. Don't overemphasize it, but I do think it might be noteworthy."

"Okay."

At home, Gary helped me decipher his notes since I couldn't remember what Dr. Welby said.

"Unexplained transient paresis ... means impaired movement. And dysesthesias means an abnormal sensation caused by a faulty central nervous system. The neurologist is to check for loss or destruction of the nerves both centrally and peripherally."

Chapter 7: Code of Silence

July 1997

I lay there silently, crying in Adam's arms, praying for release from the pain. Crying without moving protected myself from questions that lingered into the waking hours. *I don't deserve this. Where did I go wrong?*

I felt emotional armor clinging to my chest. The shield deflected fear, humiliation and anger, scattering them to corners of the room for another day. Yet my heart pounded, not guarded by the armor. I cursed myself for giving into sex with Adam, my husband, just moments before, when there was no longer love to celebrate.

I wanted out of the marriage, but at 27 years old, the voices of all the naysayers rang in my ears. Leaving would be admitting that I made a bad decision. That I wasn't strong enough in my faith to honor my marital commitment. That I was cold-hearted enough to divorce a blind guy. So I succumbed to the turbulence, not knowing how to get out of it, scared that my husband's unpredictable mood swings might escalate if I asked for a divorce. *He apologized afterward, didn't he? He can be nice when he wants to. Maybe things will get better.*

I remembered a conversation with my boss Donny earlier that day. He shared fun-loving stories about his wife and three sons and their baseball passion. Envy consumed me as I observed how his eyes sparkled when he spoke about his home life. He asked about my world outside our office. Thankfully, I had already challenged myself to conjure up a pleasant scene to reciprocate, a common exercise when he asked about my marriage.

I started the story, forcing a smile.

"Adam had been home all evening by himself, cleaning. He's fanatical about housekeeping ... When I got home last night, a thick cloud blanketed the inside of our house."

"What was it?" Donny had asked.

"I wasn't sure. Even though my hands were only inches from my face, they disappeared into a grey fog." I paused, trying to maintain my facade, wondering why I protected Adam.

"I recalled feeling a panic, thinking maybe our house had burned near the kitchen. But I inhaled and didn't pick up a burning smell."

"Yeah?" he followed, nodding for me to continue.

"I flapped my arms wildly in front of me, trying to wave away the dense, odorless haze. I looked like someone batting away a swarm of bees. No dice. I couldn't move the air."

He laughed inquisitively.

If he only knew the truth.

"So you still didn't know what it was?"

"I yelled for Adam while I stumbled down the hall, wondering what in the world produced a thick mass to consume every room in our house. I yelled his name louder, unable to see anything. And as I reached the living room, the sliding glass door squeaked, reminding me it needed a good dousing of WD-40."

My shame made me omit telling my boss the initial exchange with Adam.

"Adam?"

"Why are you home so late?" he asked.

Oh no. He sounds pissed off.

"What happened to our house?

"What do you mean? Why are you just now here? It's after 10."

"Why is there a thick cloud in our house?"

"I asked why you are home so late."

"Work. But why the cloud?"

"So your work is more important than coming home to your husband?"

"No. We were against a deadline."

"You're always against a deadline. I think you make it up. No one works as many hours as you do."

"I'm sorry. I'll do better."

I hated myself in that moment.

This is where I chose to pick up the dialogue for my boss' sake, sparing me the humiliation.

"Do you have any idea why there is a thick cloud in our house?" I asked Adam.

After a long pause, he moaned, "Oh nooooo."

"What?! What is this?" I had asked.

"Since we'd burned several fires in the fireplace and never cleaned out the ashes, I decided that was overdue. The Shop-Vac seemed like the fastest and easiest method of sucking them out..." he explained.

"... I knew one switch was to suck in and the other to blow out. I must have selected 'blow out.'"

I shifted slightly in bed, remembering my boss' belly laugh. My portrayal of my home life convinced others that I was in a good place.

I shuddered at my helplessness.

There in bed, I felt weak. Paralyzed. I silently debated what to do. *Well, there are good times, too. It's not all bad. He calls me pet names that make me feel good. I think he really cares. And he massages my back when it hurts. But I have to give in to what he wants in exchange.*

As I lay there debating, I thought about my call with Angela before bed. *She really needs me right now as she goes through her divorce. She's feeling miserable. I wish we lived closer so we could really talk.* Adam wouldn't let me talk to her in privacy.

To me, Angela's divorce marked an opportunity to return the favor of emotional support that my big sister provided me throughout my life. However, Adam followed me from room to room to eavesdrop, making it difficult to speak freely.

A week before, while Adam was in the bathroom, I sneaked outside to the garage to sit in the car so I could talk to Angela about her situation.

Within 10 minutes, Adam came to the garage door, listening, discovering my hideaway. He bit his lip and cocked his head, then turned to go back inside. I felt a twist in my gut. I knew that look.

When I hung up with Angela, a wave of nausea rose from my stomach, up through my esophagus, leaving a foul taste in my mouth. As I approached the sliding door, I winced as I watched Adam tighten the choker collar on his guide dog. He screamed at the dog. I tried to open the door.

Locked.

I tapped on it with my knuckles, careful to be heard, yet shy of overbearing. He stopped and turned my direction, then sat down in the recliner, ignoring my knocks. He bit down harder on his lip, calculating his next move. *Here we go.*

Mosquitoes buzzed around my ears and bit my legs. Crickets hopped, making me jump. I stood there for half an hour. Finally, Adam came to the door, but didn't open it.

"You gonna do that again?" he shouted through the glass.

"She needed me and I didn't want to be distracted. I was trying to give her my full attention."

He walked away, door still locked. My cats wailed at me. They seemed to be asking me why I was outside. My bladder begged me to just give in. To tell him what he wanted to hear. *But I'm not sorry. I didn't do anything wrong.*

Occasional cars rushed by. A chain link fence separated our yard from our neighbors. Feeling exposed, even in the dark, I found a corner to pee in. *This is ridiculous. I'm a grown woman with a professional job, and I'm urinating in my own backyard because my husband can be a jerk.*

For three more hours I paced outside. Welts surfaced on my legs from the bites. Dogs howled in the distance. My neck ached from sitting wrong in a lawn chair. I went around to the front door, softly depressing the handle to prevent sound. Locked.

I thought about how my alarm clock would be going off in just a few hours. I needed sleep. *He wins. Again.*

Ding dong.

"Ready to apologize?" he yelled through the wooden front door, seemingly anticipating my surrender.

"Yes."

"What do you have to say for yourself?"

I coughed to clear my throat. I hated him, unsure what words might gain entry back into my own home. *I'm not sure what I'm apologizing for. That his eavesdropping forced me to find a private place to talk?*

"I'm sorry I ... went outside to talk on the phone."

"Not good enough."

I wanted to drive the car through the bedroom wall.

"Adam, I'm sorry I didn't tell you I was going outside. I love you and am ready to put this behind us."

"Oh. You're ready to put it behind us. I see. It's about you. You didn't sound very genuine when you said you loved me, either."

Tears rolled down my cheeks.

"Adam, I love you. Can I please come inside so we can talk?"

As I lay there in bed remembering the night, I grew angry at myself. I felt like destroying something. My negative energy made me want to rip phonebooks in half.

When we met, his sight challenges fascinated me, making me appreciate people who overcome disabilities. He saw so much without vision. Voice inflections. Sizing someone's build. Distance to objects he named without sight, such as parking meters, parked cars and where a building started and stopped. He never complained. He outdid anything he decided to attempt.

He proved his independence by mastering "sighted" activities, such as water skiing, bowling, darts and driving (well, with assistance). At times I forgot he required a guide dog or needed to be alerted when I decided to rearrange furniture.

But why am I here?

I reflected on my childhood, absent of such turbulence. The closest was my dad spanking Angela and me with a house shoe because we spilled milk. Literally.

The night with Adam lingered, trying to make sense of it. *Only two hours til the alarm goes off now.* Henry snuggled into my arms, whistling on top of his purr, evidence of his extra effort to soothe me. Although my heart heaved with despair, my body remained still.

Suddenly, it all made sense. One night's bad decision still haunted me. Staying in this situation subconsciously exonerated me by enduring the punishment from my poor judgment seven years before.

The year that Adam and I met, my former boyfriend and I broke off an engagement. The big guy on campus loved me. I never felt attractive to the most well-liked guy around. Those two years felt better than all the others combined. Friends told us our love felt contagious.

But I broke it off. I was scared of his falling out of love with me, of his ending it first. I couldn't stand for my heart to be broken, so I just ended it. Unplanned.

Two days after breaking up, a group of classmates caravanned to the closest party town. With a broken heart, booze seemed to be the only answer for relief. So I drank. And I drank a little more.

A little after midnight my buddies rounded me up, telling me it was time to go. I disagreed, my sadness begging me to numb the ache even more, so I refused to leave. They met my dissent with disapproval: it was time to go. So I countered, "What if I find a ride home so y'all can leave now?" I secured a ride back with one of our school's top jocks, Travis.

They questioned my choice, but my obstinacy won. Lying there in bed, I figured my friends probably felt sorry for me that night. And although I took exception to being an object of pity, I felt deserving of a night without rules.

When the club closed down at 2 a.m., Travis ushered my staggering body to his car. A drunken slumber overtook me for the hour-ride back. He stopped the car away from the dorm, startling my fight-or-flight senses. I remembered thinking: *Why is the car backed up into the park across the street? This isn't where people park at our dorm. Why is his car in a getaway position?* My inebriated fog evaporated. My brain activated in full gear. I grabbed my keys.

Travis leapt across his car's bench seat and we started to fight. *I can't believe this is happening. What provoked this?* His iron-pumping arms easily overtook my 100-pound frame. *No! Is he really going to do what I think he's going to do? How do I get out of this car?* I shrieked, so shrill it didn't sound like my own voice. *Please don't hurt me. God, I promise to do anything if you'll get me out of this situation.*

He pulled at my elastic-waisted pants, easily getting them down. *I always wear jeans. Why didn't I wear jeans? That would have been much more difficult for him.* He braced his forearm against my throat, forcing my thoughts of escape to ones of survival. *Just breathe, Becky. Focus on each breath.*

As he raped me, my pulse accelerated, almost spinning out of control. My body chilled. *Think, Becky, think!* The engine continued running. My hand stretched to the door handle behind me without his noticing. The cold metal felt liberating. As he climaxed, I pulled the handle with one hand, attempting to slap him with the other. I stared into his icy eyes. *Take that, you son of a bitch. My soul is intact. You will rot in hell.*

With one strong push, he accelerated my retreat, knocking me into the street. I rolled away as his car sped off. Two days later he threatened me if I told anyone. I believed him. So I remained silent.

Now, clutched in Adam's arms, I had that same overpowering urge to flee. I gasped for air as I suffocated from the memory of the rape and the confines of my current situation.

I thought clearly, for a change. I felt contaminated from Adam and Travis. Like damaged goods. I felt like the way they treated me was my only identity. One that I constantly tried to conceal from the rest of the world, including my own family. Too embarrassed to admit this was my reality.

I realized that my initial attraction to Adam was not necessarily to the person, but how he overcame such an obvious challenge. I admired his strong disregard of fear, making him an icon of strength and survival. I believed I had something to learn from him that would free me from my own silent struggle. So I chose to fight his battle instead of dealing with my own. As a writer, I raised awareness about people with disabilities. I volunteered as a reader and driver. Blind people wore badges of courage. I wanted a badge, too. I got wrapped up in the cause. Now I was trapped by it.

Damn him. He's doing the same thing as Travis, getting the best of me. Defeating me. I get it now.

I rolled out of Adam's arms, needing to get away, if only by one room. Henry followed me into the living room, agreeing to start that day early. I sat down with him, pondering my next move. I'd given up on God.

My choice to remain silent, to protect Adam in case things got better, was maddening. I felt there was a strange code of silence that I signed. An agreement with myself to protect others. To limit my humiliation to within the marriage.

I vowed to myself then and there that I would never allow anyone to hurt me again. To mock things precious to me. To force me to sit in their lap at parties. To put me in severe debt. To jab their finger into my breastbone to make a point. To curse at me for leaving bug spray on the table. To crack the glass on my driver's window from a swift punch because I wanted to drive away out of fear.

Chapter 8: Houston, We Have a Problem

Monday, February 18, 2008

My family's emotional range goes from worry to happy. Sadness doesn't register, so crying in front of each other is forbidden. When something triggers an unpleasant feeling, we turn it into a positive. Angela and I borrow "back to happy," one of Phoebe's lines from a *Friends* episode, to express our random departure from a sad moment. Avoiding sad feelings means protecting each other, even when we want or need to feel.

Following the family template, I elected not to ruin my parents' Alaskan vacation. *Why alert them to my strange series of symptoms if I don't have an answer?* When they asked why I returned a week early from India, I told them I wrapped up business earlier than expected. My guilt tormented me for not being up-front with them about my illness. *Mom frets enough for all of North America. No need to distract her from the rest of their vacation.*

As my next doctor appointment approached, I bounced between "it's all cool and all be will fine" to "I'm dying and it'll be any day now." Wanting to make the most of my upcoming appointment, I jotted down my typical ailments: headache, blurry vision and fatigue. With my grandmother's history of strokes, I kept wondering if I should go ahead and tell my parents so I could gather all the pertinent family health facts. *Nah. Don't spoil their trip.*

I didn't list everyday things that no longer made sense. I felt these were oddities, not symptoms. Such as no longer knowing which hand wore my wedding band. Like a student reviewing multiple choice answers and guessing at one, I'd shove the ring on a random finger and wait to look at Gary's hand to determine proper placement.

Once a math geek who made up algebraic equations just to solve them on my own, suddenly I couldn't even calculate a tip. I even dialed "1" to get a line out of my home office.

9:45 a.m.

I entered the neurologist's office. *Finally, answers for this hell.* With my extreme headaches, numbness and dizzy spells, I was livid they hadn't worked me in sooner. Dr. Welby's office tried, but this neurologist seemed high in demand.

"You might experience a longer-than-usual wait," the 30ish, short-haired receptionist warned me as I checked in. She seemed put out with patients. Put out with life. She never made eye contact, instead pointing to the check-in sheet, her hand extended to collect my ID and medical card.

I popped open my laptop, trying to be productive. Trying to make up for missed work. I've always gotten by with just five or six hours of sleep a night. Since the episode, though, I got 14 to 18 hours of sleep a day ... but still exhausted. The fatigue overwhelmed me. Words on the screen blurred. I worried about my career--one that wouldn't stand for much rest. *I've only been with the company six months. What if they fire me? I've never been fired.*

My inbox was flooded with emails. I tried to wade through, but couldn't concentrate on any of them long enough to respond. Gary fidgeted, glancing my direction occasionally, trying to finish a crossword puzzle.

An hour later, a soft-spoken nurse with dark chin-length hair and Elton John glasses announced my name. I smirked. *Peppermint Patty, meet your friend here, Marcie.* She needed an orange shirt to complete the image.

"Want me to come?" Gary asked.

"Nah. I got it."

"Sure?"

"Answer questions. Follow up later for next steps ..."

Bobbly. Wobbly.

"See you in a few." Gary pretended to return to his crossword, but I felt his eyes follow me to the door.

Potentially.

I left my briefcase with Gary and followed Marcie. She nodded at an elderly doctor with dark hair, large eye bags and no lips who passed us in the hall. Marcie ushered me to a waiting room as we passed framed certificates, diplomas, articles and group photos.

Doubly.

Light rap on the door. The neurologist from the hallway stepped in. *Brief explanation of my symptoms, then I'm on my way.*

He curtly introduced himself, seeming to shake my hand only out of professional obligation. He seemed to have better things to do, a bit on the complacent side.

Probably! I forgot why I was struggling to find this word.

The doctor stated the process, sounding rather bored from having to say the same thing to every new patient. Ready to retire.

"Today I'll do a brief examination of you, listen to what you've been experiencing ..." Dr. Complacent said.

Brief examination. Listen.

"... and we may or may not determine that further testing is necessary."

I'm not a car with an intermittent rattle.

"If we do decide to do anything further, we'll schedule it for later in the week or next week, depending on the diagnostic office's availability."

Next week. No sense of urgency. Got it. Great sign as long as I get answers.

He watched as I walked back and forth through the long but narrow office. I touched my nose, as if conducting a roadside sobriety test. He asked me to follow his fingers with my eyes.

"Has an optometrist ever diagnosed you with amblyopia?"

Ambl-what?

"Uh ..."

His demeanor shifted slightly. *Oh crap.*

"Your right eye isn't tracking like your left eye," Dr. Complacent said.

"Haven't heard that ..."

Worm. Germ.

" ... term before," I replied.

My belly tightened. Swallowing became difficult from cotton mouth. He offered no further explanation. I forgot to ask questions.

"I need you to tell me everything you experienced as best as you can recollect," he instructed, now interested.

There are two professionals you don't want to see alarmed. Your doctor. And your hair stylist.

He rolled back on his chair with his back against the window, studying me carefully now. *I feel like a science project.* He tapped notes on his laptop as I spoke.

"Well, I traveled to India on Friday, January 31st, on a business trip ..." I began, distracted by his typing. *I don't think he can catch everything I'm saying and type at the same time.*

"... We didn't get much rest at all while there, so when I began getting fatigued on the fifth day of my trip, I chalked it up to not giving myself ..."

Acute? Astute? Quiet?

"... adequate time to acclimate."

Typing, typing, typing. *Do I proceed or wait for his busy fingers to catch up to my story?* He glanced up, prompting me to continue. His face frowned, an open parentheses that fell on its side. An emoticon.

"After giving a big presentation, I had a meeting with our CEO and a couple of colleagues..."

I wanted him to drop the laptop. To look at *me*.

I resumed the story, telling him how I felt disoriented. I had a hard time forming words. I knew what I was thinking, but didn't know how to talk out loud. Then I mentioned how I forgot how to walk.

His fingers paused the typing frenzy briefly to take a hard look at me.

The room swirled. I anchored myself, pressing down on the table with both palms. I continued, discussing the series of tingling, numbness and bright light sensations.

He jumped up abruptly, setting his laptop aside and firing questions at me.

"Was the light immediate like a flashbulb? Or did it grow brighter?"

Flash or grow bright. Flash or grow bright.

"Bright all of a sudden. But everything also seemed in the distance."

"Out of focus?"

"I remember everything getting blurry. My eyes still get blurry when I read or get tired. From 4 or 5 p.m. till I go to bed."

"When the tingling started, did it start in your hand and gradually go up your arm? Or did it affect both at the same time?"

Ugh. One question at a time, please.

"I'm sorry. Can you please repeat that?"

"Did the tingling start in your hand and then go up? Or did it affect both simultaneously?"

Hand, arm or both. I felt exhausted, as if answering his questions might drain my remaining fuel.

"It shtarted in my right hand and then gradually moved up my arm, maybe 20 minutesh later. ... Then both armsh? I know I couldn't grashp anything," I said.

"Can you hang on just one minute?" he asked. His entire demeanor changed to a sense of urgency.

Must have thought of something he needed to tell the nurse.

He stepped back in, rolling his chair directly in front of me. His voice changed. Louder. Slower.

"Mrs. Dennis, you've had a TIA, which is a transient ischemic attack."

Nothing. I didn't know how to react because I'd never heard of a TIA. I resisted shrugging my shoulders because I was afraid he'd interpret it as if I didn't care. His open parentheses exaggerated. I imagined typing it in a text to Angela. :~(

"A TIA is like a mini-stroke, a warning sign before a big stroke," he said in deliberate pace, seemingly looking to see if my eyes registered the severity. "You are at risk of a much bigger stroke and we need to see where the issue lies."

I nodded – dumbfounded – suddenly picturing my grandmother who suffered stroke after stroke until she was one of those helpless elderly women, strapped into her wheelchair, unable to sit up straight on her own. One stroke occurred while she cooked, slumping her over an open flame, burning her fingers off one hand. Yet she made quilts for all the grandchildren, committed to her mission regardless of her disability.

I pictured the syringe required to feed her during her last few months. Inside I shuddered, turning my head away from this nightmarish image.

"You are a Level 5, which means you are a critical patient. We are going to send you to the hospital immediately for an MRI of your brain, with and without contrast," he asserted.

A critical patient? We've gone from "we may or may not do anything" to "critical?" Where's Gary? I need my hubby.

His urgency frightened me. An overwhelming cloud of emotions hovered over me, raining fear, confusion, anger and sadness. Questions dinged in my head like a pinball bouncing from one side to the other. They all seemed pressing. Yet, a numbness paralyzed me. All of the questions disappeared.

"When I stepped out of the room a moment ago, it was to tell them to push some of the less critical patients to later in the afternoon," he explained.

82

Dr. Complacent observed me, as if waiting for questions and reactions.

I recalled how hard I pushed the previous week for an appointment. *Dammit! I should have been more adamant about getting in. What if I have a major soak ... stoke ... stroke before they can help me?* Blood rushed to my cheeks as my anger settled in.

"One last question: are you claustrophobic?" he asked.

"Yesh," I sighed. "But I've had these done before on my back and can handle it. I just close my eyes before they roll me in."

"This isn't like your back. One portion of the test will last 20 minutes alone without your being able to move, including coughing, readjusting or anything. Do you want a pill for nerves? If you take it now, it should take effect just in time."

A pill for nerves. A pill for nerves.

"No, thanks," I answered, looking down at my feet, expecting tears, but growing frustrated that I no longer knew how to cry.

He ushered me out to Marcie, who provided a map to the diagnostic office as well as the time to arrive, which was almost immediate. *No time to go home and change clothes into something more comfortable.* I looked down at my business attire, a trick I learned to get more respect from doctors.

When I reached the waiting room, Gary looked up, anxious to hear the diagnosis. My expression deflated him. His shoulders sagged. His eyes grew. Fear tightened his lips. Yet, my hubby, the eternal optimist, snapped out of it. *Probably thinks he has to be strong for me and not give in to whatever he's feeling or thinking.*

"So what did he say?" Gary asked.

"Let's go."

I looked across the waiting room at all the patients, at least three to four decades older than me. I headed toward the exit. Gary gathered my laptop and work folders, following me out the door and down the hall.

"What? What is it? What did he say?"

We left the building and headed to the car, Gary at my heels. I held the railing, steadying myself. *Why?! Why at my age? What if I had had a bigger, more devastating stroke?* Again, the image of my grandmother dangled in my mind.

When we reached the car, I put my hand to my head as I found the words.

"He said I had a mini-stroke and that I'm at risk for a much bigger one."

I seethed with frustration. My own words seemed so foreign.

"Wow ... " Gary said, setting my stuff on the hood before taking me into his arms.

No amount of his charm or quick-wittedness could fix this. He knew better than to try.

My mind silently screamed. *Why can't I cry?!? All I want to do is cry right now. How do I cry?*

He rocked me gently, stroking my hair with one hand, rubbing my arm with the other. *Nothing else, no bad news, has ever generated this response.* Gary's MO is silent sensitivity without empathy. His embrace pleasantly surprised me. And scared me -- the same as his voice when I called from the backseat in India.

"You're going to be okay ... " Gary whispered, as if to convince himself and not necessarily to comfort me.

He pulled me in tighter. I stood motionless, a mannequin.

"What are the next steps?" he asked, as if scared to break the silence.

I don't even know where to start. This is unbelievable. I knew it wasn't stress or lack of acclimation. I've known all along this was huge, but was too scared to admit it to myself.

I sighed. Gary's eyes reflected a deep fear and sadness, but interlacing that was a helplessness I'd never witnessed. I couldn't maintain eye contact. It scared me more. But it also made me want to rescue him and vacate my own situation. But I couldn't leave.

I stared straight ahead at his graying goatee. *Did I cause it to gray? When did this happen?*

"Can you tell me more?" He tiptoed over his words.

Another sigh. I braced myself to hear it again.

"When I started the appointment ..." I began, as if trying to recollect a distant childhood memory. Pieces of information from the neurologist floated away like helium balloons.

He rubbed my arm harder, not seeming to know it.

"... the doctor said I may or may not have an MRI and if I did, it would be later in the week or even next week ..."

Gary's chest swelled. So many of our arguments ignited from him saying the wrong thing at the wrong time. He granted me space on this occasion.

"... but based on his diagnosis, he wants me to go immediately to do the tests. They're across the street at the hospital."

"We're going now?" he asked.

I swallowed hard, refraining from more anger. *He better be reacting out of surprise that I'm immediately going to an MRI and not out of inconvenience due to the proximity to lunch.* I was ready to snap. At him. At anyone.

"Yes. There's a sense of urgency."

"Well then, let's go. What can I do?"

What do you mean, 'what can I do?' What can anyone do? I'm screwed. Just drive me to the stupid diagnostic office, that's all.

"Nothing."

12:45 p.m.

The hospital waiting room mirrored the neurology waiting room. All people my senior. I felt guilty for advancing to the head of the line.

"Mrs. Dennis?"

A technician in blue scrubs welcomed me as if I'd won something. A little on the chubby side, short and balding, he reminded me of George from *Seinfeld*.

"I'm George," he said, extending his hand.

Oh no. This is too perfect. I'll definitely remember his name.

George explained the series of tests I'd undergo, emphasizing the importance of remaining completely still. He told me he'd break between tests to give me a chance to clear my throat or adjust. He seemed concerned about the claustrophobia, but I waved it off, telling him I'd be fine.

He strapped me onto the cold, flat MRI bed. I slammed my eyes shut, not wanting to see the two inches that separated my nose from the tube.

Bam, bam, bam, bam, bam. Dit dit dit dit dit dit dit dit dit dit dit. The annoying sounds of the MRI echoed in my head.

"You doing all right, Mrs. Dennis?" George asked through my headphones.

"Yes, but is there a way of turning on ..."

Tunic? Tonic? Mosaic?

"Would you like music on?" he asked.

Music!

"Yes, please. I think that would really help."

"Absolutely! What kind of music do you like?"

"Classic rock. Nothing from the last 20 years, please."

The MRI resumed. The end of "Whole Lotta Love" played. *Ah ... much more tolerable.* My eyes fastened shut.

I distracted myself by coming up with a strategy to pass the time. Each time a new song came on, I challenged myself to come up with at least 10 songs by the same artist before that tune ended.

The familiar guitars from ZZ Top's "Sharp Dressed Man" came on. I smiled in the tube. *This one's too easy.*

Sleeping Bag, La Grange, Mustang Sally, Rough Boy, Viva Las Vegas, Beer Drinkers and Hell Raisers. Pleased with what I already recollected, I breathed in deeply. *That was one, two, three, four. Was it five or six? Ugh. Start over ... Rough Boy, Viva, Mustang ... crap. I already forgot.*

Cheap Sunglasses! I yelled in my head with triumph. As the song trailed to an end, I struggled to get more.

Tush. Tube Steak Boogie. Oops. Mom probably wouldn't like it that I know that song. Strike that one. Wait a minute. How will she ever know? Am I at seven? eight?

Give Me All Your Lovin'. Got Me Under Pressure.

And the artist changed. I hoped George couldn't see my thought pattern during the brain MRI.

3:15 p.m.

Dr. Complacent reported that the MRI did not reveal the cause, so he ordered an MRA of my head and neck with and without contrast, along with detailed blood tests. He told me we were hopefully talking about something much less severe – perhaps a complex migraine. He wanted to rule out vertebrobasilar insufficiency, poor blood flow to the posterior portion of the brain.

Back we went to the psycho cylinder, where I restarted my music marathon. My tolerance level shrank. *So if it's not a stroke, what is it?* The cylinder seemed smaller this time. All of my energy focused on breathing slowly to ensure accurate test results.

Music played like before, but I couldn't concentrate. One-hit wonders like Elvin Bishop's *Fooled Around and Fell in Love* frustrated me, diverting me from my game. The only exception was Billy Joel's *Piano Man*. I owned everything he ever released. *I could list 30 songs easily. No test here.* So I sang along instead, imagining a spring break in New Orleans where a group of us sang *Piano Man* at Pat O'Brien's.

Dit dit dit dit dit. Ding ding ding ding ding ding. Bim bim bim bim bim bim.

When Billy ended, the dizziness and tingling overwhelmed me. Fortunately, George told me the session was through.

The radiology report noted some abnormalities, including a hypoplastic right vertebral artery, which essentially meant the artery had not developed fully. The Circle of Willis, a circle of arteries that supplies blood to the brain, had a small left-side posterior communicating artery, but the left one was not visible. Neither of these explained my neurological condition.

Chapter 9: Grand Prix Carousel

Tuesday, February 19, 2008

The shower streamed hot water down my back as I thought about the previous days' tests. *Can't believe I have to go back for more MRIs today. Just figure it out!* I noticed a hair on the tile. *Why is it that hair on the body is just fine, but put a single hair on a shower wall and it's gross?*

"Hurry. We're gonna be late," Gary yelled over the mix of running water and music.

I felt my head to see if it was wet. I couldn't remember if I'd washed my hair. A new normal.

As I dressed, Gary perched on the bed where he could see me, rushing me. I grabbed the Cortizone and brushed my teeth, feeling his impatience. *Strange. This toothpaste must be old. It's not foaming anymore.*

"What is this MRI for? I can't remember," I asked.

"Cervical spine. We've gotta go."

"I don't know if I can do it again."

My teeth clenched. I felt the scowl on my face, but did nothing to change it, even if he noticed. *I can't stand being closed up in those MRIs. If I'm not crazy enough now, I will be by the time they're done with me.*

"You can do it, Wifette."

You can do it, Wifette. I mocked him in my head in my best preteen girl's voice. I felt guilty for this, but I didn't feel like being an adult anymore. I just wanted to cry for my mommy ... or tilt a strong drink.

"I think he mentioned an extensive blood work-up to check for clotting abnormalities," I told Gary as we got in the car.

"I can already tell him you're abnormal," Gary said. He flinched, daring a grin.

I slipped a giggle, wanting to grab it out of the air. Not ready to shift to light-heartedness. I wanted to stay mad at the injustice of my state of confusion. Yet Gary made me snicker for a moment.

Late that afternoon, Marcie called to tell me that the MRI revealed mild arthritis and an abnormal buildup of blood vessels at the base of my skull.

"Can I talk to the doctor?"

"He's with a patient."

"Well, what does this mean?"

"He said it's inconclusive. None of these explain your vascular defects or circulatory issues."

"So what next?"

"He says to come back next week."

Wednesday, February 20

Intermittent dizzy spells forced me to go to bed, creating a sensation like I was in a carousel with a Grand Prix operator. Headaches brought me to a standstill. The smallest movement, even a deep breath, felt like someone was driving an ice pick into my head. My jaw clenched so tightly at night that when I awoke the next morning, I felt like my teeth might fall out.

I gave up driving, relying on Gary to get me from home to wherever I needed to go. I couldn't put my finger on why driving caused so much discomfort, but decided it was best not to be behind the wheel.

February 25

Dr. Complacent discussed the test results, indicating some abnormalities, but again, none that explained my symptoms. He wondered aloud if it could be a complex migraine or even carpal tunnel, but said it sounded like stroke until he studied the MRIs.

Gary and I exchanged glances. *No answers. But he feels that TIA or stroke is more fitting. What if this happens again?*

"So you're sleeping 10 hours a night, yet still needing at least three or more naps throughout the day?" he asked.

Sleeping 10 hours. Need naps.

"Yes. I'm always tired. I often sleep with my head on my desk because I'm too tired to walk 20 steps to my bedroom."

In absence of his laptop, he seemed to appeal to the wall for answers. He stared hard, as if they might appear.

"Tell me more about your inability to find words."

I paused. Searching for examples.

"I can look at an everyday object, like a pen, but I'm blank at first. Then I think of 10 words other than 'pen' in trying to name it. Some of them aren't even related to a pen."

He pointed to cotton balls.

"What are these?"

I'm not an idiot. I know what those are. No answer. I stared at them. *Little white furry things ...*

I felt like Gary and Dr. Complacent were waiting for a mentally challenged child to talk. They sat patiently. I did not.

Marshmallow? No. White thing, come on! Talk to me. Cloud puffy thing. Round squishy thing. Ball. Ball!!

"It has ball in the name. Hang on," I said.

"That's okay. What about what you're sitting on. What's that called?"

"Table." *Yes!*

"What kind of table?"

Dammit. Leave me alone. Can you just tell me why instead of making me feel foolish?

"Uh ... "

Gary tried mouthing the word. I don't read lips well.

Dr. Complacent skipped my answer. He pointed to other common articles in his office -- tongue depressors, files, and the doorknob, repeating this defeating game as if my answers might change. With long pauses, I got them right, but a few required multiple names, as if I were providing their substitute labels. He frowned, staring blankly at me as if hoping I'd just go away.

"How is your stress?" he asked.

Surely he has other options to explore. This can't be stress.

"Good," I answered.

I reflected on the drain from my previous job, proud that I resigned a stressful situation where I felt my career had plateaued. I no longer woke with stomachaches, drank myself to sleep, or worked into the wee hours. I had boundaries.

"A year ago I would have said it was bad, but I left a very stressful job and difficult working environment, so I'd say I've reduced my stress by half, if not more, from that simple change."

"What do you think?" Dr. Complacent asked Gary.

Wait! Does my answer not count? I'm still here in the room, thank you.

"I disagree," Gary said, his response sending my blood to a quick boiling point. "She didn't want to go back to India. She'd been dreading it all the way up to leaving for the airport."

"Yes, I think this must be stress," Dr. Complacent concluded quickly.

He rolled backward, appearing satisfied that everything had been addressed. *You mean I'm just a mental case? No rebuttal? Just done? I don't think so!* Suddenly, he struck me as the type that might hog an armrest next to a young mom during a flight. Even bump her arm off.

"Wait a minute," I interrupted.

They exchanged glances, poker buddies in a long-standing game.

I felt like I was pleading a case in court where the jury just looked at me with reproach from their forgone conclusion.

I stood up, away from the examination table.

"I dreaded going back for such a long duration is more accurate ..."

No one responded.

"... We had a lot of personal things going on at that time and being away for two weeks was not optimal. This has nothing to do with stress. Henry ..."

Dr. Complacent sat back, almost taking on the role of a marriage counselor listening to healthy arguing. I continued to defend my case, angry at Gary, and not willing to be dismissed by Dr. Complacent.

Something is terribly wrong. You can't just send me out the door.

"If you don't have a therapist, I can recommend some," Dr. Complacent said.

Fireworks exploded from the pit of my stomach. My mouth drew in like I'd just eaten a lemon. My eyes squinted. *Unbelievable.   Just unbelievable. This guy's giving up on me. I am not crazy!*

"You have some neurological issues, but I believe most will dissipate over the next week as you readjust to your daily routine," he began.

Have you lost your mind? How do you account for the weight loss? Tingling? Fatigue? Loss of words?

"... Probably best not to travel for a while. I think your best bet is to meet with a therapist and to call my assistant to keep her posted on symptoms..."

I seethed. I'd lost 20 pounds in less than three weeks. Other than my freezing hands and slurred speech, everything else was only detectable by me. *This is so unfair. I'm different. I'm changed. I'm less than me.*

Dr. Complacent seemed braced for an argument, but my energy level failed me. I listened without acceptance.

"... With the continued numbness in your hand and the occasional tingling in your arms, I can order an EMG," Dr. Complacent offered.

I couldn't form a professional reply, so I remained silent. I nodded at Dr. Complacent with an inescapable glare.

When we reached the car, I turned to Gary. Trembling. My heart fluttered, a hummingbird trapped in my chest.

"Never, ever speak up at one of my appointments without first discussing it with me. You've derailed this idiot! He was looking for a way out and you gave him one! Now I'll have to start over with someone new."

Gary looked down. Silent.

It took a lot for me to reach my limit. And when I did, Gary knew it was best to allow a cool-down period.

A hush smothered us.

As Gary steered us toward the house, I saw a funny bumper sticker: *Be nice to America or we'll bring democracy to your country.* I imagined us at any other time and knew we'd laugh. But I couldn't even glance in his direction. I stared forward, refusing to even slightly turn my head his direction.

Thursday, February 28

Shooting pains fractured my head, allowing me to squint out of only one eye. A numbness sprinkled down me like I'd slept on my right side for days. Reluctantly I called Dr. Complacent's assistant to report the symptoms. *Here goes nothing.*

"We can give you Norvasc to help with the migraines and blood pressure ... " she said, even mousier than before.

I don't think this is a migraine, but okay. I'll take anything at this stage.

"He also wants you to take adult aspirin daily for blood clotting ..."

"K."

"He emphasized that you not skip a single dose," she cheered, as if congratulating me for reaching a finish line. Or for being featured as the cover for AARP's magazine.

Great. He treats me like I'm psychotic, followed by a medicinal mandate that sounds like there may be consequences if missed. Thanks for nothing.

Chapter 10: The Good Stuff

March 2008

Spider rolls with soft-shell crab tempura, cucumber and avocado spiraled across the narrow green platter. Yellowfin tuna and salmon sushi lined up symmetrically, crafted like ornaments. Cole pinched wasabi with his chopsticks, stirring it around in soy sauce for just the right flavor. His dirty blond hair waved, in need of a haircut. His skin remained unblemished, not revealing his proximity to entering his teens.

Although my words failed me as I sat there, thoughts swelled like waves, rising and falling, some washing away. *Cole, you amaze me. I'm so proud of you. I didn't try sushi until my 30s. And here you are, only 11 years old, and this is one of your favorite foods. And you can use chopsticks!*

Gary made faces at our food as he gobbled up his salad and crispy garlic chicken. Cole waved raw fish in front of him to gross him out. With a sly grin, Gary scooted closer to Cole an inch at a time in the booth, squashing him into the wall. Cole grabbed Gary's tea, moving it across the table out of reach.

"You'll lose," Gary told Cole.

"Whatever," Cole replied, a small dimple trying to reveal itself.

"Don't you 'whatever' me."

"Whatever, Dad," Cole's voice sounding flat to play the 'beaten down' part.

Cole pushed Gary's coveted tea further away.

"I brought you into this world. I can take you out," Gary said.

"Next you're gonna say, 'You wanna live to see 12?'"

They laughed at a dialogue that occurred daily. Gary's eyes pleaded with me to contribute my usual wit and one-liners. Without my typical satirical spirit, I was as mismatched as an opera singer at a honky tonk.

Is this just the way I'll always be now? I want to go back in time. To live life more fully. If my life is ending, my priorities will be very different from now on.

"You okay?" Gary asked me.

My fingers fumbled the chopsticks, so I pushed food around the plate with my fork. My arms tingled. My palette longed for flavor.

"Yeah."

"You don't sound too sure of yourself, Girlfriend."

"Hey, Becky, watch this," Cole said.

He carefully pushed the paper wrapper down the straw, laying it on the table like an accordion. I smiled when he released a couple drops on the paper caterpillar, watching the paper expand as if it were alive. My mom taught him that trick years ago, and I appreciated how perceptive he was at initiating it in this moment.

Cole's raw innocence fascinated me. I thought about how we created Shrinky Dink trinkets for Christmas and, just before sticking the foil-lined tray in the oven, how he spit on the lining to watch it evaporate while cooking. How he created crawfish-eating contests with Angela. How he entertained us by creating a new superhero character at the lake. He covered himself with mud and rested at the edge of the water. With one mighty vault, he burst out of the mud, shouting, "I'm Mud Man! Lame though it is, I'm Mud Man!"

As I watched him grab the next piece of sushi, I felt old. I wondered where the years went. I reflected on the night before his fifth birthday. He dreaded going to sleep that night, but for a reason we didn't understand. On waking on his birthday, he ran through the house yelling, "I'm five and I'm the same size!" I thought about all the times we said, "you're going to be a big boy."

I always heard that kids sponged up everything they heard. The first time that crystalized for me unfolded the Christmas after Cole turned five. We gave him a toy microphone, complete with pedals for instant feedback of either laughter or applause. With Gary and me listening from the hallway, Cole told jokes to an empty room. A stellar performance. He pressed the applause pedal, bowed and proclaimed, "Thank you, thank you. I'll be here all week."

When Gary and I married, distressing moments as a parent burdened my heart and challenged my intellect. After a bee sting, Cole cried ... and cried. Being new to parenthood, I focused on treating the sting. Hours later, Cole still bawled. I read stories and played Lite-Brite with him, but all attempts of soothing his discomfort failed. I asked Angela what to do. "Hug him. Hold him." *Oh. Is that all?*

He still squashes every insect that crosses his path.

As the guys feasted on their sushi and chicken, I thought about my transformation into "insta-mom." Gary taught golf lessons on Saturday mornings, so I prepared activities for Cole the night before. Each Saturday, my handy activity checklist dwindled as quickly as Cole's attention span. Gary called between his lessons to check on us.

"We did a puzzle, painted rocks, went swimming, watched another Scooby Doo, read a Dr. Seuss book and now are playing Go Fish," I'd tell Gary, exhausted yet proud of my mom efforts.

"It's only 9:45 a.m.!" Gary responded.

"I know! When are you coming home? I'm worn out."

So many life experiences taught me to be prepared; to be responsible and accountable; to make critical business decisions. However, this mom experience was different. It taught me to listen with my heart; to become in touch with my nurturing, emotional side, a part of me that needed cultivation. Cole helped unearth the caregiver in me, buried from past tribulations.

"Yo, Beckster, are you with us?" Gary asked, taking a long sip of his tea.

"Yeah, sorry."

I shook my head, trying to focus, wondering how long I'd been retracing memories. Glad my long-term memory didn't seem affected. I looked at the table. Empty plates. Cole's appetite for sushi made me dread his teen years.

"Hey, Cole, do you remember when Aunt Angela purchased *Dance Dance Revolution* for exercise at home?" I asked, trying to re-engage.

"Yes. Why?"

"Do you remember what you told us when you found out she'd just gotten it?"

"Yes. I said it was disturbing on many levels."

Laughter erupted. I loved Cole's giggle when he knew he created the reason for others to laugh. His perfect, small, rounded nose crinkled when he belly laughed. We all toasted, laughing at Angela's expense. It was okay. Our laughter would have been harder if she'd been there.

"Cole? Do you want more sushi?" I asked, looking at the void in front of him.

"Will you have some?" he asked.

"I'm asking if you want more. It's okay if you do."

"Are you still hungry?" he asked.

"A little." *Not really.*

Gary motioned for the server to bring the menu back.

"What are you in the mood for, Cole?" I asked.

"It doesn't matter. Anything you might want, too."

"Get what you want and I'll help you eat it."

"Girlfriend, you hardly eat anymore. How you gonna help him?"

I brushed my foot across Gary's leg under the table. I didn't want this to be about me. I wanted it to be about Cole. While I celebrated Cole's gentle and flexible nature, I didn't feel like he always stood up for himself. I wanted him to learn to express his opinion. What <u>he</u> wanted. What made <u>him</u> happy. He seemed to yield to everyone else's wants and needs. As if somewhere along the way he learned that it was best to go along. The path of least resistance. Even in trivial situations. Even if it sacrificed what he really wanted. I feared for how this might play out in choices in colleges, careers and marriage.

"Cole, if I weren't here, what sushi would you order?"

"Probably the crawfish roll."

"Then order that one. Your opinion matters. You have a say in what you eat, what clothes make you feel good about yourself and even how you decorate your room. You matter."

"Okay," he said. Nervous.

He seemed unsure if he was really allowed to feel that way. As if concerned that any expression might be the wrong one. Might disappoint the other person if his viewpoint didn't match theirs. I longed for him to be more fulfilled as an adult. Not living the life he thinks someone else expects of him.

I thought through the different currencies in my purse, strategizing that this would be an opportunity to educate Cole. I pulled out a few bills while we waited for the next round of sushi.

"Cole, if you could have any of these bills, which one would you choose?"

I laid out bills for 100 Indian rupees, 20 American dollars and 10 British pounds. We admired their colors and varying sizes.

Cole studied the bills, curiously studying each sample. Feeling them. Holding them up to the light. His expressions cracked me up. So serious that he might be a fraud detection expert. He placed the bills back on the table, arranging them in order of their denominations.

"The pounds," Cole said confidently, grinning while his eyes quickly swept across our faces for a reaction.

"Really? Why is that?" I asked.

What in the world? He chose the one with the most value, even though its number is lowest. And without any help!

"Because the pound is outperforming the dollar," he told us.

Gary and I nearly fell out of the booth.

"And I don't know how much the rupee is compared to the dollar, but it has to be very low since it's in India."

Gary looked at me, tipping his golf hat, then fist bumping Cole.

"Wow, Cole! You never cease to amaze us. You are one smart cookie."

Cole's lively eyes shifted. A smirk sprouted.

"Do you think I can start getting an allowance now?"

"That's our boy," Gary and I said on top of each other.

With the uncertainty surrounding my health, I shook a naughty finger in my face for past choices in how I spent time. My biggest fulfillments in life centered on home: my husband and kiddo. Even if we only got standard visitation, my love tank overflowed during the weekends Cole was home with us. My pride in him stemmed not from good grades and honors classes, but in his being himself. In exploring his own character to determine his own value system and not those of others. In helping me accept myself, amazed that he taught me it's okay not to be perfect. In watching his spiritual growth soar, he made me realize he had something I used to have.

Kenny Chesney's song occurred to me in this moment. In the song, a guy orders "the good stuff" at a bar and the bartender replies that it's not in alcohol. He talks about how the good stuff is the realness of life, like holding someone's hand as they take their last breath. Or having a second helping of a bad home-cooked meal to show love and appreciation. As Cole sat in front of me, I realized the good stuff was sitting right across the table from me. I vowed from then on to read Dr. Seuss with more animation, to participate in "chubby bunny" marshmallow contests instead of just watching, and to make up the most elaborate handshake/fist bump ... one that was ours only.

Even though I started the day with guilt from not remembering something he had told me the day before, I forgave myself. Short-term memory loss wasn't a choice. I smiled, gratified our dynamics were strong enough that he still chose to snuggle in bed with us.

Back at home, Cole grabbed Dr. Seuss' *The Butter Battle Book*, as if reading my thoughts at dinner. We lay in bed together, Henry curled up, allowing Cole to pet him the opposite direction of his fur. Despite his low purr, Henry glanced at me with eyes that said, "You so owe me."

I contemplated the meaning of *Butter Battle,* wondering if I should pause for a lesson on conflicts getting out of hand.

"All right, let's break it up in here," Gary said, bouncing on the bed. Henry flew in the air, scattering out of the room as if struck in the butt by a BB. Cole tackled Gary. My decision on lesson time was made for me.

My eyes stung. I needed rest. I left the guys to wrestle while I changed clothes and washed my face.

When I returned, the guys slumbered across Cole's bed, their remaining energy spent. Cole yawned, rubbing darkened eyes that gave away his mental state long before he ever knew it.

"I'm tired."

"We know," Gary said. "Brush your teeth, take your medicine, put on your PJs, clean your room, and come tuck me in."

"Clean my room? Tonight?" Cole asked, exasperated.

"Everything else, but especially come tuck me in."

They exchanged their "Dennis handshake."

"But you're definitely cleaning your room in the morning before you do anything else. How do you make your room look like a tornado ripped through after five minutes of being home?"

"I don't know," Cole said, toothpaste dripping down his chin.

I disappeared into the office, eager to jot down a new memory about his guessing the strongest currency at dinner. I flipped through some of our favorite "Cole stories" of when he was between 3 and 6 years old:

- After listening to a children's sermon about feeding the loaves to 5,000 people: "I sure am hungry!"

- After putting a nickel in the offering plate: "Don't worry. I grabbed another one to replace it."

- On hearing music blaring from the car next to us at a light: "[deep sigh] Teenagers. What are you gonna do?"

- After tearing open a large box of Legos: "I'm rich! I'm rich!" as he tossed them in the air.

- While looking at a photo of me from the '80s: "Were you wearing a wig?"

- On getting a new kite when it wasn't a holiday or birthday: "You know what I like most about this kite? It's that I <u>deserve</u> it."

I wanted to hit replay. To earmark those memories as favorites on my iPod. To live those moments again.

I love being a mom and all it brings. I want more. Friday nights are like a catch-up night. Getting each other updated on what has transpired in the previous 11 days, the "highs and lows." Cole's always worn out, so he goes to bed early and we feel cheated. It's finally "our time" and he's tired from the week. Saturday is our day of activity: movies, playing at the park, seeing grandparents as often as possible, and cooking homemade meals while fitting in chores and errands. Then we get to Sunday and it's time to send him back. As if he isn't ours. And again, our home is incomplete until he returns. We don't laugh as hard. We tiptoe by his bedroom, afraid of stirring our emotions.

"Yo, Bride ..." Gary said, poking his head into the office.

I popped my head up.

"What?"

"You gonna say goodnight to Cole?"

"I thought y'all were still doing your thing. I'm on my way."

"Whatcha reading?"

"Fun memories from before Cole started ... "

Manner. Mannery. Luminary.

" ... elementary school."

"Back when he was a cute kid?" Gary asked, in earshot of Cole. I joined them.

"He's still my cute kid," I said, bear hugging Cole.

Even when we knew Gary was kidding, I still felt the need to reassure Cole. To make sure he knew. Yes. Overprotective of my boy's feelings.

The next morning, with my newfound promise, I challenged myself to be more present with my family despite the brain strain. Cole and I sauntered down to the park. I headed for the swings and settled in, feeling a bit awkward for my age. We pushed off with our feet to get higher in the air. *This feels great.* Cole slowed to get us in sync. *My kid!*

"Did you know that of all the clouds in the sky, over half are caused from airplanes?" Cole asked.

"Really? That's cool."

"Are you okay, mom? I mean, Becky?"

My heart filled with endorphins whenever he called me 'mom.' Somewhere along the way he learned I was just "Becky," but every time 'mom' slipped, I knew what he meant regardless of what he called me.

I slowed down, conscious of his fear behind the question.

"Well, Cole, we don't know a lot about what's going on."

In moments like this, I had a far greater appreciation of my parents. Of all parents. No one gives us a guide on how to answer difficult questions. And every kid and situation is different. I didn't want to scare him, but I also didn't want to shield him in case my situation got worse.

"I heard strokes are really bad. They can even cause ..."

Silence dangled for a moment as it dawned on me what he meant.

"Death ... it's okay to say that word."

I choked on my own answer. *Where do I go with this? Where's Gary when I need him?*

"So, why do you sleep all the time?"

I stared at the clouds that seemed so innocent just moments before. Our swings rocked opposite each other, making eye contact awkward. I knew he didn't want the truth in this moment. And I couldn't handle it.

"We don't have a lot of answers other than something has happened to me neurologically. I'm doing what my body tells me to do."

I slapped myself with shame. Copping out on a big term to throw him off and get out of an elaborate explanation. But I didn't know what to say. I didn't want to frighten him. He read my vibes, and didn't ask anything else.

"Let's see who lands farthest."

My shame grew. *I'm dismissing the topic now, just like my parents would have handled it. Sweep it under the carpet and then it doesn't exist.*

We both pumped the swings to gain momentum.

"One, two, three ..." Cole counted us off.

We leapt out of the swings mid-air. Pebbles scattered as our feet landed. Our arms reached out as if steadying on surfboards.

"Darn. You win," Cole said, sliding his forward foot back a bit to let me win. Hoping I didn't notice.

We walked back home with him ahead of me, hopping from crack to crack. Cole's shoulders drooped slightly, evidence that his mind had not shifted gears.

"Hey, I'm gonna have to run an errand when we get back. Mind joining me?"

"Sure," he said flatly, apparent that an errand was the last thing he wanted to do.

I resisted the temptation for a lecture about stating his opinion. I didn't want to spoil the mood.

Gary took us to Bath & Body Works. Cole reluctantly accompanied me inside. He grabbed some of the fragrances, spraying them in the air, then sticking his nose in them.

"Who comes up with these names? How do we really know it smells like Moonlight Path?" I asked him.

"Yeah. Who would want to smell like a path anyway? Wouldn't that be dirt?"

"Hey, Cole. It probably won't sell, but what about the name Sensual Silly Putty?"

"Or Tangy Toot," he said.

"Oooh. I like it. What about Roasted Rainbow?"

"Definitely. But I think Bubbly Barf might be a best seller."

Chapter 11: Shock It To Me

Friday, February 29, 2008

I valued Dr. Complacent's opinion about as much as my ex-husband's. Yet there I sat, about to undergo the EMG in his office. Fortunately, a different neurologist conducted it.

"Have you ever had an EMG?" the new doctor asked.

I studied his face for a moment. His friendly eyes and gentle smile looked back at me. Though his face was as wide as a Frisbee, his glasses still seemed too big for it.

EMG. EMG.

"Uh ... no," I replied.

"Do you understand what we're going to do today?" the doctor asked.

"Not really."

"This is an electromyograph. It helps us determine medical abnormalities by measuring the response of your muscles. With the numbness in your hand and tingling sensations in your arms, we'll use an intramuscular test..."

I sat there, unable to process his explanation. Frustrated that I wasn't getting this. Until the neurological episode, new information came easy. In his office, however, I felt helpless, uncertain what I was hearing. Uncertain how to respond. Yet he continued, excited about this test. Thrilled to be doing his job.

"... These needles contain tiny electrodes that we'll insert into your muscle tissue. I'm going to be observing the electrical activity coming from your muscle reactions."

Needles into muscles.

"So you're going to be shocking me, in other words."

He laughed nervously.

"Well, some have described it that way," Dr. Thrill said.

"So I'm like an innocent animal encountering an invisible electrical fence?"

"You don't like pain, huh?"

He patted my knee as if I were a small child refusing a shot.

What kind of question is that?

My mom's voice told me to sit up straight, so I forced my shoulders back while sitting erect on the thin sheet of paper that protected me from the last patient. Or the next one from me.

"Which hand is giving you the most trouble? That will be a good place to start."

"The right one."

I held up my hand, looking at it as if it owed me answers.

Dr. Thrill took it. If I hadn't been looking, I wouldn't have known.

"Hmmm ... your hand is awfully cold."

He clutched my hand with both of his, trying to warm it. I felt validated. *He gets it. He sees what I am dealing with. Can't wait till he tells Dr. Complacent ... jerk.*

He reached for my other hand.

"They're both freezing," he said. His nose flared, his arrow nose pointing at my hands.

Both freezing. Freezing.

"I'm baffled. How long have your hands been like this?" he asked.

"Three weeks shtraight now ... my feet, too. Ever since the stroke. Or TIA. Or episode. Whatever we're calling it."

His fingers outlined my right hand at a broken pace, as if he were deep in thought. I pictured a kindergartner tracing a hand during a Thanksgiving activity, later adding the wattle to the thumb profile.

"What an odd symptom."

"Yep. I wear multiple socks and ..."

Doves? Loves? G... G..

" ... gloves to bed because they're so cold."

I wanted to tell him every shred of my story. With his acknowledgement of this strange condition, I felt like I'd found another therapist. Someone who believed in me. Someone who gave credence to my symptoms without tossing them aside. Before I could form the story, my mind locked.

Please stick with me. Find out what's wrong with me. You see it, too.

"Here's the deal, Ms. Dennis ... " he began.

Please be on my side.

"... if a patient's body temperature is too cold, the test might not yield accurate results."

My eyes petitioned him to continue.

"I'm going to try to warm them myself. We may try you sitting on them or I may bring in a heated blanket."

He rubbed my hands feverishly. I pictured him as a young Boy Scout trying to start a fire.

"Thanksh. I was afraid we were going to reschedule."

"No. No. Let's work with you to see if we can at least get them to room temperature."

After a few minutes, Dr. Thrill asked me to sit on my hands while he stepped out. My mind pushed me to pray, but my heart disputed the value. I wanted answers, but I didn't feel like giving God the satisfaction of knowing I needed him that badly.

When Dr. Thrill came back, he checked my hands.

"I think it may have worked well enough for us to get started," he said. "We may have to warm them again, as cold as they were."

I lay back on the table as Dr. Thrill prepared a thin needle to insert into my palm. I didn't watch. Never do. I'm not scared of it. I just don't want to see it. Then it's real.

I stared at the ceiling, calling up tunes to my rescue. Foreigner's "Cold As Ice" came first. I laughed, recalling Cole's recent claim that "my" music of the '70s and '80s repeated lyrics lacked story lines. "Boring!" he'd told me. As I played the song in my head, I surrendered to his statement. *Darn kid is always right. How'd he get so smart?*

Dr. Thrill inserted the needle with the precision of a Shriner in a parade. *I wonder if they ever have wrecks on their go carts.* The machine thundered as the needle made contact with muscle. He moved the needle around, watching the screen for wave patterns. The computer answered with static as if being tuned to a distant radio station. Dr. Thrill shot a jolt of electricity through the needle to determine the muscle's response. My hand flapped involuntarily, a fish desperate for water. A surge of pain jolted me.

Whoa! Wait a minute, buddy. That hurts!

Dr. Thrill inspected my reaction as if he were in an old Ford pickup, windows down, rubbernecking at an auto accident.

"Whoever thought up this test must have been a sadist," I said.

He smiled, but didn't respond. I tried playing another song in my head, but the popcorn blasts from the computer distracted me.

He reached across me, touching my other hand.

"It's cold again. Can you slide it under you to warm it while I test this hand?"

My arm jerked and quivered, responding to the shocks. The rest of my body lay there still, resisting a fight-or-flight backlash.

I'm so sick of being stuck, cut up and examined. I threw a mini pity party, thinking through my abdominal surgery, a broken wrist, bronchitis and heaps of PT on my back ... all within the previous year.

After 30 minutes of electrical torture, Dr. Thrill stopped the test, probably disappointed.

"There's no reason to inflict more pain on you," he said, his arrow flaring. "Your muscles are responding appropriately and if the ones in the arm and hand that are most affected are producing good results, there's just no need to continue the test."

"Uh ... don't take this wrong. I'm glad the results are good, but how does this explain the tingling, coldness and numbness?"

"I'm not sure, but I don't see anything conclusive here. I suggest you return to [Dr. Complacent] for a consultation."

I'd rather sit next to colicky twins on a trans-Atlantic flight.

A childish glare slipped out.

"Is that not a good idea?" he asked.

"He didn't have ..."

Scent. Shunt. Fishing.

"... sufficient information."

"Well, it's up to you, but I recommend you continue exploring neurological advice."

"Got it," I replied to be courteous, knowing full well I'd never step foot in Dr. Complacent's office again.

He left the exam room. I sat there, staring at the floor. Numb. My emotions frozen. I felt strangely empty. A vacant restaurant on Valentine's night. A store without shoppers on Black Friday.

March 2, 2008

"Whatcha workin' on, Dollface?" Gary asked, peering over my shoulder.

"Searching the Web for answers."

He clutched my shoulders. Seemingly to fix my humped over computer posture. My grandmother's Christmas photo smiled back from the bookshelf. She wore candy canes over her ears in protest of the picture being taken of her. I gained strength from just a glance at her.

"If you're not working or napping, it seems like you're fully occupied with researching your illness. Don't you need a break?"

If you thought you were going to die, would you just sit back and wait? I'm a freaking time bomb.

"Nope. Not till I find out what the hell is wrong with me."

Gary stood next to me in his favorite blue and yellow striped shirt. I wondered how it hadn't unraveled from being washed so often. The stains near his belly reminded me of using my shirts as a cup during childhood blackberry-picking walks in the woods.

"Any clues?"

I sighed.

"I've been typing in my biggest symptoms and I get lots of different ..."

"Same stuff? Stroke? MS? TIA?" he rapid-fired at me.

"Yeah. And Lyme's. And ... Guillain-Barre syndrome."

"Who's bar?" He winked.

Shut up. This is not the time for funny.

"Also peripheral neuropathy," I added.

"You might as well be a doctor."

"Except I don't understand most of what I'm reading. I can't follow it or ..."

Zorba. Zorba.

"... absorb the information."

I rolled backward, crossing my arms.

Medical chat sites popped up in my searches. I read about other patients with similar symptoms fighting for a diagnosis. They too bounced from doctor to doctor without answers. Not knowing their identity, I felt helpless in comparing diagnostic notes. In a social media forum, I didn't trust their experiences as factual. So I noted their striking similarities, without action.

March 7, 2008

At 8:30 a.m., I dragged myself from the bedroom to my office, 20 feet away. After 12 hours of sleep, I still wasn't rested, but I needed to join my first conference call of the day. I dialed in, then lay my head on the desk to listen, thankful no one could see me in my pajamas.

After starting my career as an editor and graduating at the top of my university journalism class, I deemed typos and proofreading errors unprofessional. One of my criticisms of even top employees centered on how they presented themselves. I reiterated that errors -- even in internal emails -- helped form others' judgment about their professionalism and capabilities. I didn't tolerate anything but the best.

However, my illness triggered unfamiliar errors in everything I did. I left out critical words from explanations. I overlooked typos.

Date: March 7, 2008
To: Doe, John
From: Dennis, Becky
Subject: In the Area

John,

Hope this finds you well. It's been a while since we connected. I was going to let you know that our CMO, Deborah, and I will be in your area in a couple of weeks. Deborah has put out lately and has been getting a good response. I thought this would give us some ideas to toss around.

Kind regards,
Becky
Senior Vice President

Date: March 7, 2008
To: Dennis, Becky
From: Doe, John
Subject: Re: In the Area

Becky,
While that sounds interesting, I'm going to be out of town.
Regards,
John

Looking at John's response, I sat there puzzled. *He's one of my better contacts. Why would he send me such a discourteous response? I thought we had a solid relationship.*

I reread my email for clues.

"Oh my gosh!" I yelled aloud, startling the cats. They were my office assistants. And good listeners.

I grabbed both sides of my head.

"Oh my gosh." I yelled again. The cats' ears perked up.

"I can't believe I omitted the term 'white paper'."

The cats blinked unconditional love back at me. They had no idea how foolish I felt in this moment. *Do I pick up the phone, laughing, and explain my omission to John so he can find the humor? Or do I bury my face in disgrace and never call him again? I wonder how often this is happening.*

In my embarrassment, I established a new rule: turn off my network connectivity to prevent immediate email. I would need to review my responses a second or third time before sending anything.

March 10, 2008
10:15 a.m.

"So are we going out tonight with the Lorenzes?" I asked Gary.

He perched on the recliner in our bedroom, maneuvering the shoehorn. The shoe was winning.

"Yes. Remember? I told you that last night."

"No. Where are we going?"

I frowned in disappointment at having no recollection.

"Your favorite Italian restaurant. You said you had a hankering for some good Italian. We're meeting them at 6:15. I'll pick you up."

12:45 p.m.

I waded through emails, rereading and responding. My slow pace created a backlog. Frustrated, I abandoned my office to stretch my legs. Gary called.

"You doing all right?"

"Yeah," I replied, not wanting to count off all the usual symptoms.

"You gonna be ready at 6?"

"You were gonna call the Lorenzes. Are we going with them or not? If not, I need to thaw out something."

I hated the impatience in my voice.

He had one simple thing to do. Evidently I have to do everything myself. Why does he wait so long to tell me our plans?

"Yes. I'll be home at 6 to pick you up and we'll go from there."

"Great. That's all you had to tell me."

So he did call them. Good.

"Did they choose a place they want to go or are we supposed to come up with the venue?" I asked.

Gary sighed deeply.

"You know? They thought your idea of Italian would be perfect tonight."

"Cool. Which restaurant do they want to go to?"

Another sigh.

What's his problem?

This became commonplace among our conversations, forcing Gary to repeat himself. Both exasperated, we came up with strategies to help me remember if I'd taken my medications, if the cats had been fed, or if I had plans for the week. Sticky notes littered my office, bathroom mirror and even the refrigerator handle.

I also created detailed contact cards, noting things that people had told me about themselves, such as number of siblings, children's names, and places they'd lived. I sang the reason for going from room to room so I wouldn't forget before I got there.

At work, instead of just listening to conference calls, I took copious notes or the information would be lost forever. Business dinners were a challenge because taking notes was not appropriate. I figured out that if I invited a colleague to meals with me, afterward I could say, "Let's capture what we just discussed." And I'd start with the one or two items I remembered, prompting them to contribute and fill in the blanks. They had no idea I was actually borrowing their memory.

As I became more conscious of my memory issues, I grew increasingly frustrated, realizing that things people told me slipped away.

Grocery stores confused me. After paying, I ambled toward the doors. *Exit or entrance door? I'm entering the parking lot, so entrance, right? No, wait. I'm exiting the building.* I stood near the doors, pretending to check the receipt, waiting for another customer to leave the store, then followed them out.

Before this disorder struck me, I regularly walked six laps around the park at the end of our block. Although fatigue prevented me from continuing this routine, I managed to get in a few laps from time to time. I never knew how many, losing count despite memory tricks.

Many walks never commenced because I couldn't find the front door key to lock the house behind me. After checking the mail one afternoon, I noticed the key, still in the door from the last walk. *Oops. Wonder how long that's been there. Glad we live in a safe neighborhood.*

Problem solving in its simplest form challenged me. I guessed at which side to put the stamp on an envelope. One morning I stuck my cup under the water dispenser on the refrigerator door. Water spilled everywhere. I tried again, with the same results. So this time I leaned over, making sure the cup lined up directly under the dispenser. Same thing, except with water sprayed across my face. *Maybe it's broken?* After about five attempts and a puddle around my feet, I realized the cup was upside down. *How can I perform my job if I can't even fill a cup of water?*

Chapter 12: Mirror, Mirror On the Wall

March 13, 2008 Journal Entry

How can I be discussing such traumatic events in therapy, yet feel numb? I feel few feelings. My mind seems vacant, as if detached. However, when I look in the mirror, I look so sad, like my emotions are worn physically, but no longer internally.

March 18, 2008

"Wanna hear something weird?" I asked Angela.

"You and weird go together."

"Thanks, B," I told Angela, using my favorite nickname for her. Short for 'bitch.'

"So try me."

"I get so confused."

"It's been that way since you were born, Beck. Nothing's new."

I paused, waiting for any remaining jabs. I pictured her driving to work, with rotting banana peels on the floorboard and empty water bottles rolling in mass with each turn.

"So this morning, when I finished fixing my hair, I turned around with my back to the mirror. I just stood there, knowing when I finished my hair, I was supposed to turn around."

"Yeah?"

"But I didn't know *why*. I studied the items on the lavatory, eliminating each item I had already used."

I laughed, allowing her to see humor in it.

"When I saw the handheld mirror, I realized it was to look at the back of my hair. But I couldn't figure out how to use it. I looked like a cat chasing its tail."

"That *is* weird. But we expect stuff like that from you."

"Funny."

Whether important or mundane, routines confused me. *Maybe Dr. Complacent was right.* I pictured the cowlicks on the back of my head, horrified as I imagined the divots in my hair after weeks of ignoring the back of my head.

March 19, 2008

I fretted over our decision to cancel our long-awaited trip to D.C. with Cole and my parents over Spring Break due to my health issues. Every-other-weekend parents get a raw deal. We can't make up for lost time. I felt ashamed of forfeiting the trip just because I needed to sleep. I felt like I was letting everyone down. My mom had been looking forward to Cole's fifth-grade Spring Break since he was 5 years old. This was the same age as the grade she taught, and she hosted annual D.C. trips. But I couldn't imagine traipsing around D.C. if I couldn't even walk around the block.

March 21, 2008

"Hi. This is Becky," I said.

Beeps sounded for each participant joining my conference call. My heart beat fast. *I have no business leading a call. I can't even hold thoughts in a cohesive fashion.* My eyes glanced through my notes, hoping to be able to keep up.

"Hey, Becky. How's the weather down in Big D today?" one of my clients asked.

"Itsh pretty shunny, ssssho I'm hopeful it'll be nishe today," I answered.

I silently reprimanded myself for getting my tongue twisted. Frustration seeped into my thoughts, throwing my confidence.

"We're in the teens, so I'm envious," my client said. His usual jovial tone sounded awkward.

What if they think I'm drinking cocktails at eight in the morning? Why else would I be slurring words? Anyone who's been to happy hour with me knows I enjoy a martini. I hope they don't think I've gotten out of hand. I felt like my reputation was at stake.

"Y'all seeing much of an ..." I started.

Stick? Click? Joystick?

"Much new business?" I finished, changing my sentence.

"We can't complain. Just signed a couple of new engagements. Hope to include your team in one of them," he said.

"Great. We appreshiate the conshideration."

Uptick! The word was 'uptick'! Have I completely lost it?

Another beep sounded.

"Hello? This is Deborah joining. Sorry if I'm late."

Deborah's voice relieved me, like finding my kid in a crowded mall after a brief disappearance. Although I was prepared, my fear rose. I second-guessed myself, afraid to slur more words or lose my train of thought.

"Deborah, why don't you give them the shtate of the market according to your view," I requested.

I avoided as many words as possible with an "s" in them.

"Uuuhhh, sure," Deborah said.

She sounded confused about why I was handing the meeting off to her on the fly. We tag-teamed quite well, however, usually we discussed who would lead and who would be the wingman in advance.

Deborah put on her customer voice, sounding cordial and professional, a stark contrast from her forceful internal tone. After living in London several years, she adopted an accent that sounded more British when there were clients on the line. I pictured her while she spoke, her brown eyes deep in thought with her hands waving expressively. Probably multi-tasking by responding to emails even while leading a discussion.

March 24, 2008 Journal Entry

Well, I guess I was right about Dr. Complacent. He thinks I'm neurotic. When I called to give his assistant the latest update, she told me that he really thought I'd benefit better from a psychologist and maybe I should go a different route. She sounded nervous, as if he'd told her that the next time I called, she should tell me not to call anymore. I was so humiliated. These symptoms are very real, but what if I'm crazy enough to bring them on?

March 26, 2008

The whirring sound of Gary's car needing an alignment distracted me on what seemed like our daily journey to a doctor's office. We parked and filed into the elevator as if clocking in for the day. Gary found his typical chair toward the back of the waiting room and pulled out his stack of crossword puzzles.

"What's a five-letter word for pop?" he asked, holding the paper in front of my face.

And even though I knew he intended to lighten the mood, to divert my attention from medical mysteries for only a moment, I pushed the paper out of my face.

"You know I can't think of words. Is this to ..."

Laminate. Amilate. Agitate. Hum. Hum.

"Humiliate me? Sorry to burst your bubble, but your wife is damaged goods."

"Burst! That's it. You got the word!"

I seethed. *How can he be so cheerful all the time? Can't he see I'm not the same wife he married?*

"Ms. Dennis?" the nurse called just before I caused a scene.

I followed her to the scale, which I hated for different reasons now. The pounds still dropped.

Dr. Welby greeted me warmly, like a long-time friend. Amid the chaos in my life, I welcomed his calming geniality. I returned his smile, suppressing my inner thoughts.

"Says you're back because you're still undergoing neurological phenomena," he said.

"Yes."

"And did you get any resolution or guidance from [Dr. Complacent]?"

He scrolled through the latest paperwork in my chart.

"Not really. He basically dismissed my problems as stress. There's no way this is stress."

I wanted to thrust myself to the floor and throw a temper tantrum. I wanted to plead for answers. Yet I remained professional, afraid he might agree with the stress theory.

Dr. Welby's friendly eyes met mine as if detecting my exasperation. I felt like a burden for presenting such peculiar symptoms. Even though Dr. Welby treated me with respect, I was afraid my manifestations weren't believable. I shied away from detail with the doctor I trusted the most.

"I'm sorry he treated you that way. I hope I don't give you that feeling."

"No, no. Never. He actually referred me to a *psychologist*. Basically said it was a complex migraine caused by stress."

"You know, I thought I was sending you to one of the area's best to begin with. Now I'm concerned about sending you down the same path you've been on."

"So what do you suggest?"

"There's a neurologist at MGH in Boston that I'd highly recommend, but of course there's a cost associated with that, with no promise of getting any further conclusion than what you've already gotten."

"Options are good at this stage. I feel like I'm ticking ... unsure when I'll explode."

My lips tightened from anxiety. Gary calls these my "business lips" because they disappear under stress. Dr. Welby crossed his legs, seeming to signal his willingness to hear me out.

"[Dr. Complacent] put the fear of God in me about another episode, then sent me out the door with no answers."

"I'm sorry."

"I sleep all the time. My face tingles. My right hand still has numbness. I'm ... "

Stop, Becky. Don't say anything about dropping words. You'll reinforce the 'crazy syndrome.'

"I'm just afraid of becoming like my grandmother. Stroke after stroke until I'm helpless."

"Hold on."

He left the exam room, returning with a profile of Dr. Martin Samuels, a highly regarded neurologist in Boston.

"You'll have to make the decision to go up there for yourself. I've seen him at conferences and he's considered leading edge. He may look at your case differently."

"K."

"I sense your frustration. I wish I had more answers for you, Becky."

"It's just that I'm so distracted by everything. I'm scared of it happening again and with more ..."

Sensitivity? Instantly? Serendipity?

Dr. Welby waited patiently. Concern consumed his face.

"Intensity."

My fear boiled deep like lava within a volcano.

The Boston doctor's profile picture stared back at me, thick eyebrows and a pleasant smile that made him look like someone you'd want to be friends with. His photo seemed to promote confidence without arrogance. I tried reading through his credentials. MGH. Harvard. Brigham. American Academy of Neurology. My muddled mind rejected any further reading, too tired for more information.

Gary abandoned his remaining crossword blanks, removing his reading glasses as he jumped up in the waiting room. He grabbed his phone and hat, which sat by his car keys to remind him of his belongings. He has a system for everything. Never loses a thing, dang him.

"Well?"

"He gave me a referral."

"When do we go?"

"He's in Boston."

"Boston?"

"Yep."

"You gonna go?"

"Dunno. I trust his judgment, but we live in such a huge metro. There's bound to be other good doctors in Dallas."

"You'd think."

I thought through my options.

"Let's book it," Gary said.

"I'm gonna sleep on it. Like he said, no promise of resolution."

"Whatever you wanna do, Girlfriend."

April 3, 2008

"Hey, did you get my voice mail?" said Angela.

"I got it but haven't listened to it," I said. "What's it say?"

"You're just not going to listen to it?"

"Leave shorter messages."

Angela left two-minute voice mails all the time. She sounded so conversational that sometimes I responded, forgetting it was a recorded monologue.

"Are you coming this weekend or not?" she asked.

"Dunno. Up to Gary. He has to drive Little Miss Daisy here."

"Any new stories?"

"Ah. Today was hilarious. I sprayed my hair, but the more I sprayed, the more limp it got."

"Did you remember to look in the mirror when you turned around."

"Yes, B."

"Good girl."

"So I couldn't understand why it got limp instead of firm. So I wetted it and started all over again. Same result. More spray, more limp."

"Is it time for new hair spray?"

"No. I was saturating my hair with *body* spray instead of *hair* spray."

"These are getting better over time."

"Visit me when I'm in the nursing home."

"You owe me dinners, then."

We laughed. Our Aunt Rosemary fought over the restaurant bill each time the waiter presented the check. She rationalized that each dinner meant a nursing home visit when she grew old since she didn't have kids of her own to visit her.

April 8, 2008 Journal Entry

I hosted an event in New York City with the rest of my leadership team today. Our CEO wanted me to take the group through the last few slides of his presentation, but my mind went blank. This was not like me. Normally I would not read bullets on a PowerPoint slide, but feeling as if my thoughts had otherwise dissolved, I had no other choice but to read the bullets. I was angry at my mind, desperate for some way to demand it to collect all of my thoughts and put them back in their proper place. I was extremely disappointed in myself. This was an opportunity to shine, but my prepared message disintegrated as I spoke.

And at lunch, one of my contacts arranged for me to sit with one of her executives. This was a great opportunity to position the company, but the tingling in my lips and across my face was so strong that I was distracted, fearful that I was about to have another episode. I couldn't form words, so I just sat there as if I knew nothing about the industry, feeling stupid. These were things I couldn't explain to anyone else.

I'm scared of losing my job. When asked how I am, I feel like I have to smile as if everything is normal since my issues aren't visible.

April 10, 2008

"I'm gladjur back, Girlfriend," Gary said, kissing me on the lips. "You sounded tired when we talked last night."

"Yep."

Gary grabbed my bags, depositing my briefcase in our office and throwing my suitcase on the bed so I could unpack. I was glad to be home, surrounded by Gary and the kitties. Looking forward to Cole coming home the next day. Henry played hard to get, punishing me for being away for a few days.

"How are you feeling?" Gary asked.

I stared ahead, too fatigued to feel anything. Yet glad to be home. Glad meant comfortable in my surroundings. Access to things that held value to me. But not excited, or thrilled. Not gratified or cheerful. I just felt like I existed now in a different place. One called home.

"Uh ... fine, I guess."

I wondered if Gary ever thought about leaving me. Or if I should just leave, sparing him the "in sickness" rather than health.

"I'm happy you're home. Henry missed you. He's been pacing all over me at night. I don't know how you can get any sleep with him in bed with us."

Henry strolled in, as if on cue. Although a skinny guy, Henry's long fur gave him an appearance of a large cat. His weight dwindled from 13 to 8 pounds, while his failing kidneys stole his beauty. His bones protruded. His once soft and groomed fur now appeared greasy. I dreaded losing him and I felt guilty every time I left the house.

"How was Henry while I was gone? Other than keeping you up?"

I collapsed on the bed, contorting my legs around the heavy luggage. Henry jumped on the bed, content I finally settled into one place. He snuggled into my arm, curled up with his back to my side, one arm propped over my arm. Although he closed his eyes, his ears followed our conversation, rotating like radar. He reveled being the center of attention.

"Pretty good. He threw up twice. I got his treatments done, but I had to chase him all over the house. Dang ya, Hank," Gary said. Henry opened one eye in acknowledgement, seemingly pleased.

I thought about asking about the mail, bills, any voice mails. But I didn't care.

"Talk to Cole while I was away?"

"Yep ..."

Gary lay down opposite me, propping his head up. He swirled his keys around one finger. Boots on, as always.

" ... said he wants crawfish this weekend. No surprise. Made all A's on his tests this week. No surprise. Disappointed because he got the part as Satan in the school play."

"Satan?"

"Yeah. It's more of an acting thing to music," he said. "No speaking parts but acting out a voice-over."

"Hmm. Doesn't sound like his kinda thing," I said.

"No. Said he'd tell you about it this weekend."

"I miss my kid."

Gary hoisted my suitcase off the bed, realizing I didn't feel up to unpacking. I appreciated his perceptiveness. Not waiting for me to have to ask. I hated asking him to do things I used to do myself: driving to appointments, picking up groceries, grilling, lifting heavy objects. The two things I hated most: 1) missing out on full weekend visits with Cole while my body forced me to sleep; 2) his picking up the wrong items at the grocery store. Generic fabric softener? Please.

Chapter 13: A Dose of Validation

April 26, 2008

"Gary, please pick up more ground turkey on your way home."

"I thought we had some."

"It's not good."

I cradled the phone with my shoulder as I dumped out the meat in the trash.

"Again?"

"Do you mind?"

My she-devil instincts never worked so well. *Just pick up the freakin' meat. I would go if I could drive.*

"Sure, sweetheart."

Liar. There's nothing sweet about me.

"And don't go to Albertsons. They don't have good meat anymore."

"Where would you like me to go, Dollface?"

"Tom Thumb."

"Anything else you need?"

"Nope. Just turkey meat. Get two pounds so we have another good one on hand."

"See you in 22 minutes."

Why does he do that? Is there a prize for calling the exact number of minutes it takes to get here?

I caught myself spiraling down. *This isn't me. I usually find it endearing that he specifies the minutes.*

Grocery bags littered the island. Gary pointed to the "packed on" date, showing me the new meat was packaged the same day. In typical Gary fashion, he picked up all sorts of other things, including Super Glue, batteries and a 24-pack of toilet tissue.

"You just got tissue last week."

"We can always use it."

"What is your obsession with toilet tissue?"

"Never goes bad."

He grinned, shaking me out of my funk. I pictured our bathroom, where he built a tower design from the large volume of toilet tissue rolls already on hand. I couldn't imagine where he was going to stash this new pack. He disappeared, I assumed to build his new tissue project.

Turkey sizzled in the pan. Garlic powder, chili powder, onion powder and oregano lined the countertop. I added each, stirring and browning the meat. No smell, so I added more. And more.

"Smells great, Girlfriend."

"No. This meat is bad, too."

"What? It smells awesome. I'm starving."

"I'm throwing it out."

"Why? Really. It smells great."

I hovered over the pan, inhaling deeply. Nothing.

"What do you smell, exactly?" I asked.

"Garlic mostly. How much did you put in?"

"More than usual. The meat seems to just absorb it. There's no smell."

Gary folded his arms across his belly, waiting for me to move away from the stove so he could load up his plate.

"You don't have to eat it, but I'm digging in," he said.

He scooped a healthy portion while I omitted the meat from my spaghetti. He "oohed and aahed" at the taste. I wondered if he was just trying to make me feel better about my cooking. I sat dumbfounded, not knowing if the meat was good. I didn't want him to pacify me by eating it.

April 28, 2008

"One of my colleagues handed me a Styrofoam cup at the office," I said.

"Yeah?" Angela replied.

"And you know I don't grasp very well with my right hand anymore."

"Right."

"I was afraid I'd drop it, so I clutched it tight enough to know I had a good grip on it."

"Uh huh."

"And I crushed it. The water went sloshing everywhere. Even though I was embarrassed, I just had to laugh."

"You have *man hands*."

Still, the image of my deteriorating grandmother continued to haunt me. *Is this all permanent?*

April 30, 2008

My optometrist's assistant smirked, waiting for my typical smart-ass comments. She sat upright with perfect posture, fingers laced together under her chin.

"Did you come in to give us grief or do you have a reason to be here just a couple of months after your checkup, Miss Becky?"

I wanted to joke, but as fear seeped in, I got that familiar urge to cry.

"I had a medical problem when I was overseas."

"Oh goodness. Are you okay?"

"I don't know. Kinda scary."

"Bless your heart. Here, have a seat. He's wrapping up with his last patient."

"Anything you can talk about?" she continued.

What do I say about my neurological weirdness? I feel ridiculous. Did I have a stroke or not?

"Well, I had a neurological episode while I was overseas, similar to a TIA or stroke."

"What? A stroke? You're so young!"

"Yeah ... "

"Oh my gosh. That must have been so scary."

She covered her mouth with her hands, the epitome of a Southern Belle. I found her adorable.

The optometrist himself came to get me, omitting normal office procedures.

"Hey, Sweetie. Come on back."

His voice softened and he abandoned our typical banter. He directed me to an exam room, where he closed the door. I felt like someone about to hear her own obituary.

"Hey, Beck. Let's talk."

He rubbed my arm, unconcerned with doctor-patient protocol. He pivoted on the round chair, seeming to anticipate grabbing me if I lost balance.

"N-k."

"Tell me what's going on."

His casual demeanor soothed me. He leaned in, interested. His grayish hair accentuated his blue eyes. His chin appeared as if someone pressed a finger in it for a few minutes, leaving a perfect dot indentation. *Serene. On all occasions. How can I be more like him? What I'd give to sound AND seem chilled at all times. I bet his kids confide in him more than in anyone else in his family.*

Dr. Serene talked to me as if we spoke daily. I wanted to crumble. He represented a safety net. My mind begged to tell him how difficult life had become. But I looked back at the situation with Dr. Complacent and became scared.

I explained the story of how the 'stroke' unfolded. He listened, taking notes and expressing empathy through his nods, hard blinks and slow head shakes.

"But the reason I'm here is that my vision blurs by about 4 p.m. every afternoon. I'm having some ocular migraines, as well."

"Those are both classic post-stroke symptoms, Beck."

Ugh. There it is again. So have I had one or not? Is this confirmation?

"Let's run a couple of tests to see what we're working with. Do you feel up to doing these now or are you already fatigued with the blurriness?"

"I'm good since it's morning. After about 4 p.m. I'm toast."

In the technology-equipped rooms that lined his office, Dr. Serene tested for early onset glaucoma and cataracts, among other eye diseases. Being a patient with near-sightedness and astigmatism, I never needed his scanning equipment to test the health of my retinas. But I trusted him, so I followed his tech to a small room where she conducted a visual field test and recorded a panoramic view of the back of the retina. I suspected nothing, so I sat in an examination chair, expecting to greet Dr. Serene just prior to being discharged. He walked in, wearing an expression that said 'bad news.'

"I see some changes in your visual field test," said Dr. Serene. "It seems your stroke or neurological event may have occurred in either the left parietal or temporal centers of the brain. Talk to me about your memory."

Validated. I don't want to have damage, but this is nonsense. Why can't anyone see what I deal with daily?!

"It stinks. I've had a hard time retaining even simple things since this occurred."

"Those same centers in the brain that control your vision also process your memory. Makes perfect sense."

"And my taste is messed up. I don't taste much, so I forget to eat. Gary has to remind me."

"Your taste is really coming from a change in your sense of smell. An olfactory dysfunction, which is damage caused by the stroke."

"Huh."

I felt a strange sense of relief from his explanations. Although the word 'stroke' scared me, it made more sense than stress or a migraine. I felt less deranged.

"What does your neurologist say?"

"I don't really have a neurologist I'm confident in. A friend of mine suffered a major stroke a couple of years ago and I'm going to go to her cardiologist for another opinion. Maybe he'll have more answers about the cause. That's what disturbs me most now."

"You're young, Beck. You deserve to know. To have answers ... Well, I know some in the area if you want a referral. If you don't like the path you're going down, come back to see me or just give me a call."

"Thanks, [Dr. Serene]. I really appreciate you helping me get a better understanding."

"Anytime, Beck. You just give me a call if you need anything and take care of yourself. Lots and lots of rest."

"Can't help from doing that."

When I reached the car, I just sat, not turning the key. Driving still scared me. I took short jaunts, not wanting to bother Gary for every two-mile trip.

I feel temporary. I need to live life fast ... knock things off the bucket list. Australia. Open my photography business. Build an amazing flower garden. I'll be danged if I'm completely disabled before doing the things I want and seeing the places I've always dreamed of seeing.

Chapter 14: Speak English

June 10, 2008

Commercials flickered across the screen as the theater came alive. Cole sat between Gary and me, sipping his root beer, sporting his 3-D glasses. I put mine on, feeling nerdy. Gary and I enjoyed a legitimate reason to view *Kung Fu Panda*, a nice break from adult realities and my illness. I dreaded the day when Cole no longer took an interest in animated films. Or when a chocolate shake didn't solve all his problems.

"We getting popcorn?" Cole asked.

"Ab-so-toot-ly!" I answered, initiating the 'Dennis handshake.'

We back-handed a high five, followed by a palmed slap, then pointed the finger gun at each other. *Gary has his moments of brilliance. He certainly did well when he made up this handshake.*

"I hope this is better than the last movie," Gary commented.

"You mean *Kingdom of the Crystal Skull*? The geriatric version of *Indiana Jones*?" Cole asked.

"Stop it! I love Harrison Ford. He's not old," I protested.

Gary and Cole locked eyes and laughed. I puckered my lower lip.

"You're in denial, Girlfriend," Gary said.

I crossed my arms and turned my back in defiance of their Ford bashing. They snickered.

Gary and Cole took turns knocking each other's elbows off the armrest. I rolled my eyes, invisible to them from the colored cardboard shades.

"Stop it!" Gary teased.

"You started it, Dad."

"No, you did."

"Dad!" Cole's voice sang, typical of a preteen.

"Am I going to have to separate you two?" I asked.

They "Dennis handshook" in the victory of forcing me to say my line.

Our server appeared with dinner-ruining amounts of popcorn. Disney's dreamlike melody rippled through the speakers, hushing the loud whispers. Vibrant fireworks burst around the Magic Kingdom, signaling previews on the way. Cole looked left and right, making sure we were paying attention.

First in the lineup: *Bedtime Stories* with Adam Sandler. When the trailer ended, our heads craned in search of a family vote. Thumbs up all around.

Second up: *Beverly Hills Chihuahua*. Halfway through the trailer, we gave it a thumbs-down in unison.

"I was afraid Dad would like that one," I whispered to Cole.

"Shut up. I can hear you," Gary said across Cole.

I grinned, celebrating the moment in silence. *That felt good. A glimpse of me. I haven't felt sassy for months.* Feeling "me" felt like I was fishing a gnat out of a glass of water. The closer I got to the feeling, the more I seemed to push it away.

Journey to the Center of Earth rushed from scene to scene. Rocks crumbling. People falling. Dinosaurs chasing. Venus flytraps biting. Sound boomed in my ears. I squinted, trying to filter the amount of information coming toward me. My head pounded in response to all the stimuli. My eyes closed, hiding behind the blue and red cellophane lenses.

"Well?" Cole asked as the screen darkened.

I gazed their way, blinking hard. Cole's thumb up. Gary's down. I hated being the tie breaker. I hesitated.

"Comes out in just a couple of weeks," Cole said. He scooted to the edge of his seat, plunging his hand into the popcorn.

Maybe I'll be better by then. Too much for me now.

About half-way through *Kung Fu Panda,* I noticed the guys' fingers on autopilot, dipping into the popcorn. Yanking their hands back when they grazed each other.

" ... will never fulfill his destiny ...," Grand Master Ooogway, a turtle, predicted in the *Kung Fu Panda* movie.

A mom hushed her young son. He cried, loud enough to compete with the theater's speakers. I squeezed my eyes shut for a moment, as if trying to reboot.

" ... but a peach cannot defeat ..." Master Shifu replied.

Hmmph. Usually kid movies are easy. But I'm lost.

"We are noodle folk. Broth runs through our veins," said Mr. Ping, the adoptive father.

Cole's head snapped my direction, smiling. He fist-bumped me. *Ahh. His new phrase for the week. I need to try to retain it.* I matched his grin, admiring him, reflecting on how easy it is for him to memorize all the lines in a movie. Even with just one viewing.

Noodle folk. Broth through veins. Noodle folk. Broth through veins. Noodle folk ...

June 12 Journal Entry

I feel a heap of emotions just beneath the surface. Inaccessible to me. Not sure if they'll haunt or console me. It's like I'm lying on my back in the grass. Staring at distant stars and then trying to shoot them. I'm pointing in the right direction but they're so far away I can't reach them. Yet they're so visible on a clear night that I feel I should be able to aim at them and remove them one by one. I need visibility and distance to make this go away.

For days now I've felt like I'm going to explode. I'm a 4th of July fireworks stage. Ready to be lit, but not yet on fire. There's an energy building up inside me that I can't explain. I want to feel my pain out loud. I'm in chains without a key to unlock them. I want out!

June 15, 2008

Moisturizer, body spray, deodorant, powder, mousse, cosmetics and hair spray lined my bathroom sink in the order of how I applied them. If the product missed the morning lineup, it also missed being applied.

Gary's process improvement habits rubbed off on me, helping me adjust to daily routines. My pills, which I counted out on Sundays into a daily container, sat on top of my cosmetics to prevent being overlooked. As soon as I touched them, I stopped on the spot to take them. I replenished pills the same time each week to help me determine if I'd skipped a day.

Delinquency notices filled our mailbox for the first time. I lost track of a task as easy to remember as brushing my teeth. I felt humiliated. *It's not that we don't have the money to pay the bills. I just can't remember if I've paid them or even received them. How did I used to do this?*

June 17, 2008

I sat in silence, alone in the new patient room of a new neurologist. After a few Web searches, I selected this doctor because he was closer to our home and I thought that since he was about 15 years younger than Dr. Complacent, he might have a different perspective.

My eyes rested as I sat on the scratchy paper. The doctor knocked while entering the room. *Why bother knocking if you're already entering?*

Sitting erect, the doctor scanned my chart without a greeting. *Hello. Patient in the room. I'm conscious.* I thought silence might help him focus on my health history. So I sat in silence, watching him. I wondered if he didn't shake my hand because he was a germophobe. *Yep. Probably so much of one that he covers the toilet seat after his own family.*

His long crooked nose twitched while he studied my charts, distracting me. I wondered if mine did that. His punk hair suggested a Hollywood movie star. I imagined a role for him as a professor. But the nose twitch came straight from a Hanna-Barbera cartoon.

Focus, Becky.

Dr. Studious scanned the volumes of reports and MRIs. I studied the art: bold colors with thin stripes. It repulsed my eyes. *Ouch. I can't do stripes anymore. Maybe this shouldn't be hanging in a doctor's office.*

Dr. Studious took a deep breath, indicating a conclusion on the horizon. I sat up straight, ready for an explanation.

"Hi. Sorry for the wait, Rebecca," he said, extending his hand.

"Hi. I go by 'Becky,' unless I'm in trouble."

"And the reason for your visit?"

Reason. Reason. Visit.

"Uh .. yeah. I had a ..."

Stroke? Complex migraine? Panic episode? How do I fill in the blank?

"... neurological event a few months ago and am still having issues, trying to figure out exactly what the cause is."

Issues? How about 'I'm screwed in the head now?' I can't function like a normal person. Everything I do is with tremendous effort!

"I see."

His nose twitched enough to bat away a fly. I felt my own nose in lock-down mode in hopes of not mimicking his.

"One of the doctors thought it was a TIA or stroke, but then determined it might be a complex migraine."

"Yes. I see that in the notes."

Long pause. More twitching. I wanted to reach across and rub his nose in case that might stop it. Maybe he didn't want to offend his patients by touching himself. I imagined Gary in a crude moment: "Scratch it if it itches. Even in your britches."

"I don't think a complex migraine is plausible because it exceeds the duration of a migraine," Dr. Studious began.

I nodded. *So we can agree Dr. Complacent is an idiot.*

"You're still experiencing symptoms after two months, so it definitely rules it out."

"Okay."

"Although the MRIs show abnormalities, there isn't a large mass affected that's indicative of a major stroke."

He provided a few theories, suggesting that mini-strokes were still up for grabs as a verdict. My mental capacity felt overloaded, so I only caught segments of his theories.

He suggested a clot may have bled out on its own. My family history concerned him. He spoke at length about the left parietal lobe being affected because of the unexplained numbness.

"What should I do if I have another episode?"

"Get to the nearest hospital as fast as you can."

What?! I thought I was getting an explanation. You mean I have to continue living in fear?

"Have all of your history documented, including medications. Have a couple of people who know your situation always on standby."

"So you think I'm in danger of this happening again?"

I became just as frightened as my first appointment with Dr. Complacent.

"Well, I don't think it's a migraine at all."

My heart sank.

"Although your MRI doesn't look like a stroke, your experience in Asia and some of the symptoms certainly point to one. I'd suggest playing it safe with the adult dosage of aspirin. Get rest. Eat well. Avoid caffeine."

"That's it? I haven't had caffeine in 17 years. I'm allergic to it. Is there any other explanation?"

Talking, talking. I had a hard time processing his words. I would have brought Gary to this appointment to help me decipher it all, but I still fumed from his comments in Dr. Complacent's office.

" ... reduced blood supply to your brain ..."

I'm not getting this.

" ... critical blood chemicals are out of balance ..."

So I did have a stroke?

" ... arteriovenous malformations ..."

Please talk in English. I can't understand.

He never examined me. I sat there, untouched, a useless clearance item at a five and dime.

On departure, I didn't feel connected. I felt twitched. No clear path for next steps. He seemed to simply fulfill the "second opinion" role, offering nothing further. *So it's a maybe stroke.* Fear crept back into my consciousness.

June 19, 2008

"Got a new one for ya," I told Angela.

"Shoot."

"I took my laptop into the kitchen to sit at the table and work while I boiled eggs."

"K."

"My thought process was that if I sat in the kitchen, then I'd remember that I was boiling eggs so I could monitor them."

"Uh huh."

"Some time later, I wondered why in the world I was sitting at the table when all my work stuff was in my office. So I got up and went back to my office."

"Uh oh."

"About 30 minutes later, I was sitting in my office when I heard a loud racket, followed by lots of clanging."

Angela laughed slightly.

"Scared that someone had broken in during the middle of the day, I panicked. I swallowed hard, scared for my life. I debated between calling 911 or grabbing my pistol."

"No!"

I told her how I followed the cats' eyes that darted back and forth between me and the kitchen. I slowly tiptoed toward the kitchen, but the cats seemed inquisitive instead of scared. Their demeanor calmed me, encouraging me to abandon the pistol idea.

When I reached the kitchen, there was an open flame with nothing on it. A dent in the ceiling marked where the lid to the pot shot in the air from the pressure of the eggs exploding. The pot was on the floor, caked with detonated eggs. Black shells lined the kitchen island and white egg remains splattered across the floor, cabinets, stovetop and even the lights above.

"You're kidding!"

"No. I felt so dense."

"You mean you had no recollection of boiling the eggs?"

"Not until I saw the mess."

"But you had a strategy in place to remember the eggs. The clanging noises didn't tip you?"

"Nope. This is my world since all this started."

June 20, 2008 Journal Entry

I work so hard at concealing how difficult everything is now. I can't concentrate. Everything seems to take double the effort than before.

June 22, 2008

Without conclusive answers, my search continued. I remembered Rhonda, my account executive from a previous employer. Roughly my age, Rhonda suffered a debilitating stroke a couple of years prior. Her speech, walking and movement in one hand were significantly impacted. I dialed her.

"You had a stroke?" Rhonda asked.

"Well, I have doctors in different camps. I don't know, to tell you the truth."

"Can you describe what happened?"

As I chronicled the experience and my lingering symptoms, it helped me gain more clarity about what was happening to me. Food no longer interested me. I was just figuring out why.

As I talked about memory loss, Rhonda quipped, "Yep. That's a real bitch. You think you're following along really well with something and when the person stops talking for you to respond, you're just standing there feeling stupid, not being able to recall anything."

"Exactly!" I said.

I felt relieved in an odd way to identify with someone else who had lived through a similar tragedy.

"My old band director would call it 'Standing there with your teeth in your mouth,'" I told her.

She laughed, urging me to continue describing my experience. I told her about my odd variety of symptoms, including periods of disorientation and confusion.

"What about fatigue?" Rhonda asked.

"I sleep as much as 16 hours on bad days," I told her.

"I don't recall needing naps, but that seems to be the only major difference other than the severity of my situation," she said.

Rhonda required extensive speech and physical therapy after her stroke, having to relearn to walk and talk. I was thankful my condition wasn't as grave, but it seemed every day I noticed more symptoms.

At the end of my lengthy description, she highly recommended her surgeon, about 30 miles away.

June 23, 2008 Journal Entry

There's an energy building up inside me I can't explain. I feel like my emotions are going to ignite. They sit beneath the surface, not quite detectable. I feel needy and dependent. I just want to be me again.

Chapter 15: A Sense of Normalcy

June 24, 2008

"Are you losing more weight, Becky?" my therapist asked.

I stared at the carpet, with its tightly woven maroon and black threads. The design reminded me of the diagonal pattern I programmed on my Commodore 64 in junior high. A looping program that repeated the letter "H" in wavy lines. High-tech stuff.

I considered my therapist's question. I could tell him what I thought he wanted to hear: I'm working out, eating right, watching my weight. But I wasn't trying. I couldn't even walk around the block without passing out. The pounds flew off me. Not that I minded going from a tight size 12 to a loose 6. But I wanted an explanation. Without one, I felt embarrassed. What if Dr. Calm and Dr. Complacent were right? What if the symptoms were psychosomatic? I bounced back and forth, even with the new neurologist's and optometrist's assessments.

My therapist crossed his legs. He lowered his head slightly, as if encouraging my answer. I felt his eyes looking at me while I debated internally. His patience reminded me of James, my next-door neighbor from childhood, a man I considered a second dad. Always pleasant. I pictured James and my dad working on a "15-minute project" that lasted three hours. Like fixing a ceiling fan. Or finding the source of an oil leak.

James' patience increased with time. So did his jokes.

"Yes. I'm losing weight," I finally answered.

"I can tell," Dr. James said, studying my face to discern if this was good or bad.

I'm paying him to help me be more honest with myself. So why do I feel the need to sugarcoat my health issue with him, of all people?

My embarrassment won. I was afraid he might consider me a nut case given my wishy-washy diagnosis. So I fought to maintain normalcy despite being trapped in a constant fog. *I need him on my side if I'm going to finally let go of my demons. And fast ... in case death is imminent.*

I didn't elaborate.

For the previous three years, I told jokes and provided printed cartoons to entertain Dr. James, 50-ish with salt-and-pepper hair and thin-rimmed glasses that conveyed intellect. When he introduced a serious topic, I responded with one-liners and irreverent stories about my career. Sometimes I cancelled appointments, not returning for months. But I kept going back, uncertain why or if I'd finally "go there."

My closet undoubtedly contained skeletons, but I deemed that door inoperable. On the rare occasions I opened up, he asked, "And how does that make you feel?"

"I don't know."

"Try to associate with a feeling."

"Uh ... "

"It's okay. Take your time."

I tapped my foot and crossed my arms. My eyes bounced from books to a VCR to a Freud action figure to a stray nail on the pale gray wall.

"I've got nothing."

"Does it make you sad? Angry? Disappointed?"

"I don't know."

If graded, I was flunking therapy.

He had encouraged me to journal, even if I didn't think what I jotted down meant anything. So I did, feeling like a little girl filling a puffy pink notebook with secrets.

My pen rested on the page, asking my brain for something profound to say. I closed the journal. The next day, I'd write a paragraph, then close it, feeling like I checked a box for the day.

After a few months, I looked forward to the evenings, where I retreated to see what was really on my mind. My pen took the lead. I reread it later to see what my pen thought. I learned that my heart hurt.

That I still grieved the tragic deaths of childhood friends. That I mourned for never having a child of my own. And that I raged from the injustices of the rape and toxic marriage. And I discovered my critical internal voice beat me up more than a group of cruel-minded junior high schoolers picking on the ugly fat girl.

What I didn't know was that with each wisecrack, a sense of trust grew between my therapist and me, making me ripe for respite from my silent rage.

"Becky, if you were falling, what direction do you think you'd fall?"

"Up."

He sighed heavily, adjusting his glasses, seeming to decide if he should smile or throw his hands in the air. I loved it when I achieved that.

"I ask a bullshit question, you give me a bullshit answer. Fair enough."

Funny. James would have responded the same way.

Without Gary in the room to blame, I felt naked. Nowhere to hide. *Didn't we find this guy because of marriage issues? I'm not sure why I'm here alone.*

Work woes filled the hour. My angst over having to lay off highly qualified employees ... people ... friends ... packed several sessions. When my career catastrophes and jokes subsided, I sat there helpless.

"Becky, do you mind picking something out of your journal to read to me?"

"Uh ... sure."

"It doesn't matter what it is. It's up to you. Doesn't have to be highly personal. Just pick something that has meaning to you."

When Dr. James wanted to get serious, he exaggerated a shift in his chair. Always to the right. He lowered his voice, becoming raspy. His speech slowed when touching a delicate topic. His eyes squinted ever so slightly. My belly ached in response.

I thumbed through the pages. *Sex moment with Gary? No! Fear of losing Henry? Maybe. But that might be too sappy. He might think I'm a weirdo if I'm so absorbed by the fear of losing my cat.*

"Okay. I've got something."

"Great. Read it slowly and with as much emotion as possible."

I exhaled. Tapped my foot a few more times. Strained to look at the clock. *I hate it when he puts the clock just outside my peripheral vision.*

And I read ...

I took Cole to my grandparents' house today. They died when I was in my teens, so it's been years since they actually lived there. But they had the best trees for climbing - magnolia trees. We went to the house and I knocked on the door to ask if he could climb their trees. The lady was very nice and eager to let Cole go up.

I asked Cole if he was ready to leave and he called me over to the tree. He said, "Becky, I think you need to climb this tree before we leave." I paused briefly. For that split second, I thought of how ridiculous it was for a nearly 40-year-old to be in a tree and wondered what the current owner might think.

I felt Dr. James' eyes inspecting me for a hint of emotion. I avoided looking up. I hated silence, so I grinned.

"Just wait, Becky. Try to resist saying anything funny for a moment. Try to feel what you just read."

My heart fluttered.

"Are you feeling anything?"

"I don't know."

"Tell me what that passage means to you."

My voice cracked. I could feel a lump growing. I chugged some water and tried to clear my throat.

"I'm afraid of dying. I feel like my time is limited. I want to see my kid grow up. And it touched my heart that he was perceptive enough to see meaning in my climbing that tree."

"Good ... good for you."

A moment passed. White noise seeped in from just outside the door. The lamp flickered. I tried waiting him out, but the silence screamed for me to speak.

"For what? Being a lunatic Jack in the Box who doesn't know when she's going to pop?" I asked.

"No. For recognizing the meaning. You admitted you're scared. That's a big step, and you're clearly feeling it at this moment."

His facial expressions matched the sadness and disappointment that I denied.

"But I don't want to."

And that's what I did. I sidestepped any negative emotion to avoid the reality. To avoid the finality of what threatened disability, or worse, death. Yet the uncertainty nibbled at my self-doubt. *What if stress is causing all these things after all? I'll look like an idiot. But there's no way. I know something is wrong. Terribly wrong.*

Cole's observation of the tree-climbing moment sent me two directions. He detected something amiss, which prompted a growing fear in me. Yet his tenderheartedness touched me. I felt like a college football coach - thrilled for the win, but dreading the frigid Gatorade cooler over my back.

June 27, 2008 Journal Entry

Since the stroke, my emotions seem excruciatingly numb. I want to feel the happiness of how proud I am of Cole, of how comforting it is that Gary drives me everywhere and never complains. But I can't figure out how to muster up the right sensations associated with feelings. I feel a complete void.

I am less confident. I worry about being disabled. Since then, I have lost passion for hobbies that require greater concentration, like reading. I haven't finished a book since then, even though I usually read one a week before. I don't feel the same and I certainly am looking at life differently.

The more jokes I printed and brought to therapy, the more Dr. James anticipated my emotional avoidance. He read them, laughing heartily, his eyes checking my temperament like a concerned big brother.

"Becky, tell me something that made you feel angry this week."

Silence.

He knows I hate silence.

More silence. My agitation grew.

"I hate not driving. I've lost my independence."

"Tell me more about that."

Can't we just bullshit? That's far more enjoyable.

More silence. He waited me out.

"I don't feel comfortable driving, but I don't know why. Gary is having to drag me everywhere. It makes me frustrated."

"What do you feel when you feel frustrated?"

"Frustrated."

He cleared his throat, uncrossed his legs and faced me straight on.

"Becky, when you have to relinquish your driving abilities, do you feel angry? Sad? Like a disappointment? Helpless?"

"Yes."

"Which ones?"

"D. All of the above."

My toe tapped rapidly, shaking my leg. I sank deeper into the couch, bowing my head slightly.

"I see. So you feel helpless, sad, angry and that you're disappointing someone. Is that someone Gary?"

"I guess. He's the one who has to suffer."

"Is he suffering?"

Dr. James' eyes darted back and forth as if watching a ping-pong match in fast forward. I watched him, admiring his ability to listen while crafting a plan in his head.

"Well, I'm not able to drive myself. It's disrupting our lives. I drive here and there on short jaunts, but I'm tired all the time and my vision is off, so it's best that he drive."

"And you feel like you're a disappointment because Gary is driving you while you're recovering from the stroke?"

Stroke! There it is. Maybe he doesn't think I'm crazy. All along I haven't talked about it much because I don't want him in the same camp as Drs. Complacent and Calm.

"It's just such an inconvenience. He needs to be teaching a golf lesson or practicing for a tournament, but then I need him to drive me to yet another MRI or doctor appointment."

"Does that make you feel like a bother? Because he's helping you?"

"Sacrificing for me is more like it. I don't want to be a burden. I feel so temporary."

His questions continued to unravel my spool of health exasperation. My heart cried out to be discovered. To trust without the fear of judgment.

My foot shook violently, but I didn't realize this until I followed his eyes, fixated on my feet. I felt like paper maché, seemingly tough on the outside, fragile if poked.

Dr. James revealed the sadness and helplessness hiding behind my anger. The helplessness from my illness time-warped me into remembering previous helpless situations. *If I'm going to die at an early age, I have to let go of the demons.*

We plunged into deep waters, splashing my emotions up in the air. With shame rubbing its naughty finger as I spoke, I talked about the horrific details of the rape. I hinted at the injustices suffered during my "starter" marriage. And although relieved to be unburdened of these secrets, I dreaded their aftershocks.

July 3, 2008 Journal Entry

If I look back since the stroke, it's as if I sat among a pile of large rocks. The first one I was able to lift. I threw it as far as I could from shore into the water. As the ripples from that rock reached me landside, I examined what each of them meant - what caused the ripples, how long they lasted and how big they were when they reached shore. Once that one ripple subsided, I threw another and watched for the same effects.

Regardless if the rock was jagged-edged or round and seemingly soft, they churned up deep feelings. I'm tired of wondering what's wrong with me. Wondering if I'll ever get answers that make sense. The more rocks I throw in the water, I realize that I want ripples to lap at my feet, giving me a soft landing. I want to let go, no longer tormented by the unknowing or what caused the rocks to form in the first place.

July 22, 2008

As I sat in Dr. James' waiting room, my nerves fizzed like a shaken soda. After revealing so much in the last few sessions, I grew nervous about having to return to memories marked by tears and torment. To relax, I whistled Eagle's *Seven Bridges Road* and swapped one-line texts with Angela, laughing at some of our dad's quirky sayings.

"It's wake up and live time!" Angela texted, recalling how our dad threw the covers off of us to kick-start the day.

"Good gosh a mickey," I texted back.

"Well, I'll be John Brown," she shot back. I never understood what he meant, nor who John Brown was.

"Ooooooohhhh solo me-o. Cha cha cha!" I sent, laughing loudly as I pictured Dad with shaving cream all over his face and neck, peering around the bathroom door to make sure we heard him sing the only phrase of this song he knew.

"Sounds like a party in here," said Dr. James as he leaned against the doorjamb. He smiled as if wanting in on the joke.

I blushed, grabbing my purse and bottle of water.

"Hey there. Just exchanging texts with my sister while we laugh about our dad's peculiar sayings."

"Sounds fun."

"Yep."

"I've gotten good mileage out of your joke last week," he said.

I smiled. Maybe too big.

"Your proctologist called. They found your head," he repeated, slapping his leg, then clapping as he snickered.

This is a good start. This isn't so bad. What else do I have in my bag of tricks?

"Is there anything in particular you wanted to start with?" he asked.

"Nah. Can't think of anything," I told him.

"Makes sense. I didn't expect any more from you."

My head snapped in his direction. My eyes bugged out like Tweety taken by surprise. I noticed my mouth open and thought of Angela's opinion that my mouth is always open.

"What?" I asked.

He laughed cautiously to make sure I realized he was joking.

"Wow. You got me. Doctor: one. Patient: zero, but will get you back when you least expect it."

"Consider my guard up. Knowing you, I suspect a zinger will fly in at any moment."

But it won't. Where did that part of me go?

With a caring smile, he looked back at me as if he read my thoughts. He settled into his leather chair, rolling slightly toward me. I examined his pressed button-down shirt, wondering how his shirts stayed wrinkle-free, even toward the end of the day. He dramatized his effort to silence his phone. *I guess he wants me to follow suit since my AC/DC Back in Black ringtone interrupted us last week at an inopportune time.*

Then an uncomfortable silence settled in like a storm cloud, hovering, threatening. I avoided eye contact, scanning the wall as if a teleprompter might offer me some words.

"Tell me what your experience was last week," he began, his tone deep and low. The rasp told me he meant business.

"It was uncomfortable," I said.

"Can you elaborate?"

Deep breath. *Wait. I have jokes prepared.* My tapping foot gave away emotions that bubbled to the surface with his one question.

"I'm just tired of not knowing what's happening to me. I know I need to get out all the junk that haunts me, but I'm distracted by what's going on with me neurologically."

"Then let's start there."

"K."

More toe tapping. The tingle across my face surged, making me feel it was visible. I tried looking in his direction, but the thin stripes on his shirt hurt my head. I felt an ocular migraine coming on.

"Whenever you're ready. Take your time, Becky."

Pause.

"Something is wrong with my right hand, but I don't know what. I can't explain it. It feels numb on the inside and I can't type with my right hand without having to constantly fix typos. I slur words a lot. My head hurts. My hand is freezing."

"Can I feel your hand?"

My hand extended toward him. *This is awkward. We've never touched before.* I felt like I was doing something wrong. His boundaries clearly banned touch in any manner.

"Wow. It is cold," he replied as he clutched my hand on either side.

"Yep. One hundred percent of the time."

"And this has just been since the stroke?"

"Yes. Or whatever it was. I can't get any real answers. Doctors tell me the same thing. Same with my friend Rhonda, who had a major stroke."

"So you feel helpless?"

Why can't I just be pissed off? Why do I have to have a different feeling? I feel angry. Period.

"I guess ... Can I show you this joke?"

Chapter 16: The Race Is On

July 10, 2008

Rhonda's thoracic surgeon listened to me repeat my story in detail. His easygoing demeanor made him appear like a regular guy who had decided to throw on a doctor's coat. His athletic build showed that he found the time for physical fitness.

"Your story is quite different from Rhonda's," he said.

"I'm not here to rationalize how they are the same," I said.

I paused, coaching myself not to take offense. Still stung by the dismissive conclusions of Doctors Calm and Complacent, I felt my guard go up automatically when anyone challenged my story.

"I'm trying to determine whether I should keep searching for answers or if, in your expert opinion, you feel I'm out of the woods," I said.

He winced, clearly disturbed by my story.

"Let's keep searching. Something is definitely wrong here. Women your age at your level of physical fitness don't just have episodes like that if there isn't an underlying issue."

More validation I'm not ready to be locked in a pyscho ward.

"It's possible that you have a patent foramen ovale."

Patent. Wait. What about a patent?

"Come again?"

"A hole in the heart ... this is actually more common than people imagine."

"Oooh, K."

He seemed to smile to ease my concerns. I enjoyed how friendly he was, a nice change of pace. As fit as he was, I imagined him jogging, no headphones on so he could greet every person he passed.

"Unless they have a medical problem, most never know they even have this. But I'm thinking that a blood clot passed through this hole in the heart, potentially caused by a paradoxical embolism," Dr. Cordial said.

Blood clot. Blood clot. Something about a hole in the heart.

I shifted, becoming fidgety.

"I'm lost," I admitted, wanting to stay on track.

"In your story, I think the severe pain in your leg before flying is our suspect. Have you heard of deep vein thrombosis?"

"Yes."

"We're going to run a few tests to see if those two things came into play here."

"K."

"Another possibility is an arrhythmia-based problem or mural thrombus in the ventricle ..."

Slow down. Speak English. I have no clue what you're saying.

" ... but I'm leaning toward the hole in the heart and deep venous thrombosis. We're going to do a very careful cardiology workup."

His face flushed the more excited he got about my diagnosis possibilities.

"I don't understand what you said, but Rhonda trusts you immensely, so I'm going to take your word."

"Our number one priority is preventing another episode."

Oh shit!

"Is it possible to have another one?"

"Well, until we know what caused this, there is always the possibility. But try not to get consumed by that until we determine what it is. We're going to move fast."

Wait. It's possible to have another episode. But don't get worked up? Yeah, right. I couldn't wait for my next session with Dr. James.

Dr. Cordial ordered two more tests. First, a Doppler study of the lower extremities to check for blood clotting or phlebitis.

Doppler. Doppler. Isn't that a weather study?

"I'm also going to order a transesophogeal echocardiogram. It's also called a TEE," Dr. Cordial said.

I sighed, unable to keep up with the conversation.

"A TEE examines the heart from several angles to detect blood clots, masses and tumors in the heart ..."

I thought about my dad's mom, who loved her independence into her 80s. I thought about the day she turned over her car keys to my dad, deciding for herself it was time to quit driving. I admired her, wondering if I'd reached my limitations 40 years before she did.

" ... TEEs also identify congenital heart diseases or tears or valvular heart problems. I'm going to refer you to a cardiologist to conduct that test."

The questions didn't form. I accepted the course of action, feeling like he searched for more explanations than most of the others. *I like him. He's trying hard. New info! I'll try anything.*

July 25, 2008 Journal Entry

I'm so distracted by what happened to me. Now I have multiple doctors with multiple opinions: some think it's stroke, some migraine, and some just think I'm mental. Now I have a new doctor saying there could potentially be another incident. Scares me that it could happen again. I live in fear that if it happens again, it will be with greater intensity or consequence.

Each day, I reflected on my sweet grandmother who had stroke after stroke, remembering how sorry I felt for her. It was uncomfortable to be with someone so intelligent, only to have to remind her of words like "cup." She would go through an alphabet of names before she could recall mine. I didn't want to be my grandmother.

Chapter 17: Four-Letter Word

July 29, 2008

"[Dr. Cordial]'s office called," I told Gary as he walked in the kitchen.

I stood there, wondering why I was in the kitchen. Untouched *Newsweeks* and PGA magazines fanned across the island. Henry's puffy tail swept a table leg as if pointing to the kitty treats. Gary reached to turn on the lights.

"Why are you in the dark?"

"I don't know."

My eyes searched for hints. The light seemed too bright, so I turned it back off.

"So what did the doctor say?" Gary asked, flipping the light back on. I strained my eyes.

"They said they're happy to report that the leg scans came back normal."

"What does that mean?"

"Means we know nothing. So there must be a hole in the heart if the leg scan was normal."

"Sorry?"

"Cuz I have a hole? Or because we still don't know."

"Yes."

I pouted. Mad at the world. Henry did figure eights around my legs. His thin frame saddened me. I grabbed the treats.

"Anything I can do?" Gary asked.

"Make it all go away?"

"What exactly did they say?"

"That there was no evidence of an obstructing deep ..."

Minus. Minnows. Vinos.

" ... venous thrombus, whatever the heck he said."

"And that means?"

"Basically they said that given my symptoms and lack of cause, they strongly recommend I get a second opinion from a neurological perspective."

"Starting over again, huh?"

"Yep."

Gary approached me. I longed to have him embrace me, but I wanted him to make the first move. He got closer and made a silly face to cheer me up.

"I'd switch places with you if I could. I love my girlfriend," he said.

I crossed my arms, trying to listen while recalling the reason I stood near the fridge.

"I feel so helpless watching you go through all of this," he said, his voice cracking.

He reached for me. I uncrossed my arms and accepted his embrace.

"I don't know what to do for you. You don't deserve this. You talk about the time bomb feeling and how it impacts you. And I try to be strong for you, but I'm just as scared of losing my wife."

I looked at Henry, knowing I was losing him, too.

I repeated Gary's words in my head. "Just as scared of losing my wife." I tried to be in his shoes. Helpless. His wife melting away and he didn't have answers. He couldn't tell me if or when it would ever get better.

Forgiveness settled in for all of his shortcomings. Even when he slammed on the brakes after ignoring brake lights in front of him until the last minute. Or when he intentionally drove through mud puddles after my rare car washes. His hazel eyes reddened. From my five-foot-six perch, I stared straight into his goatee. I squeezed my arms around him, lacing my fingers, feeling the familiar coldness in my hands.

"Thanks for that. I don't bring up even half of what I'm going through. I feel completely different. Like I'm trapped in someone else's head ..."

He squeezed me tighter.

"I know," he said. And I knew he meant it. Felt it.

"... It's like ..." I choked. I paused, anticipating a cry that never materialized.

"... I'm partially vacant inside."

Henry circled my feet again. The closer Gary and I got to each other, the more jealous Henry became. For the last few months, he squeezed in between us at bedtime, intentionally separating us. I let go of Gary and scooped up Henry, resting him in my arms like a baby.

"I don't think you're vacant inside," Gary said, stroking Henry's head and my arm.

Henry's eyes batted at me. I felt like he tried to tell me things would be all right. I batted mine back. Not agreeing, but thanking him for standing by me.

"Not vacant, huh? That's the nicest thing you've ever said." I enjoyed finding my sarcasm more than I did finding words.

"I just don't see everything you feel is all. I see you sleep all the time. I see you struggle with words. I know you're ... "

I touched my head to Henry's.

"... You're perfect the way you are, even if you aren't as perfect as you want yourself to be."

I placed Henry squarely on the kitchen floor, looking around again for clues to my location. Unpaid bills sat on the table. I knew I'd missed due dates. Again.

I snuggled against Gary.

"I love you, Hubinator."

He chuckled, shifting me backward, then kissed the point of my nose.

"I know. Who could help from it?"

July 30, 2008 Journal Entry

Having an exploratory heart procedure done tomorrow. Stroke somewhat confirmed. Now looking to prevent future episodes. It's all too urgent. I'm not sleeping well.

I can't focus. My mind is everywhere. I feel bad when I can't remember things my family and friends tell me. I feel like a bad friend. As if what they say isn't important enough to me to retain. I'm embarrassed and ashamed when they ask, "Don't you remember? I told you last time we talked." Makes me want to isolate myself so I don't let anyone down.

July 31, 2008

The hospital staff welcomed me as if I had signed up for an expensive wine tasting. I looked around in hopes of that being an overlooked perk.

"Looks more like a hotel lobby than a hospital," I told Gary.

They directed us to a sitting area, where we settled into leather chairs plush enough to belong in an upscale home featured in a magazine. Minus their orange and avocado '70s colors.

"Yeah. And it lacks the usual pungent medical stench," he said.

Oh good. I figured it was my lack of smell.

Sun rays beamed down directly above as if someone shined a spotlight on me. I could imagine an announcement: "Here she is, ladies and gentlemen. The patient with no answers. She looks normal, folks, but she isn't. Today we find out if she's really a ticking bomb. Ready to go off at any second. We have quite a show for you today."

We retreated to our own worlds. Gary sifted through his stack of folded Lifestyle newspaper sections, all turned to the crossword puzzle. I thumbed through my Blackberry, trying to stay tuned in to work.

"Ms. Dennis?" a nurse called.

"That didn't take long," I told Gary.

I made my way to the nurse, hopeful to get answers. *It's not that I want a hole in my heart, but it sure would be good to get resolution.*

"Hi. My name is Dawn," she said, extending her hand.

Dawn's long black hair swept across her shoulder. She struck me as someone who put her family first and rarely did anything for herself.

"Ah! That'll be easy to remember ... that's my best friend from college. And she's also a surgical nurse."

Dawn. Dawn. Dawn. Dawn.

"Small world," she said. "You're Rebecca, right?"

"Only if I'm in trouble."

"Oh, I see. I'll be sure to call you Becky."

"Thanks. I'll try to fly right."

The nurse's stride doubled mine. I sprinted to catch her, feeling like I was catching up to grab her baton in a race. Raising my eyebrows, I glanced back at Gary. He shuffled behind us, not participating in the race. She paused every dozen steps, turning toward me, as if reeling me in.

As she dashed pass the nurses' station, she greeted everyone, not waiting for a reply. They all checked in with each other, rolling their eyes.

When I reached the room, the nurse stood inside the door, shaking the creases out of a crisp gown.

"I'm sorry, I've already forgotten your name," I confessed.

She frowned, the corner of her lip portraying pity.

"Dawn," she said softly. "Like your college roommate?"

I looked down. Ashamed of my failing memory. Saying nothing.

"After you change, have a seat in the hall and I have some paperwork for you to finish. Will your husband be keeping your personal items?" she asked.

"I don't really trust him with them. Is there a locker or something?" I jousted, trying to shake the temptation for my mood to sour.

"What?" she asked, her eyes dilating. Her head spun toward Gary for his reaction.

"Just kidding."

"I don't want her nasty stuff anyway. No telling where it's been," Gary piped up.

Her lower lip puckered. Her head turned away from us, studying us from the corner of her eye. Instead of handing me anything, she just tossed the gown and storage bag on the bed and left, pulling the door closed.

"Guess we confused her," I said, taking off my shirt.

"Yeah, baby. This is the best part."

"Shut up. We're in a hospital."

"Doesn't matter to me."

"Bite me."

"Where?"

I never did ask what they do if there is a hole in my heart. Or maybe they told me and I can't remember. Will they suddenly operate to repair it if they find one?

We sat in cold plastic chairs in the waiting room, me filling out what seemed like a second mortgage while fighting away goose bumps. Gary continued his crossword. I felt naked, the only one in a gown.

"When was my surgery to remove the ovary? Two or three years ago?"

"What's a four-letter word for numbskull?"

"Gary."

I win.

"Girlfriend! They better patch that hole fast. Maybe that'll take the mean out of you."

"Never."

I grinned, pleased with myself. I assumed answers were on the way, so it boosted my spirits. Gave me energy.

Dawn arrived to escort me to the procedure area.

"Any reservations about today's procedure?" she asked.

"None other than when happy hour starts."

"We'll try to get you out in time for that."

"Guess I'll go ahead with the procedure, then."

"Good idea."

Medical personnel scattered around the sterile room like a kindergarten class, everyone claiming their favorite toy, not paying anyone else attention. Dawn instructed me to stretch out on the surgical table.

What if I gag? I'm scared of the tube they say I have to swallow in order to get the probe into my esophagus.

A thin man stepped in with such a smooth face that I pictured him shaving multiple times a day. His hand extended as soon as he entered the room, as if he were eager to meet a celebrity. His deliberate pace and gentle expression comforted me among the chaos and hard table.

"Ms. Dennis, I'm Luke. I'm a chaplain here at Baylor."

"Hi," I said. More dryly than intended.

Is this when I admit I'm not right with God? When I say that my heart's in the right place, but I have too much baggage to claim that God's on my side? I believe, but please don't make me have to pray here and now. Just let me be.

"Do you have a living will or directive?" A low hum preceded his words.

"I have a will, but not a living will."

"We strongly recommend that all of our patients undergoing this procedure have a living will. You know, just in case."

"Hmmm. Guess we can do that."

"I can assist. I'll be right back." The hum again. Interesting.

Nurses and medical staff hustled around me. One of them asked all the please-don't-sue-us questions.

"Ms. Dennis, why are you here today?"

"Because the wind wasn't strong enough to fly a kite and I'm allergic to caffeine, so Starbucks was out."

"I see your sense of humor is intact."

"Glad someone does. Could you please tell my husband?"

"What procedure are you having done today?"

"They couldn't find a brain, so now they're hoping to at least find a heart."

"I need to get your medical history, including any procedures."

"How long do we have? This could take a while."

She recorded a list of procedures and health issues too long for someone my age. Right ovary removed, hip dislocation, heart palpitations, avascular necrosis in the hips, tendon sheath ganglion surgically removed, hysterectomy, knee surgery, gastritis as a child, perforated septum. *This is pathetic.*

Luke reappeared as I wrapped up my health monologue. His thin nose reminded me of my seventh grade English teacher. At any moment, he'd rub his nose as if scared that something might be dangling. Then check again. And again.

"You might want to keep this in a safe place and remember to bring it with you for future procedures," Luke said, holding out the living will.

"Oh, yeah. I look forward to those. Can't wait to get back here."

"Is there anything you'd like to discuss before they begin?"

"I've always wondered why I get the chair that doesn't work in conference rooms."

"I'm sorry?" His confusion humored me. A couple of the technicians paused, listening.

"Yes ... I seem to always get the chair that sits too high. Me ..."

Cavorting. Covering. Cowering. Towering!

"... towering above everyone else. My feet dangling in the air, unable to reach the floor. But I never can manage to operate the chair."

He grinned slightly, probably disappointed he drew the short straw for today's smartass.

"Afraid I can't help you with that one, Ms. ..."

He stared at the living will we just signed.

"... Dennis."

"Then I think I'm good."

"May I pray for you?"

For what? That I don't gag when they shove the scope down my throat? That I don't have another stroke during the procedure? That they find a hole in my heart?

"Sure," I resigned. My mom's voice rang in my head, calling for politeness.

As he prayed, I rewound to my pre-rape enthusiasm for church. Some of my best friends were ministers and youth directors. I wondered if that part of me might ever heal.

"Amen," Luke said.

"Thanks," I said, feeling embarrassed for my awkward response. Luke's eyes seemed to pity me. And not for my reason for being there.

"Tennis anyone?" I asked the medical team at large, enjoying my unconventional attitude. Regardless of being in a hospital, I felt more alive than I had since the episode. I found my long-lost friend, my sense of humor. It felt great.

Despite my attempts to stall, the technicians and nurses carried out their well-rehearsed duties. One hung the cardiac monitor on me. Another clipped a pulse oximeter to my finger and started an IV. One guy sprayed my throat with a local anesthetic for numbing before propelling the probe down my trachea. *That's just not natural. I don't even like swallowing pills.* But the most unattractive part was a mouth guard that seemed too big for the NFL's bulkiest player.

"This is for you to rest your teeth and protect the probe during the procedure," a nurse explained.

The cardiologist entered the procedure room. The congenial atmosphere shifted. A flipped switch. It reminded me of how elated I was the day I bought my convertible Miata. I sped down the highway until a bug so big it seemed prehistoric shattered on my arm, bursting into a million pieces across my face, shirt and driver's door.

My brief office visit the day before consisted of a co-pay and my telling my story one more time. The cardiologist offered no theories. His description of the procedure felt robotic.

His glasses struggled to reach his ears, accentuating his round face. They appeared as if they might spring off from the force of stretching. A crease in the middle of his forehead told me he constantly searched for his sense of humor.

"Your story yesterday was quite worrisome. I'm hopeful we'll get some answers for you today. Certainly sounds like a TIA or stroke," Dr. Deadpan said.

"Nnn. Hnn," I murmured through the mask.

Answers. I want answers.

"I agree with [Dr. Cordial]'s assessment. Let's get started. Any questions before we begin the TEE?" he asked.

I wondered how he could look at me so seriously while my mouth stretched out wide enough to fit three cue balls. The crease on his forehead expanded and constricted as he talked.

"You may hear swishing or gurgling during the procedure ..."

He paused, as if I might be able to force out words in response.

"... The sounds are your blood pumping through the heart. We're going to inject a liquid that's like 7-Up. If bubbles go through the heart, then we've detected the hole."

Great! Can we get started? I don't have a Steven Tyler-sized mouth here.

Anesthesia knocked me out. So quickly that I couldn't count to three.

Rhythmic beeping. Pressure on my arm. I opened one eye, shielding myself from full exposure to the light. Dr. Deadpan stood nearby, arms crossed.

"Take your time waking up," he said.

He seemed gentler than before. Almost like a dad. I felt bad for judging him too harshly before. The medical team had vacated the room. Off to the next patient.

The blood pressure monitor beeped again, squeezing my arm, then exhaling out its air. *Ah! No mouth guard. I can talk if I want to.*

Dr. Deadpan approached my bedside. I looked forward to knowing something. I imagined how expectant parents feel when learning the sex of their baby.

"We didn't find a hole," he said without emotion. As if he was telling me that my pen had fallen out of my purse.

Whoa. Wait. That's not possible. I must not have heard him right. No hole?

"You did *not*?"

"No," he said flatly.

"Uh ... is that a good thing?" I asked, knowing it wasn't. Knowing I still didn't have answers.

Dr. Deadpan stood over me. I felt powerless. Scared. *Where's Gary? Where's Dawn? Where's someone on my side?*

"Well, it doesn't explain [Dr. Cordial]'s theory."

"So I'm starting over again on the cause?"

"Right. There was no way we were going to find anything anyway. A stroke never has bilateral symptoms like you had."

And he walked away. Collecting his $6,100 procedure fee.

I lay there dumbfounded, steaming from paying a doctor who knew the outcome before the procedure. But did it anyway.

I felt failed by the medical system. Failed by God. Failed by life. And crazy. Scared to discuss the neurological phenomenon much further. *I don't think anyone believes me anymore. It's humiliating to talk about my symptoms without proof that anything is wrong. I don't know how much longer I can suffer in silence.*

June 30, 2008 Journal Entry

I'm scared of being disabled. And there are no answers. Why can't anyone tell me anything definitive?!?!

Chapter 18: Annoying Habits

August 1, 2008

The highway-side crawfish stands attracted long lines of locals from southern Oklahoma. Cutoff denim shorts, flip flops and tank tops signaled their weekend crustacean celebration. Most clung to their Coors Light Styrofoam coolers, stained from previous crawfish boils, while anticipating their turn to order. Masking tape carefully pieced the lids into country perfection. We passed the "Church of God Fireworks" trailer, a landmark that cracked us up every year. We joked that it needed to sit next door to the "Lutheran Liquor Store" and "Baptist Brothel."

"Are we going to Beaver's Bend?" Cole asked.

Going to Beaver's Bend. Beaver's Bend.

"You got it."

"Yes!"

His head raised as he tossed aside his Gameboy for the first time during our four-hour journey. *He misses out on so much. I used to want to know exactly where we were going. To look for wildlife. To see how people outside of Longview, Texas, lived.*

"How many years now?"

Years. I counted on my fingers.

"This makes your fifth year to be here."

"And yours?"

"Gosh, Cole. I think it might be 35 now."

"Wow. I hope I get to tell my kids that someday."

Gary and I stole a quick glance. We grinned. *We're doing something right.*

"Will we get to skip rocks and hunt for crawfish?"

Rocks. Crawfish.

"Of course."

"Shoot the BB gun?"

"Yep."

"Canoe?"

"Absolutely."

"Play Spite and Malice?"

"Only if you promise not to beat me again at my own card game."

"No way."

"You're such a mean-spirited kid."

I reached for his foot behind my seat, attacking him with "the claw." He loved it as a little kid when my hand formed a monster-looking claw that had a mind of its own. I'd argue with my hand, begging for it not to strike as he giggled and dodged. *I miss those days. I sure hope I'm around to see many more phases of his life.*

"Putt putt?"

Silence. My mind played back memories of my being at Beaver's Bend as a kid. I still remembered being small enough that Mom bathed me in the sink. And after the bath, Dad took me by the hands, placed my feet on top of his, and danced me around the cabin.

Tall pines lined the highway. Roadkill seemed like mile markers. I didn't want to look, but my eyes couldn't avoid seeing what they used to be.

"Putt putt?"

Gary patted my hand.

"He's asking you a question."

"Oh, sorry, Cole. What?"

"Can we play putt putt?"

"If we have time. Short visit this trip."

"Bummer. Jet ski?"

"Nah. We drug it up here just to make sure the trailer wheels still worked."

"Gosh, Girlfriend!" Gary finally piped up.

"What?"

"You can do that smarty pants stuff on me, but spare the kid, wouldja?"

"I don't mind, Dad."

Yes ... another glimpse of me. Too bad for them.

After dinner, Cole's eyes strained to stay open. He lost interest in our Trouble and Connect Four games, and when we suggested bedtime, he gratefully disappeared.

Gary retired to our bedroom, bummed that the cabin didn't have a TV. My book, the same one I'd been reading for six months, sat on the nightstand, daring me to pick it up. The story interested me, but my concentration allowed for only a couple of pages at a time. Gary grabbed a crossword and we retreated to our own worlds in silence for a while.

"Tired?"

"Not really," I said.

"Cole took his medicine, right?"

Medicine. Cole's medicine.

"Right."

I remembered!

Gary made a "T" sound. I rolled my eyes.

"You never put a 't' on the end of your words," he said.

"Why does that bother you so much?"

"Just pronounce it righ ... T."

"You do things that are annoying, too."

"Yeah? Like what?"

I started laughing, shaking my head to refuse what would be a losing game.

"Come on, try me. I bet you can't think of anything."

A harder laugh. I snuggled up to him, but his unclaimed challenge prevented him from being in the snuggle mood.

"Come on, just one."

"Okay, fine. But remember, you're the one who started it."

"Go ahead. I bet you can't do it."

"How about when you splash water on your clothes hanger titties as a shortcut to ironing?"

"That's not annoying."

"You asked. It is to *me*."

"Well what about you? You play music almost 100% of the time in every room in our house. Even the bathroom. That's annoying."

Game on. I learned how he noticed every little thing about me. How I was too lazy to remove toe nail polish, so just painted right over the dings and scratches. How I only knew a couple of lines of lyrics to any song, even my favorites. How each bite had to be a perfect combination of each ingredient on my plate. How it took me hours to pack for a two-day trip despite how frequently I traveled. How I don't replenish toilet paper rolls. And how I wouldn't eat the last bite on my plate, even if I liked it.

Silence wasn't an option. So I reciprocated, teasing about how he did a horrible British accent. How he tips generously, even for bad service. How he stood on our driveway at the alley for half an hour, squirting weed killer on weeds no one would ever see. How, instead of learning how to back a trailer, he backed it up sideways and then picked it up once it reached the water. And how his numerous pairs of reading glasses, all smeared with thumbprint fog, littered our house and cars.

Gary tried not to grin. His eyes looked surprised, as if he never knew I noticed those things. Silence dangled between us for just a moment and then we cracked up. Our shoulders shook and bladders strained. Snorts slipped out like unexpected gas. Whispers gave way to hearty cackles.

Unfamiliar cabin sounds silenced us momentarily as we listened to see if we'd woken up Cole. Gary checked the clock, pointing out that daylight was just a few hours away. I nestled into his side, fighting giggles, wide awake.

I turned over and flipped on my iPod. Kenny Loggins sang "And now I know my life has given me more than memories. Day by day. We can see in every moment there's a reason to carry on." *Interesting timing. I feel like I've been granted a stay during this little trip. I'm feeling more me.*

"See? You can't turn music off," he said.

"I'm not even remotely sleepy now. You don't appear to be either."

"So you just turn on the tunes?"

"Yep. Helps me wind down."

"And up."

I didn't respond. I was afraid that if we kept it going, I'd be cranky the next day. I wanted to be my best for Cole.

"You know what else is annoying about you?" Gary asked.

"Annoying? All the things you've cited about me so far are just cute little OCD tendencies."

"Same thing."

"No they're not."

"How you find a song in everything someone says."

So much for sleep.

"Everything is beautiful," I sang loudly.

"See?"

"In its own way ..."

Gary rolled his eyes and turned away from me, pulling the covers to his side of the bed. I pulled them back, starting a tug of war, giggling like a school girl.

"Shhh. You'll wake Cole," he said.

"Wake me up before you go-go. I don't even wanna go solo ..." I sang even more obnoxiously.

"And you don't know the words to any of the stuff you sing. Learn the words!"

I laughed harder.

"You know you like it. It's endearing," I said.

"Annoying."

"Endearing."

"Stop. You're killing me," he said, trying to be serious.

"Stop! In the name of love. Before I break your heart."

"It's 'before you break my heart.'"

Even though the clock read 2 a.m., our ribbing left us full of energy. Bugs kamikazeed into the screens, attracted to the faint light from our bedroom. The sheets twisted across our bed. I didn't want the night to end, even if I learned more of my nuances that supposedly annoyed him.

"Want some popcorn?" I asked, peering over Gary's shoulder, still turned away from me.

"Now?!"

"Yes."

I pouted, then raised my eyebrows, which involuntarily formed my dimples. He rolled onto his back, facing me again.

"My girlfriend. Popcorn. Two in the morning."

Yes!

"Think it'll wake Cole?" I asked.

"We're on vacation. If it does, we'll have a pajama party," he conceded.

"I love you."

"I know."

I raced into the kitchen to throw a bag in the microwave before he changed his mind. *I want this moment to last forever. I don't care if I'm not perfect. I'm alive. And he loves me. And I'm here with my kiddo. I just want to make the most out of everything I do from now on.*

The microwave counted down and I stopped it before its beep. My memory thrusted me into the kitchen as a child. My parents always hustled to our long-awaited first microwave to stop the cooking before the irritating end beep. Something about that alert prompted us to halt conversations, leap over butcher blocks, and suffer bad bruises to prevent it.

"You just had to have a crunch, didn't you?" Gary asked.

"What is it about a crunch that's so satisfying?"

"I don't know. Think it produces food endorphins?"

"Oooh. Endorphins. Now there's a ten-dollar word. I'm so proud of you."

"Shut up."

"Whatever."

Chapter 19: Phoning Home

September 10, 2008

"Hey, Sweetie. How's my baby feeling?" Mom asked. Her parents christened her Polly. They chose the perfect name.

My mother's biggest crime in life: being caught wearing white pants after Labor Day. If Ed McMahon showed up on her doorstep before she applied makeup or fixed her hair, I'm certain she'd just forfeit the money. Estee Lauder floats in the air of each room she exits. She over-thinks everyone else's sense of comfort, so she reseats us--regardless of which room, determined that everyone have the perfect view of the lake at my parents' lake house. No sun in the eyes. The right temperature. And of course, something to drink. Her worry doesn't stop at people. She once quit using her front door for a month to prevent disturbing a bird that made a nest in her perfect home-made wreath.

I pondered her question. If I answered truthfully, I'd break the family rule of feeling something other than happy. If I cherry-topped my response, I'd give in to the rule, denying my reality. Yet my parents called daily to check on symptoms, winning a prize for Best Worriers. Each call ended with, "You know, you should come here and see our doctor. He'd be happy to help if you'd just call him."

I pictured "here," my hometown of Longview, Texas. A town just shy of 80,000 people with a drag strip that attracted teens from even smaller area towns. One hour from Shreveport. Two from Dallas. And nothing to do but drive backward to see if it truly took miles off the odometer. Drivers of oncoming cars raised one finger off the steering wheel as a means of waving. Everyone knew everyone. And if you didn't yet, you would soon.

Longview claims a couple of entertainers: movie star Matthew McConaughey, and Duane Propes - bass guitarist for country music band's Little Texas. They were both friends and classmates from the '80s, when my frizzed hair resembled Jon Bon Jovi's.

I'd known the doctor my mom suggested since second grade, when his family moved in a few doors down. Their son just happened to be my age. The first time I met the dad, I noticed his dimples, then pretty eyes, then mustache. The order never changed. Well, maybe it was left dimple, then right dimple. He reminded me of Magnum P.I. with a smile that lit up his face and put me at ease.

To my family, Dr. Magnum seemed like the ultimate package deal: a family man, rancher, neighbor, vineyard producer and oh, by the way, a cardiologist.

Like a beaten-down teenager, I gave in to my mother's plea to call him. After spending countless afternoons in his home as a kid, I saw Dr. Magnum and his family as relatives. People who knew our warts and struggles, but loved us just the same. When we were kids, their son John and I instantly became friends. We rode bikes, swapped comics and played Missile Command on Atari.

As I dialed their home phone, I pictured Dr. Magnum's dark mustache, Elton John frames and receding hairline that, when combined, gave him a scholarly appearance. He was so reserved and soft-spoken that it seemed everyone else held megaphones. I felt the need to whisper around him. *I really hate to bother him. I'm sure he won't mind, but I feel ridiculous calling a cardiologist at home, even if he is a long-time friend of the family.*

He listened to my story, asking for every shred of detail I could remember. His soft tone challenged my hearing as he peppered me with questions. I pressed my cell phone deep into my ear.

"My chief complaint is that no one seems to know what the hell happened to me, therefore, no one can assure it won't happen again!"

I thought that if I sounded exasperated enough, someone might come to my rescue.

"I know you're frustrated, Becky. And you have a right to be."

Thank you! Amen!

"What you describe sounds like a stroke until you get to the bilateral weakness. A stroke is going to only affect one side."

"Okay."

I felt helplessness creeping in. I tried pushing it away.

"I know you don't want to go down a whole new path, but do you know if they've ruled out Multiple Sclerosis?"

Childhood flashbacks distracted me while he spoke: my Rubik's cube, displayed proudly on a shelf after solving it time after time. My baby-blue 10-speed that navigated a five-mile radius where I knew the streets better than any cop in town. *Gosh, I wish that bike had had an odometer.* Fried SPAM on the dinner plate. My tongue responding to the anticipated dangerous amounts of sodium.

"I don't remember MS being mentioned to date. If it has, I don't remember. My short-term memory disappeared overnight."

"Given the weakness and tingling, this seems like a credible diagnosis to check into. Do you want me to recommend some people for you to see there? Or do you want to come here for me to look into this?"

I pressed my lips firmly together in a half-ass attempt at a smile, as if he could see me through the phone. *He's kind to offer.*

"Uh ... I think I've got it from here. I was looking for a gut check. You've been very helpful."

And I don't think out-of-town doctor visits are viable. I'm missing enough work going from doctor to doctor, doing test after test. And the constant napping.

"I don't mind, Becky. Call me anytime."

"Thanks for your support, really."

As our call ended, I imagined bedtime as a child, singing Lawrence Welk's "Goodnight Song." My parents joining in with dancing, another flavor of happiness. Their fingers conducting as if tracing the pattern of flashing railroad lights. Then a belly laugh escaped as I pictured the framed photo I gave my dad at Christmas one year. A photo of Angela at her worst: mouth wide open, hair messed up and clueless expression. I recalled the bursts of laughter as my family passed the frame around, high-fiving me until it reached Angela.

October 18, 2008

When I woke, the bed was empty. Vacant of cats. Gary was long gone, running a golf tournament with a 6:30 a.m. shotgun start.

I looked out on the porch. Carson's and Trooper's tails swished as they watched a cardinal land on the swing. Their ears twitched as if being orchestrated. My stomach churned. *No Henry.*

When I reached the guest room, I saw Henry stretched out.

"Henry Boy," I whispered. "How's my sweet boy?"

He lay limp, in a puddle of urine.

Tears dripped down my face, a foreign, but welcomed, substance. My lips quivered. I could hear my heartbeat pounding in my eardrums.

"No. Not yet ..."

Henry's eyes opened, acknowledging me, yet he didn't have the energy to lift his head. I reflected on the day I got him. He walked out of the pet carrier, lay down on the carpet and propped his head up on a shoe. No sniffing. Not a hint of fear. Just chilled out.

Henry seemed to be aware of when I needed consoling. I found it amazing how much dignity a cat could convey. And in this moment, I knew he was ready. The saying was true. I cleaned him up and held him to me, choking on my tears, rocking him gently.

"I love you, Henry Boy. Thank you for holding on so long. You'll always be in my heart." And I let him go.

October 24, 2008 Journal Entry

After the disheartening TEE experience, the possibility of a whole new direction of MS and losing Henry, I can't handle doctors for a while. If it's MS, I'm not ready to know. I'll just live with the "time bomb" feeling.

I'll just follow the "back to happy" rule. I'll just keep all the manifestations to myself.

Chapter 20: Dangling Above Earth

October 2008

With my failing health, my "give a damn" finally broke. My employer still benefitted from my strong work ethic, but my choices changed. I quit looking at email after 7 p.m. Work stress quit dictating my moods. Phone calls to loved ones increased in frequency and duration.

After being grounded by doctors for six months, I itched to be in the air again, exploring the world. I needed out like a teenager locked in a car after a 10-hour family drive. I called Angela, my traveling companion.

"We gotta get outta here," I said.

"Yep. We're overdue."

I swallowed hard, wondering if this might be my last trip.

"Have the doctors signed off for you to travel again?"

"Domestically. Yes, but no one's really managing me closely anymore. Let's just go."

"Where to, Beck? Hawaii? Didn't you tell me it's on your bucket list?"

"The top of my list is hang gliding, followed by Australia ... but I could do Hawaii."

Just the thought of seeing Maui's coast, mountains and vegetation improved my spirits. I imagined the sights, eager to focus my camera on such a diverse terrain.

October 3, 2008

On our flight to Maui, I jotted a few notes in my journal.

I'm six hours into an eight-hour flight, a bit nervous that I may have another stroke or mini-stroke. I'm getting up a lot to stay active on the flight, as recommended. I'm so damn tired of the fear and conflicting information. I still don't understand how someone in my health, at my age, etc. can experience this.

I find myself working harder at overcoming language issues the more I'm aware of them. Will it always be this way? Why are there so few answers? I just want reassurance that I won't have another episode.

I'm so glad Gary didn't mind me vacating the daily stress of my health and going to Hawaii with Ange. I will miss him, but I'm so thankful for "sister time."

October 4, 2008

On the Road to Hana, a historic highway through the tropical Maui rainforest, waterfalls jetted from every hillside taller than a two-story building. This part of the island averaged more than 300 inches of annual rainfall. Ferns sprouted like weeds, turning everything a vibrant green. Roads followed beach lines until treacherous cliffs prevented even a simple footpath. The ocean below looked like a blue color palette. Black lava braced against tall breakers. Seagulls plunged into the water, kamikaze insects attracted to a bright light in the dark.

After months of being out of order, my sense of smell and taste returned at random moments. Some tastes didn't register at all. Things I loved no longer tasted good. Pungent, once-disgusting foods like blue cheese topped my new favorites list. I relished smells that most people abhorred – like creosote – because I detected their strong reek *and* associated them with the correct source. At this moment, I savored the familiar salty ocean aroma synonymous with the liberating feeling of being on vacation.

"My research said to plan on two-and-a-half hours for the drive," Angela said.

"K."

"Your endless need for Kodak moments have us at four hours, and we're not even half way there."

"I'll share the photos with you."

If anything, the 'stroke' seemed to ignite my right brain, including my passion for photography. I spent more money on expensive equipment. My home office looked more like a photographer's studio. I could also sightread music for the first time in my life. My band directors would have been so pleased if this part of my brain functioned back in my school days.

"Short hike?" Angela asked.

"Sure."

On the way to Puohokamoa Falls, we stopped to check out the rainbow eucalyptus trees. Banana trees dwarfed us. Sunbeams pierced through the vegetation. Fruits resembling red and yellow X-rays of a rib cage dangled from leaves. I snapped away at the unique foliage, despite Angela's weariness of my rapid-firing Canon.

"Oh my gosh! You've gotta see this," Angela yelled from the distance.

She stood still, staring into the sky. I followed her gaze.

"They're breathtaking," I finally said.

"It's like being in a Willy Wonka forest. The colors are amazing."

Eucalyptus trees soared 100 feet high. Yellows, greens, oranges and purples painted themselves up and down the smooth bark. Branches canopied near the top.

"It was definitely worth the walk," I said.

"You're worn out, aren't ya?"

I lowered my head and felt like sulking. *Here we are on vacation, surrounded by beauty and I need a nap.*

"It's all that photo taking," she said.

"Whatever."

"Let's head on. You can get a nap in the car."

"And miss out on stuff? I don't think so."

Angela drove. I moped, unable to control my declining mood from the fatigue.

Palm trees lined the beaches. Oncoming cars crossed one-lane bridges while we waited. Angela pulled over just beyond the bridge.

"What's up?" I asked

"We're stopping."

"But this isn't a scheduled stop."

"Now it is."

She handed me a corkscrew and a jacket and started toward the beach. Waves crashed against the lava rock. I followed, toting my camera bag, too paranoid to leave it behind. Large palms zig-zagged, dancers in the breeze. Angela threw her jacket in the sand and plopped down.

"Nap time," she said, smiling.

She popped the cork, prompting other travelers to crane their necks toward us. With no cups, we shared the bottle. I exhaled a long, deep breath and stretched out. *I don't care what others think of us. I really don't care if they think we're just a couple of winos. This is the life. Enjoying a bottle of wine on the beach under a tree with my lifelong best friend.*

"Thanks, B. Means a lot," I told Angela.

"Listen to the waves."

She understands me. Gets me. She knows I can't press any harder. I wanted to acknowledge her thoughtfulness, but the words didn't fit.

"I get so run down and I don't like to be the party pooper, so I don't say anything, but then I get grumpy," I said.

"You don't have to explain yourself. Stop talking."

Waves. Don't have to explain. I struggled to listen. Fatigue choked my thoughts.

Angela was the only person who could get away with saying this. From anyone else, I'd feel dismissed. Like they weren't taking me seriously or didn't care. I succumbed to the fatigue, drifting off to the constant swashes that teased our feet.

The next day, Angela woke me back at the hotel room.

"Sleep good?" she asked.

"Like a coma."

I lay there, trying to bookmark my dream so I could come back to it.

"Nervous about today?"

"If I'm honest. Yes. But I'm not backing out. It's high on my bucket list."

The ride up through the Kahikinui Forest tested my nerves as I glanced back down the mountainside with the ocean peering through the trees. We parked at the summit's bald spot.

Pilots spread out parachutes and harnesses. I stared at the treetops directly in front of us. *I'm about to run and jump off a perfectly good mountain.* My heart fluttered, a bee on the wrong side of the window, trying desperately to get out. The tingling intensified across my face, common now for high-stress situations.

"Yo. Isn't your pilot smoking weed over there?" Angela asked.

Pot Pilot eased his way over to me like a mellow cat wanting a stroke across the back. His hair curled like a messy blond version of Kenny G.

I snapped on my helmet. *If we don't make it, at least I was doing something I enjoyed before another stroke wiped me off the map.*

"It's going to seem strange, but all you really need to do is run down the mountain as fast as you can and as hard as you can," Pot Pilot yelled through the wind.

I studied the slope of the mountain.

"Whatever you do, don't stop running until you're in the air peddling like Lance Armstrong."

I resisted the temptation to ask if he really thought we'd clear those trees just in front of us. *He's a pilot. He must know what he's doing even if he's doped up.*

Pink flags shifted directions as a gust hit us in the face.

"Run!" he screamed.

A bolt of energy surged through my body as I ran down the mountain toward the treetops. The glider lifted into the air. Running became harder with the wind's resistance. Pot Pilot yelled to keep running, just short of swatting me like a horse in a tight race.

My feet pedaled the air.

"Hurry ... tuck your legs," he shouted.

Seconds later, Pot Pilot found a thermal and increased our altitude. A peace fell over me as I looked down at our 3,000-foot descent. My heart rhythm slowed as if he'd shared some of his toke. My worries sailed away with the wind. *This is a piece of Heaven. I'm living life and that's all that matters.*

"Stretch your legs out. You'll love the shot later with your feet dangling above earth," he said.

My hands clutched my pocket camera. I looked below at our car that looked like a Matchbox toy. I straightened my legs, and shot the photo, which is still one of my favorites today among the hundreds of thousands in my collection.

Over the coming days, we zip-lined 3,500 feet along eight cables throughout the lush valleys near Mount Kahalawai. Each zip frightened me as I tried playing back the instructions. *Twist left to go right? Touch the cable or not? Didn't he say something was dangerous? What was it?* Panoramic views distracted me from the landing platforms on each zip, twisting me into more crash landings. Angela enjoyed my lack of grace. I felt more alive by taking risks, wanting to "live it up" in case ...

On the last day of our trip, we finally made it out to our hotel's beachfront. The mountains provided a serene backdrop to the perpetual waves. A red sailboat drifted by, reminding me of a photo I took during our excursion across Lake Como in Switzerland.

"We can't leave without naming the photography business I'm opening when we get back," I said.

"You really gonna do it?"

"Yep. Been thinkin' about it all week."

With all my expensive equipment, a gallery on display, and friends constantly asking for me to shoot them, I decided I'd test this hobby gone wild.

"How about A Step in Time?" Angela offered.

"I like the 'time' aspect of it."

"Or Just Shoot Me?"

"Goes with my sense of humor," I said.

"Or something that suggests 'say cheese' or 'smile on three.'"

Three. Three. Three. Three.

"Oooh. I've got it ... On Three Photography."

"Yes. That's it. Glad I could help. I'll send you my bill."

"As soon as I've paid for this trip."

Chapter 21: Answers!

October 15, 2008

My blurry vision and ocular migraines persisted, prompting a visit back to my optometrist, Dr. Serene.

"Can you put your finger on the issue?" he asked. "Is it more than blurry vision as the day goes on?"

More blurry. Finger on the issue. More blurry. Finger on the issue.

I tried to imagine him in an angry situation. Someone breaking one of his basketball trophies. Getting cut off in traffic. Lost luggage after a grueling flight. Nothing. I could only hear his soothing voice assuring me he had my back.

"It's definitely more. I notice it mostly when I'm driving."

"You're driving now?"

"Yeah. Maybe I shouldn't, but it's such a burden on us for me to not drive."

"As long as you feel safe on the road."

"Mostly ..."

Pause.

"... When I'm in the left lane, which I always am, I feel like cars are coming into my lane as I pass them."

I didn't mention my urge to curse every car that I passed because I thought they were pulling into my lane. However, after several months, I knew they couldn't *all* be coming toward me.

"Let's repeat the visual field tests and I'll see you afterward," Dr. Serene said, lifting his chin and peering through the bottom of his lens. His signature move.

His assistant seated me in front of a machine. I leaned in, zeroing in on the center target. She handed me a handheld button. I thought about Gary. Always in search of a remote control to "see what else is on."

"Each time you see a light or flicker of movement, click the button. That's all you have to do. The computer will map and calculate your visual field," she said.

I envied her petite figure. She looked healthy. Happy. I felt withdrawn. Uncertain of what was next.

Dots darted. I clicked. Squiggly lines appeared. I clicked. Nothingness. *Maybe the test is over.* More dots. Less defined. I clicked. Nothingness. *The test that never ends.* A stray speck. *Hmmm ... not sure if it's click-worthy, but I'll click just in case it gets the test over faster.*

His assistant escorted me back to an exam room, where I sat, studying the two fingers on my right hand that stayed stuck together now like conjoined twins. They slowed my typing. They were the only physical sign of change.

Ten minutes later, Dr. Serene returned to my exam room, altering his tone to one appropriate for a bereaved spouse.

"Becky, your results show that you are blind in a quarter of your right eye."

What?!? That can't be right.

"You're kidding."

Uh oh. Karma for all those blind jokes.

"I wouldn't joke about something like that. It's called a right homonymous inferior quadrantanopia."

"A whatsa-topia?"

He repeated the medical term. I sat in disbelief.

"I couldn't have drawn it any better myself. Yours is a textbook case."

He pointed to an image on the printout, darkened in a quarter of the circle. He touched my shoulder gently.

"At least there's a clue to point to," I said, looking for resolution. I tried distracting myself from the feel of defeat. I thought of Cole's latest funny comment: "I want my last words to be ... 'I hid the million dollars ...'"

Dr. Serene cleared his throat, sat back in his chair and jutted out his thin chin. He tilted his head. His tone softened further.

"In the most simplest form, it's as if your right eye is missing vision from 3 o'clock to 6 o'clock."

The shaded image stared back at me, shaming me as if I received a poor school grade.

"Could I have missed a few clicks?"

"Not with this pattern. It's too telling."

Dammit! I want answers, but not reality.

"And that's why it appears cars are pulling into my lane?"

"Exactly ... Because the cars disappear on you, it probably feels like they've gotten closer than they really are."

I crossed my legs, grabbed my chin and looked to the ceiling.

"I can't believe I didn't figure this out earlier," I finally said.

"Don't be hard on yourself, Sweetie. You need lots of rest. With a stroke, it's no wonder you're fatigued and having vision issues. They're classic post-stroke symptoms, just like we talked about a few months ago."

I'm not crazy. He sees what I see. I felt so thankful someone else saw what I was dealing with. I felt closer to answers. Less crazy.

"So can I drive?" I asked, raising my shoulders to my ears and bracing for a 'no.'

"If you're comfortable and feel safe. You're going to have to be the judge. Be right back. I'm going to bring some books to help you understand what's happened in your brain."

I texted Gary: "Some answers. Will be late."

Dr. Serene returned with textbooks. He spent the next hour with me to help me understand more about the brain, the Circle of Willis, how the carotid arteries worked, and, based on the area of my blindness, from which parts of the brain my issues might be stemming. Great information ... except I couldn't retain most of it.

"Beck, you really need to be in the hands of a good neurologist," he said, tapping his finger on my charts.

I loved it when people felt close enough to me to just simply call me 'Beck.' This made me like him even more.

"I'm all ears if you can suggest one. I'm definitely ready to try someone else in that field."

"I'll call you in a couple of days. There's someone I have in mind, but I want to personally walk your chart over to him and give him your history and ..."

Gosh, he's nice. What doctor walks charts over and takes this much of an interest?

" ... I'll ask him to check the internal carotid artery in the optic chiasm."

Optic chiasm. Optic chiasm. Wait. I don't have to remember this if he's going to talk to the neuro himself.

Chapter 22: Swimming in an Exasperation Pool

November 5, 2008

A large-framed doctor greeted me, shaking my hand while making eye contact. He pulled back his frosted, receding hair with two fingers as if there were more there last time. His pleasant face and blue eyes cast a sense of familiarity. I pictured him bouncing a grandson on his knee, shutting out the rest of the world. No computer distracted him. *I like him already.*

"How can I help you?" he asked. His gentle tone neutralized his intimidating size. He must have played football back in his day. His bulky frame suggested offensive tackle. He leaned in and scratched his bare chin as if it sported a goatee.

"Well, I'm looking for answers. I believe [Dr. Serene] spoke with you on my behalf."

My knees bounced. My teeth bit the inside of my lip. I held my breath. *Please help me find answers.*

"So how many doctors have you seen before me?"

"You make 11."

"Well, from what [Dr. Serene] tells me, you've had a lot of struggles. Let's see if we can't get to the bottom of it."

"That would be ideal. I'm tired of wondering if it will happen again and if so, if it will be with more intensity, or even deadly."

He asked me to tell the story, so I embarked on the agonizing journey, starting with the disorientation, tingling and loss of ability to walk and talk. I wished I had recorded it so I could just hit play. Telling it wore me out, trying to remember everything. And not knowing what was relevant for a doctor and what was just coincidental.

"Your story is fascinating," he said.

Deep breath. *I wasn't shooting for fascinating.*

"You've seen another neurologist, right?" he asked.

"Yes ... [Dr. Complacent]."

He made a face, turning up his nose like he'd just eaten a sour grape.

"I get a lot of his patients. Arrogant son of a ..."

He paused, catching his potential unprofessionalism. I didn't care. I appreciated his candor.

"Well, I'd have to agree with the direction you're headed," I said. "He treated me like a head case when he couldn't figure it out. Said it was stress. Called it a complex migraine to get me out of his hair."

"That's awful. A young woman loses vision, ability to walk, numbness, and you've lost how much weight?"

He frowned a big, childish frown. As if someone tripped him while carrying his lunch tray in a junior high cafeteria. He looked like he wanted to get even.

"I've lost nearly 30 pounds now. Although that's the only thing I'm really not complaining about."

I forced a smile as I swam through my exasperation pool.

"You've had a horrible experience. I can't believe he just sent you out the door."

His raw honesty relieved me. I felt validated in my reaction to Dr. Complacent's treatment toward me.

Dr. Candor ordered new tests, including a CT of the spine, a thyroid test and a new set of MRIs. These tests served as a new baseline as well as to rule out Dr. Dimple's suggestion of MS. And within a few days, I resumed my music game as I lay motionless in the MRI tube.

Ah ... the Doobie Brothers ... a favorite. Listen to the Music jammed above the dit dits and bang bangs.

I prayed to my grandmother. *Momo. Help. I'm sinking. I can't seem to articulate my full experience to anyone. I hate these tests. And I hate feeling temporary.* I wasn't sure if I should say "amen."

China Grove, Black Water, Jesus Is All Right. Hmmm .... What A Fool Believes. Takin' It to the Streets. Ugh. Harder than I thought. It

Keeps You Runnin'. And the song changed. *Dang it. Not even close to 10 this time.*

November 21, 2008

Dr. Candor bit his lower lip, frowning. I sat across from him in a chair. Our conversations didn't entail exams, so I felt less like a patient than someone doing consulting work with him. A fresh change of pace.

"Well, you've gone and surprised me," Dr. Candor said, squinting his eyes as if he were making out the answer on my face.

"What does that mean?"

"Your MRI revealed lesions that were not present back in February when the original tests were run."

"Hmmm ...."

"The MRI also showed thickening in the ethmoid sinuses, but since we're in high allergy season, I don't think it's relevant. Your thyroid and spine CT were both normal."

"Okay. ... What does a lesion mean?"

"In its simplest form, it's abnormal tissue in the brain. Tells us that there was some damage caused from your experience back in February."

I sat. Stunned. My legs no longer bounced. I felt like a weary passenger staring at the conveyer belt in a remote location, willing my bag to be next. Or arrive at all.

"Follow me. Let's go look at your MRI together."

Dr. Candor ushered me to his office. A new experience. I'd never had a doctor leave the exam room and invite me in his office. I felt special. A participant in my diagnosis instead of a helpless victim.

Brain images flashed across his screen until he got to an image with what he called "lesions."

"This is in the area called the centrum semiovale."

Why don't doctors speak English?

"This might explain some of your memory disturbances, headaches and visual field defects. Even the lack of function or feeling in your hand."

"So, will I have another ... whatever we're calling this episode?" I asked with hesitation in my voice, wondering if I really wanted to know the answer.

"With everything I see in your charts, it doesn't look like a full stroke, yet I can't rule out mini-stroke or some other type of neurological event."

His eyes softened, as if he was saying this to his own daughter.

"You're awfully young to have been through all this and while I can't promise you you're out of the woods, I'm going to work with you as closely as you want to ensure we stay on top of it."

"I appreciate it. I guess I need to absorb what you just told me. I'm not sure what to ask at the moment."

"Let's repeat the MRIs every three months to see how you're trending. And I'll ask [Dr. Serene] to continue repeating the visual field tests."

Chapter 23: Living Life Fast

September 8, 2009 (19 months after onset)

After cashing in hard-earned miles from my countless business trips, Angela and I flew across the world to Australia in first class. I felt odd being there, far from my childhood roots of driving across the country, dragging the pop-up camper behind us, and making our own turkey sandwiches from the lukewarm ice chest.

With Henry gone, travel was more appealing even though I still felt bad about missing time with Gary and Cole. Henry's passing erased that nagging fear of not being there at "the" critical moment when he died. I stretched, turned on my side and imagined Henry curled up next to me during my most intense moments since the neuro phenomena. My breathing sank into waves of blended exhaustion and tranquility.

September 12, 2009

Outside our cabin in Yarra Valley, I breathed in a remote scent of thick grass, happy to smell anything. No chemicals - a nice change of pace from Dallas. The sun batted its eyelids across the fields. A kookaburra surprised us with its shrill cackle as it took flight. Kangaroos kicked and punched each other like Ali versus Frazier.

We sat in awe of valleys filled with kangaroos, some with joeys stuffed in their pouches. Wild cockatoos flocked from tree to tree.

Work thoughts evaporated into the cool Australian air. *I'm here. I'm finally here.* The guilt of another big trip so soon after the last one vaporized as I enjoyed crossing one more item off the bucket list.

One by one, kangaroos approached us, rooting through the mildewed grass. Our slightest movement prompted them to hop away, triggering an impulsive "boing, boing, boing" from us for sound effect. Life was good.

"I don't know which is better, Beck," Angela pondered quietly, wide-eyed as she continued to take in the sights of the kangaroos.

Which is better. Which is better. What are we talking about?

"... the kangaroos or all the colorful fish at the Great Barrier Reef."

"Oh. I think this is far better. Much safer."

We laughed, recalling our snorkeling experience just two days before. Stingrays rippled without effort, drifting in a different course of direction from all the other ocean life. Miniature orange Nemos darted in and out of large purple sea anemone. Spiky blue starfish stretched themselves over peach coral. The underwater world soothed me.

I took the lead, snapping photos without the disturbed water from fins or bubbles. Hoping to get at least a couple of keepers, I clicked a few extra shots. Well, 384 to be exact.

With my head cocked to one side, I angled my camera toward a deeper area we hadn't seen. The large variety of coral formed a tall wall. *What an awesome backdrop to zoom in on this kissing fish.* A large fish floated underneath me. *That fish looks sleek. And long.*

And ... Shark!

I froze. Sayings like "stop, drop and roll" and "look both ways before crossing" floated through my head. Totally useless. I didn't want to yell or splash in fear of calling attention to myself. *I should make sure Angela is aware and safe.* My instinct told me to keep an eye on the shark while signaling to the others. *But I'm this close*, my louder photography voice yelled as I ducked my head back down and swam closer. I snapped the shot. Then I paddled backward, trying not to rush in fear of causing a commotion.

I surfaced near the others, who were pointing down.

"Did y'all see the shark?"

"Yes, you idiot," Angela said. "... He's been stalking you the past few minutes. While you were in your own world taking a zillion pictures, we were watching him track you, not knowing how to get your attention. My gosh, you make me crazy sometimes!"

"Sorry," I said, laughing, not able to help myself. "I won't charge you for the picture."

"What picture?" she asked, confused.

I smiled bigger.

"Wait ... don't tell me you took the time to get a picture of the shark?"

"Yep! Once I saw he was moving ahead, I went after him just like I did with the bears at Lake Tahoe."

Angela sighed, then looked away.

"You kill me. I don't know why I do these trips with you. Mom and Dad are gonna kill me when I come back alone someday. And I'll be responsible for killing my baby sister the rest of my life because of your daredevil decisions."

The thing about being close to someone, really close, is that you know when they need a wind-down phase before the situation explodes into something bigger. This was one of those times. I kept my mouth shut.

That night, back on Dunk Island, she forgave me as she flipped through all the reef shots. We enjoyed a bottle of wine as sun rays withered beyond the palm trees. I missed Gary. And I grew tired of the need to explain to everyone that Angela and I were sisters, not lovers.

"Hey, I need your help," Angela asked. "Have any ideas for what we could be for Halloween this year?"

"Give me a minute," I said.

Kamikaze coconuts dropped with a vengeance, reminding us to stick to the sidewalks. Couples splashed through the water's edge.

"You going with your buddy?" I asked.

"Yes."

"K. Got it. You can be Mounds and he can be Almond Joy."

Silence.

"What? What do you mean?" she asked.

I stayed silent. And before I had a chance to explain, she started cracking up. "It's perfect!"

September 16, 2009

Angela stuck me with the driving again as the sun ducked behind the mountains and wildlife assumed the right of way in every direction as if on cue.

"What are those things in the road?" I asked.

"I dunno. Some of them are huge."

"They look like wild pigs. I think they'd do damage at a high speed."

"And the small ones might be Tasmanian devils. You know they're on the endangered species list, right? You don't want to live with knowing you killed one of the few remaining ones."

"Thanks, B."

Our car crept through the dark unknown, dodging odd animals. Silence fell between us.

I'm in Tasmania. Tasmania! I'm so lucky to live one of my dreams. I'm living life. I'm not giving up. It's been so damn hard. It's not fair how hard I have to work at things and no one seems to notice.

"You OK, Beck?"

"Yeah."

"I can feel your emotional shift. Talk?"

"Nah. Just glad we're here."

"I'm not letting you off the hook."

I debated, not wanting to ruin the mood.

"I'm scared, Ange," I finally said.

"Talk to me."

"I'm scared of having another stroke, or whatever it was. I'm not the same. I get so confused. I picture Mammo, stroke after stroke. I hear her laugh, trying to speak, but not being able, so she resorts to laughing again."

I paused.

"... I can feel her squeeze my hand firmly, a grip that tells me 'I may not have words to say out loud, but inside I'm very much alive. Inside I have many words. I'm still human and have feelings even if I can't speak. And I love you. I love that you come spend time with me and embellish on your stories just to make me laugh. And I know it's hard for you to see me this way and I'm sorry for that.'"

"You think she was capable of thinking all of that in her condition?"

"I know she was. And then I picture her in the nursing home cafeteria being fed with a syringe. I'm scared of being that person. Why can't anyone tell me what the world happened to me? I'm different now!"

"I'm sorry," she said just above a whisper.

"I also picture Mammo holding her hand out as far as she could from her body, admiring the watch that loosely dangled from her thin wrist."

"Diddydaddy's retirement watch?"

"Yeah. That one. She got a dreamy look in her eyes when she'd look at it. I always wanted to know her most important memories. And then it'd nearly kill me when she pulled her wrist to her chest, as if Diddydaddy's soul touched hers at that moment."

We sat quiet until we pulled up to our cabin at Cradle Mountain.

"I love you, Beck."

I felt the tears formed in my eyes. I wanted to preserve them for use at a later date.

"Thanks, Ange. I love you, too."

"Back to happy?"

I regretted leaving the moment too soon. I thought about my therapist and felt like I just let him down by not allowing myself to embrace my emotions longer. I was finally beginning to understand that ditching my feelings kept the wounds fresh.

We settled into the one-room cabin. Two green club chairs flanked the fireplace, with a round table in between. A smoky hue filled the air, evidence of the last occupant. A double bed lined the far wall, just underneath a bay window. Angela tossed her bags next to the sofa bed.

"Fire?"

"Do I have a choice?"

"No."

"Then, yes, I'd love one."

I tossed my legs over the arm of one of the club chairs, sitting sideways as I watched her start the fire.

"Remember our furniture forts when we were kids? How we tore up the living room, stacking cushions from every chair and sofa and covering them with blankets?" I asked.

"That was the coolest. And the tunnels. Don't forget the tunnels," she said.

I stared ahead, worn out. Listening to the crackling fire.

"Why did Mom and Dad store the cereal boxes in the highest cabinet in the kitchen?" Angela asked.

I pictured us dragging a chair from the dinette to the kitchen, stepping up on it, then climbing up on the cabinet and reaching on our tippy toes to snag the Frankenberry or Fruity Pebbles boxes. We tapped on the side of the box with one finger, trying to wedge it out between the adult Raisin Bran and Grape Nuts boxes.

"I never thought about it," I replied.

"But it's not as if they didn't expect us to eat cereal. Dad plainly laid out the spoons, bowls and napkins the night before, so he knew we'd be getting the cereal down."

"Right. And then the sweet note that said, 'Mornin', sweethearts! Enjoy the cartoons. I love my girls.'"

"The notes! He is all about the notes."

"And Mom with the Eskimo kisses."

"See? You have a good memory, Beck."

I held my breath for a moment, trying to hide my anger. The fire logs hissed. I crossed my legs, then my arms, and stared at the fire.

"I can remember my bike combination from second grade, but I can't remember the name of the town we stopped in an hour ago."

In the solitude the next morning, I thanked God for getting me to Australia, not sure if I really wanted Him to hear.

Our first stop in Tasmania that morning was Crater Lake. Snow-capped mountains reflected across the water. We bundled up in our new cheap coats and took off by foot, the sun bright enough to take the edge off the bitter cold.

Waterfalls roared in the distance. Palm trees, beech trees and button grass outlined the lake. A natural aroma filled the air. An eagle flew overhead, its wings outstretched, sailing across a cloudless sky. Stones crunched under our feet on the path.

Happiness swelled in me as I admired the beauty of the dense rainforest around us. Thick leaves and moss-covered rocks and logs featured every shade of green. *Crayola would have to come up with more greens if they visited this place. I can't believe I'm finally here. I feel at home here. Nothing else matters.*

A slow trickle meandering through the mossy rocks relaxed me even more. I let go of my health fears. I felt significant among our surroundings, as if I was meant to be there.

A bench welcomed us from our hike around the lake. We straddled the wood plank opposite one another, holding each other up with our backs.

"Is that a pademelon?" Angela asked.

In the bushes, three feet away, a pademelon sat looking at us, as if pondering our conversation. This creature resembled a cross between a kangaroo and a rat. He seemed unfazed.

"I believe it is."

"You know, kangaroos come in large, medium and small," Angela said.

"Yeah?"

"The kangaroo is large. The wallaby medium. And the pademelon small."

"And you know what else?" I asked.

"Do tell."

"The pademelon got robbed when it came to names."

Chapter 24: Piano Man

November 2, 2009

"You don't have anything to prove to anyone," Gary said.

"I went back to India in February and you didn't say anything then," I said.

"I still think your illness came from something there."

"I could have had a stroke anywhere in the world. It just happened to be there."

"I'm just saying," he said.

I shrugged. This conversation got us nowhere in the past. I didn't want to have it again. I continued folding my clothes.

"How long you gone?"

"Ten days," I said.

"I'm ready for you to have a non-traveling job."

I sighed. Another dead-end. Even though I agreed with him, I didn't know what else I could do to match my income. I felt stuck, ready for a change, but not knowing how to apply my skills to any other industry. I knew I'd never make enough at photography. Too much competition from professionals who perfected their shots with PhotoShop.

On the first morning of my return to India, I met my assigned driver, Shaikh. I remembered him from past trips.

"I'm heading to the office," I directed, as if there were anywhere else in India I might need to visit.

"Yes. Vedy gud."

And that was the extent of our conversation. I pressed my right foot on the floorboard as we dodged traffic. Taking in the sights, I felt blessed to have a roof over my head, clean clothes on my body, food to eat, a bathroom, a bed, a job. I felt blessed that my health, even in my struggles, gave me more opportunities than most of the people I saw between my hotel and our office. The poverty forced my eyes shut as the images broke my heart. The hardened faces of women carrying heavy baskets on their heads. Children knocking on the windows of slowing cars, begging for money. Yet I enjoyed side excursions where I photographed wild monkeys and the historical Kanheri Caves dating from the first century. A stark difference to Texas.

During the weekend, Neeraj hosted a party at his house for the executive team. On arrival, male servers dressed in long, red and black achkan coats approached guests bearing large trays of samosas, steamed momos, pakoras and bharu kababs. The hosts and locals donned colorful, collar-less kurta and kurti shirts, flowing with diagonal stripes. I looked down at my khakis and button down. *Boy, do I look American. Maybe I should have at least bought a sari.*

No one talked business. Beers, liquors and wines lined the buffet. My colleagues from Romania, England, Sri Lanka, India and the States shared stories about concerts, books and upcoming vacations. *I never imagined myself so comfortable a million miles from home. We're all the same, just from different origins.*

Drinks flowed freely. The pianist took requests from guests who sang along, some off key, some ready for prime time.

"Becky, do you have a favorite?" Neeraj asked.

The room silenced for the first time that evening.

"Come on, Beck. What's your tune?" one of my UK colleagues asked, patting me on the back.

"Madonna? Britney Spears? Miss Jackson if you're nasty?" Peter teased.

I rolled my eyes at Peter, then checked in with Deborah. She looked amused at my dilemma, nodding her head to encourage my selection.

"How about *Piano Man*? Do you know any Billy Joel?"

"Good one, Becky. Come lead us," Neeraj said.

Lead us? Gary says I should never sing in front of anyone. And never, ever dance.

Visions of Piano Man on Bourbon Street danced in my mind. *I can do this. Just play like I'm with my buddies in New Orleans. Sing loud. Sing bold.* Even without a harmonica, the pianist played a great Billy Joel. My Romanian colleague danced like he was rowing a canoe. I'd never seen someone have so much fun singing off-key and clapping off beat. About a dozen of us swayed while we sang, our eyes half-closed as if we were on stage. I locked arms with Lyndon and Peter. Everyone followed suit, belting out the lyrics in different dialects.

At the end of the week, Deborah and I treated ourselves to the Hyatt spa. My back begged for deep tissue relief from tension and lots of sitting. A short, petite, pleasant woman greeted me, motioning for me to follow. Light music chimed overhead. Therapy fragrances stung my nose.

She pointed to the massage table. *A bottom sheet, but no top one.* I felt a hand rag cover my backside after I lay down. She applied the same amount of pressure as a five-year-old girl might if stroking her dolly. I arched my back slightly, trying to lean my muscles into her fingertips. *How many more days until I get back to my regular therapist for relief?*

Finally relaxed after forgiving her for only teasing my back, she asked me to turn over. She held the small towel to cover my mid-section while my breasts stared up at the ceiling, nowhere to hide.

"Do you have another towel?" I asked, gripping the other towel to indicate what I was referring to.

"Please relax," Abha replied. I knew my efforts for an additional towel were futile, so I swallowed my pride and modesty, and tried to return to a relaxed state.

The stomach is not on my list of body parts to be touched by anyone, not even Gary. But it topped her list. Suddenly she gained the strength of a man. Her fingers sorted through the dab of flab I tried so hard to conceal from the rest of the world. I forced back a grin as I pictured myself lying there, imagining the laugh that Angela would get later from this.

Once she finished fondling my flab, she moved my breasts around. I guffawed uncontrollably, opening my eyes to tell her that my breasts weren't considered part of the scope of her work. Other than mammograms and dreaded yearly trips to the gynecologist, I was proud to say that no other female hands had ever come in contact with my breasts.

This petite, dark-haired, gentle-looking woman threw her hand up with the universal sign for stop. She insisted on finishing her job, so I resigned and let her massage my boobs, which she shifted side to side, like buoys being tossed about on white-capping water.

Chapter 25: A New Inspiration

January 20, 2010

"I'll be home in 17 minutes," Gary said.

"K. I'm headed out to see [Dr. James]," I replied.

"What's for dinner?"

"I thought we'd rent a pizza."

"Rent one? Think they'll want it back?" He laughed.

"Ha. You know what I meant."

I caught myself before spiraling downward. Dr. James worked with me on not bottoming out each time I encountered a post-neuro experience. Like dropping full cups of water, forgetting to start the dryer after loading it with clothes (every time), forgetting how to figure out time zones or even not zipping up. Or the one occasion when I caught the toaster on fire. Okay ... two.

I thought about Halloween a couple of months back. We took Cole to our friends' house so he could trick or treat with a buddy. While the kids scrambled for Snickers and Starbursts, the adults threw a block party with homemade chili as our entry fee. Since the bash was several streets away from our friends' house, they instructed that if we needed a bathroom during the party, to use the house directly behind us. Friends of theirs.

An hour into the cul-de-sac gathering, nature called. Feeling a little odd going to a stranger's home to use the bathroom, I knocked. No one answered. I looked back to our friends, the Totzkes. Dave waved, nodding for me to go on in.

As I washed my hands, I heard a thud. *Probably Gary just behind me.* I opened the door, and a couple stood there. The man raised his shoulders like a cat in a standoff. I forced a smile.

"What are you doing here?" the man asked.

Though a shade taller than me, he felt like a giant. The woman rammed her fists into her hips.

"I ... uh ... was using your restroom."

"Who are you?" he said.

"I'm Becky."

My own last name failed me.

"And why are you in our house?" he asked, stepping closer. His five o'clock shadow looked intentional. Like a teenage boy proud to grow facial hair.

I got scared.

"Our friend said you wouldn't mind if we used your bathroom. He's just outside. A friend of yours."

"What's his name?"

No words came to me. I pictured Dave, nearly seven feet tall. A friend for several years. He owned a moving company. He swept playgrounds with his metal detector, finding lost keepsakes. His sons played with Cole many times. His wife, Kelene, with big brown eyes and a perfect smile, taught school, loved animals and shared great stories. Yet neither of their names emerged. Not even the beginning letter.

Horrified, I stood there blinking, unsure how to explain. The woman's face scowled at me. I felt like I was about to be bitch-slapped. *Should I make a run for it or should I explain that I have memory issues?*

Their front door opened. Gary walked in as if he lived there.

"And who are you?" the man asked, his head snapping Gary's direction.

"Oh. Apologies. We're friends of the Totzkes. They said you wouldn't mind if we used your house for the bathroom or an ice refill," Gary said.

The man and woman exchanged glances with each other, smiling. The man shot his hand toward Gary, shaking it as if they were long-lost friends.

"Oh! The Totzkes. Well any friend of theirs is a friend of ours. You're welcome to anything you need," he said.

January 22, 2010

My friend Rhonda, who referred me to Dr. Cordial, became a great source of information during my recuperation. With a petite figure, Rhonda hardly seemed the type to endure a stroke: late 30s, enjoying life, good health. Like me. Yet her surgery to remove a clot in her carotid artery produced clear evidence of her diagnosis.

In conversations, Rhonda's face beamed as she shifted from business talk to her young children. I hoped mine revealed the same intense love for Cole.

Like me, Rhonda received cursory insight on the cause of her life-changing stroke. I tried picturing her recovery efforts with her children at home, how difficult it must have been to tend to their needs in a challenged physical state.

The emotional side of the aftermath of a neurological episode opened an unfamiliar cruel world. The mounting number of lost abilities crushed my hope of being "normal" again. I repeated things said to me. My confidence, fragile as it was, was shaken from questioning myself about what was and wasn't related to my illness. Nothing seemed the same.

We met for lunch, where Rhonda freely shared her medical knowledge, trying to help me make sense of something that remained unexplained.

We laughed at some of the ridiculous advice we got from doctors.

"Try to eliminate caffeine," Rhonda said, repeating what our doctors said.

I nodded my head, snickering.

"They always tell me 'you need to exercise regularly,'" Rhonda said.

"Yes. And then I ask why the hour a day I was working out didn't prevent it," I said.

"That shuts them up, doesn't it? And then they probably tell you to be sure and take an adult dosage aspirin each day."

"Exactly. And I ask if it means I'm at risk of having another stroke."

"And they just lower their voice and don't answer the question. They just say ..."

"Precautionary steps," we said in unison, toasting each other's water glasses.

January 27, 2010 Journal Entry

Gary and I got into a huge fight tonight about his role two years ago in misleading the neurologist. As I begin another trip to India, I want to tell him that I'm afraid of being away from home with all of these issues. I'm still so tired. I can't imagine what the jet lag is going to do to me. But I feel like I can't tell Gary since he led the neurologist to believe I was stressed out of my mind. It really pisses me off. For a year I've felt I've had to contain my feelings because he'll blow them out of proportion.

However, he accused me of deliberately misleading the neurologist about my stress, which made me feel I was married to Adam all over again. This upset him, but it should have. How dare he! And now he wants to call my doctor - a year later, to set the record straight. Too late! I don't want to see Dr. Complacent again, and I definitely don't want Gary butting into my healthcare again!!!

January 29, 2010

"Good to see you again, so soon," I told Rhonda, giving her a hug.

Her blue sweater fit her frame as if sewn just for her. I visualized my closet, filled with oversized, long-sleeved button-down Polo tops. Nothing cute like what she wore. Angela and my college roomie Dawn pestered me to update my wardrobe.

"Hey, Kim. Thanks for joining us," I said.

We knew Kim from our same demanding outsourcing industry. I looked forward to visits with her, when she would entertain us with her sarcasm and commonsensical narratives about people we knew. Her fascination with Rhonda and my medical stories seemed to hypnotize me, making me feel like a temporary hero.

"Becky, have I ever seen you anywhere but here at this restaurant?" she asked, swishing her brown hair that dusted her collar.

"I've been accused of loyalty to an extreme before," I answered.

"Tell me you're getting something other than the salad this time."

Kim's eyebrows volleyed up and down. She hit her jovial stride faster than usual.

"Nope. I'm in love with the Maguire's salad."

"You probably own their dressing so you can replicate their salad."

I blushed.

"Busted."

"You're kidding!"

Rhonda and Kim laughed. I faked shame.

The restaurant filled. Glasses clanked. Loud voices and laughter spilled over the booth. Kim and Rhonda spoke with animation, but I couldn't distinguish their voices from the others. My face tingled. I quit trying to listen, just nodded as if I followed their dialogue.

"Oh my gosh!" Kim burst out while touching her fingers to her temples.

"What? Did you forget something? Happens to the best of us," Rhonda said, winking at me.

"I meant to tell y'all that Dr. Jill Bolte-Taylor is coming to Dallas ... ," Kim said.

I leaned in, picturing my copy of Dr. Bolte-Taylor's bestselling book, *My Stroke of Insight,* which guided me like a health bible. My copy looked like a college textbook. Color-coded sticky notes marked pages with highlights and underlined passages.

" ... She's being featured at an upcoming Tate Lecture Series at SMU. Y'all should be my guests," Kim said.

I felt like Rhonda and I belonged to a secret club. And the head of that club was Dr. Bolte-Taylor, a Harvard-trained brain scientist who experienced a massive stroke in 1996. I recalled how reading about the unfolding of her stroke resembled mine and triggered the first time I had been able to cry. At the time, Angela wrapped her arms around me, bursting into tears. We both sobbed and shook, fearful of what was happening to me.

February 7, 2010 (Two years after onset)

My excitement for the lecture built like a kid waiting for Christmas. I re-read Dr. Bolte-Taylor's passages[3], the ones that held personal meaning. They hit so close to home, I could have written them myself:

"I felt bizarre, as if my conscious mind was suspended ...

"As I walked, I noticed that my movements were no longer fluid ...

"... let me sleep and sleep and sleep some more. Again, we both trusted that my brain knew what it needed in order for it to mend itself...

"... a serious gap in my information processing and often I could not articulate what I was thinking.

"... my emotions had been relatively flat. I had been observing the world, but not really engaging with it emotionally."

To cope with my memory struggles, I jot down questions and notes at random moments. My cell phone contains a list of topics related to my neurological event. My nightstand is stacked with journals to grab my thoughts before they flee forever. Some reflections randomly wake me, demanding I record them before waking for the day. The alphabet game helps me scan for names. Sign language even helps. I form the first letter of a word I need to remember during a conversation. When it is my turn

---

[3] Jill Bolte Taylor, Ph.D., *My Stroke of Insight* (New York: Penguin Group, 2008), 38-112

to speak, I look at my hand at the letter formed, sometimes helping me recall the topic I want to comment on.

February 17, 2010

My gut told me that none of the diagnoses fit my situation. So in the absence of a proper diagnosis, I clammed up except with Rhonda on occasions, even though it distracted me every waking hour of the day.

While there were strong similarities in Dr. Taylor's and Rhonda's stroke experiences, theirs didn't match mine. The MRIs, although abnormal, didn't seem conclusive despite lesions in a few areas. There seemed to be multiple issues. Nothing I read or heard quite fit my situation.

At work, despite my ongoing muddled thoughts and fatigued state of mind, I pushed hard. And I was successful. I increased the U.S. sales pipeline by 700 percent, half the company's growth in new business. I should have been proud of my accomplishments, but I was too tired to care. Naps with my head slumbering against my desk made me see myself as 'a failure,' 'weak' and 'subpar.'

I continued to schedule calls in groupings, making myself available first thing in the morning, then at lunch and then again late afternoon. I felt grateful for being able to work at my home.

February 23, 2010

The Bolte-Taylor lecture date arrived. I welcomed it with a long-lost giddiness. A teenager before a first date. Kim made arrangements for us to meet beforehand for dinner. I felt fortunate to have friends who tried to understand me.

My mom and Angela drove in from East Texas to attend the lecture, knowing how important this was to me. And Dr. Welby, my steadfast physician, joined our dinner as well, intrigued to be part of the event.

After polite introductions, our conversation accelerated from business chitchat to global travel.

"I'd be interested in hearing what you think about all the proposed legislation around healthcare," my mom asked Dr. Welby.

Oh, not now. Can't he just be a person joining our party tonight? He's here as a friend, not a doctor.

But Dr. Welby took the bait. He became animated, sharing the conflicting interests in pharmaceutical companies that tried influencing his day-to-day decisions. His face reddened. He moved his hands as if conducting a full orchestra in front of him. He admonished the drug companies' antics, exposing common practices that he refused to accept as medical solutions. *This is yet one more reason why I like him so much. His ethics are beyond the norm.*

Jazz muffled our exchange as it bounced off the hard floors. My difficulty tracking voices among a crowd distanced me from everyone. The wait staff seemed to have second jobs as they were nowhere to be found.

"Isn't the lecture starting in 10 minutes?" Kim asked.

We all grabbed our cell phones. *When did phones replace watches?*

"Oh my gosh! Yes. We need to go," Dr. Welby said.

With the lecture about to begin, we paid the bill and sprinted to the McFarlin Auditorium on the SMU campus, arriving just in time to claim the last available seats in the nosebleed section.

In my anticipation of the lecture, I viewed video clips of Dr. Bolte-Taylor online. I knew what to expect. Long blonde hair with a natural look. Boston accent. Despite her intellect, she forced herself down a few notches for us normal people. Her opening recounted her stroke experience, giving me goosebumps. *I know this. I've been there. It's traumatic. It's horrible to know what you're thinking but not be able to express one lousy word of it.*

Dr. Bolte-Taylor paced the stage confidently, lecturing like we were a college class. Her explanation of neurons, lobes and blood vessels made her more animated. She seemed to celebrate the beauty and amazement of her experience, admiring the brain's highways, roadblocks and bumper-to-bumper traffic. Her energy grew as she celebrated her brain's incremental steps toward recovery, such as relearning the alphabet and realizing the world was multi-dimensional. She peaked when she talked about choices. Choosing between happy and sad. Choosing to schedule a set time to throw a pity party, then letting go of it the rest of the day. Choosing to allow her right brain to push through, overriding the rigidity of her pre-stroke, left brain tendencies.

I questioned my own critical thinking and giving in to frequent frustration. Here was a person from whom I could learn, someone who made a conscious choice not to yield to negativity that might have prevented significant progress. This aspect of her lecture surprised me. I wasn't expecting to be uplifted. At 40, I felt like I was starting life over. Her speech motivated me to surround myself with encouragement and get back to the spiritual journey that I had abandoned.

March 2, 2010

"I'm so bummed I didn't get to talk to her," I told Dr. James. "I even took my copy of her book, all tattered, dog-eared and underlined."

"Why not reach out and contact her?"

I made a face. Not meaning to.

"There's nothing to lose, right? You're a good writer," he said.

"She probably gets hundreds of emails a day."

"So write something compelling in the subject line and see if she'll respond."

So I took his advice that same day. I wrote and rewrote and then edited my message, trying to make it short enough to keep her interest, yet long enough to relay all the appropriate information. A close friend helped me revise until we narrowed it to the bare necessities. We couldn't get it any shorter than two full pages.

March 3, 2010

The next morning, I sauntered into my home office, booting up the laptops, anticipating the usual onslaught of messages from my overseas colleagues. I checked work email first, eliminating the messages that didn't require action. Then I switched to personal email.

She responded!

Like an unemployed college grad seeing their first job offer, I reread her email many times, almost memorizing it. She recommended a couple of institutions that she believed were experts at finding the cause. She described the difference between TIA, which has symptoms lasting for only 24 hours, and full stroke, which has lasting effects. She believed mine fit in the full stroke category, based on the limited information I included in our correspondence. My thoughts zigged and zagged, trying to decide whom to tell first.

I grabbed my cell phone and quickly texted my therapist.

"Emailed Dr. Bolte-Taylor. She responded! Said it sounds like a major stroke from brief description. Suggests I go to a major medical ctr like Mayo or MGH. Says to stay ahead of the fear."

"This is great!" Dr. James texted back instantly.

My hopes soared. I immediately contacted one of the clinics. *I will get answers. I don't care how much it sets us back. I'm going regardless.*

Within a few hours, the clinic responded to my application to see one of their neurologists.

"On wait list for one of leading U.S. neurologists. Could meet internist immediately but chose to wait on specialist," I texted Dr. James again.

"WOW! That's great! I'm impressed you contacted them so fast! This is exciting!"

"Yea ... usually takes me weeks to feel motivated enough to want to take action on anything. This is so uncharacteristic of me."

"Ha ha ha ha," he texted back, making me laugh out loud at our bond. I never imagined trusting a therapist to know me so well. I thought about the three years I wasted with him, dodging anything but laughter.

Again, I reread Dr. Bolte-Taylor's email. Two golden nuggets energized my motivation to continue searching for answers. "Stay out of the fear. Hunt until you find the answers."

At her suggestion, I divulged, for the first time, more of my internal experience to Drs. Welby and James. *I have to reduce my fears. Time to reveal more of this ongoing ordeal, even if they think I'm nuts. I can't live like this much longer.*

Chapter 26: Living Inside Myself

March 9, 2010

Our childhood Sundays meant waking to the smell of blueberry muffins. Dad buttered them, carefully replacing the tops as if the dabs magically appeared inside. Angela and I failed to adopt Dad's morning-person outlook. We smiled anyway. Dad craned his neck even though he hadn't put on his tie yet. Mom whisked in and out of the kitchen. No makeup. Hair bobby-pinned into a tight helmet. She took one bite of her muffin in between each morning task. Lacy dresses lay on our beds, already selected by the time we returned to our rooms.

Church started at 8:40 a.m. At 8:50, our family scrambled for a place to sit, preferably while the congregation stood for a hymn. Angela and I sat separated by a parent to prevent our inevitable giggles. Methodists like their routine. We stood up. We sat down. We recited creeds by memory. We sang traditional songs from tattered hymnals with musty smells. We listened to elderly soloists whose voices reverberated in contrast to the smooth organ pipes stretching to the ceiling. We recited the Lord's Prayer, while I looked around to make sure everyone else had their eyes closed. We fought the nods during the sermon. Dad left us just before the offering to usher.

Sunday school followed, where we were divided according to age groups. My class hosted the most popular kids in school. Some considered me a friend. Some considered me an object of ridicule in opposition of my being a tomboy. I hated Sunday school, but that's what we did. It was Sunday.

My mom's parents anticipated our arrival after church. My balding grandfather sang *Hello Dolly,* greeting us as he danced in his slippers. My fragile grandmother giggled, clapping her hands to his rhythm, admiring the love of her life. I smelled pot-roast aromas. My dad's mom joined the gathering, bringing custard for dessert, one of my favorites.

She called me one of her "favorite little brats," sealed with a loving wink.

At the dinner table, Dad bowed his head. We held hands, bowing with him.

"Our gracious Heavenly Father ..."

He tightened his squeeze on my hand. I wasn't sure if it was because he was telling me he loved me or because he meant for me to stay serious for as long as the blessing.

" ... bless this food to the nourishment and strength of our bodies and our bodies to thy service. In Christ's name we pray."

We said "amen" in unison, a signal to plunge into the home-cooked meal.

Until I found the Lord during a summer retreat between 8th and 9th grade, my religion took place on Sundays and at bedtime. However, a visiting youth director helped me discover meaning beyond childhood rituals. I felt different inside. A spiritual energy grasped me and walked me to the altar, where I cried softly, asking God to forgive me for being a sinner and to please bring Jesus into my heart. Angela and my buddy, Judd, knelt beside me, placing a hand on each shoulder.

For the first time, I felt whole inside. I didn't know I was half.

I made promises to God. *I'll be a youth director. I'll be there for some kid like me who needs extra nurturing. I'll mentor to stimulate kids' creativity and spirituality.*

My grandfather died that Wednesday.

One of my best friends, Marian Arnold, died in a car accident four days later. So did her brother. She was 14. He was 12.

My newfound faith didn't waiver. I didn't blame God.

Eighteen months later, another best friend, Chad Palmer, died in a hunting accident. He was 15. His death crushed me. I never told anyone, but I often pictured us married someday. He made me feel special. I could be myself. Nothing to hide. Nothing to prove. But his death made me pray even harder. I was afraid that questioning God meant disobedience.

My last two years of high school, I led my church's youth group as vice president and president, helping plan Bible studies and youth retreats. My closest friends grew with me. Christianity was cool. We met Wednesday nights for even more faith fuel at Bible studies. I wondered if my band friends felt awkward around a Jesus freak.

When I cut class, I landed at the church, hanging out with my youth director and a couple of our pastors. *I'm in a church. How can this be wrong?*

After my first year of college, I felt certain about youth ministry as a career. My home church hired me as their first summer youth intern. Serving on the staff with the church leaders who raised me made me feel honored. *I'm on the inside now. I get to hear what all goes on in church staff meetings. I'm one of them! I've wanted this so long, and here it is in front of me.*

With the youth minister, I planned mission trips, designed youth week retreats to recruit followers and created fellowship agendas for Sundays. *If I could just graduate from college sooner, I'm ready to just do what I want to do.*

Eight months later, the rape ripped apart my soul. I didn't just question the rapist. I questioned all of mankind. And my mission in life.

Three years later, in our toxic marriage, Adam used religion as a weapon. Holding the Bible, he repeated "women must submit to their husbands" in a context useful to him. He condemned me for never being "Christian enough."

In a defiant state of guilt, I became bitter toward God. The series of intense emotional torments triggered the questions I held at bay for so long. *Why do You, God, allow so many horrible things to happen to good people? I've been devoted to You, yet why does this happen under Your watch? Why do You keep ripping things away from me?*

I left the church. Done.

My family pleaded for me to return. I blew them off with vague explanations. After Dad's prayers at meals, I wondered if I had to wait a little longer before indulging in the food. I felt less deserving of anything blessed. Their pleas for me to forgive and forget, to just move on infuriated me. *They'll never understand.*

After three or four years, they gave up. Other than occasional holiday visits or to take Cole to church so I could check the "I'm doing the right thing" box, church became a place for people with something to prove.

Stepping away didn't make me happy, either.

In 2006, severe abdominal pain led me to see my gynecologist. She conducted surgery within two days to remove a cyst the size of a grapefruit, as well as an ovary. In this vulnerable position, my stance toward God softened. So I prayed. Not to Him directly, but in general.

This time of need is humbling. Regardless of my "status" with God, I know I'd prefer to have His support. I ask for Him to give me the ability to put trust in my doctors. I ask for strength to overcome the inevitable pain. And I ask for mercy to consider the contents of my heart, regardless of the outcome. I don't promise anything. This is not a plea to watch over me in exchange for something I'm going to do different.

I am who I am and have always been ... a good person doing the best I can with what I'm given. In the spirit of wanting to get past my anger, I ask for the courage to acknowledge the past and let go now that my feelings toward God are in the open.

I still feel like a kid - one with a sense of humor, one who enjoys occasional mischief and one who loves to discover something new. I've been lucky enough to see God's world and I know that regardless of where I am on this globe, He has created good people. We are all the same - trying hard, seeking to understand and wanting to do what's right.

Complications from internal bleeding lengthened the surgery by two hours. The doctor told my family, "We had to literally lift all her organs and set them aside to find the bleeder. Also, the cyst was much larger than we expected. We had such a difficult time getting it through the incision. She's going to have a difficult recovery."

My faith idled. I was scared that if I got tight with God again, a wave of adversity might strike. Things like bleeders and large cysts. Lost friends.

Somehow my career soared despite the string of setbacks outside the office. No one could break me. I'd proven that.

But my neurological event broke me in many ways. I felt defeated. Unable to keep up with conversations. Unable to absorb new information. Fatigued at all times.

With the uncertainty of my condition, I accelerated disclosing truths that haunted me to Dr. James at each session. I didn't want to die with them weighing me down. My chest tightened and hands tingled. My stomach had that fight-or-flight feeling, causing a dull ache. Dr. James waited me out. I wondered what he thought. I felt like I was on stage.

As I revealed the pains of my past to my therapist, my harbored secrets unwound violently, like getting rid of a stomach bug. Dr. James didn't flinch. I felt like he'd silently been rooting for me all along. Like he knew I was too scared to open up, too afraid to say these things out loud because then I could no longer push them away. I was afraid of baring my fears and pains, exposing a fractured self. A figure of shame and pity. I feared judgment: Why didn't you leave with your friends at the club? You wouldn't have been raped. Why did you stay in the toxic marriage for so long?

Dr. James acknowledged that someone with these experiences might feel shame and humiliation. I agreed in silence, feeling like my heart bore a large hole. With Dr. James' guidance and a lot of dread, I dissected each and every ugly part of the rape. As I relived the terror, I forgave myself for one wrong decision, realizing finally how powerless my 100-pound body was against an animalistic athlete. Again, Dr. James didn't flinch. He encouraged me to get it out, to release the nightmare that silently held me back. Misplaced blame, he said.

Unlike the previous trials in my life, my neurological challenges made me think life was ending ... and quickly. I felt I needed to be at peace with myself ... and with my faith.

"How are you with God these days?" Dr. James asked, as if he had an ability to read my mind.

As we crossed the delicate threshold into religious territory, my body shivered. I bowed my head, but in a guilty fashion instead of the praying stance.

I hated where I was. My intent was always to lead a family on an amazing journey with Christ. Knowing and trusting that He "had our backs." Praying openly before each meal, before bedtime and at trying moments when our faith gave us unwavering strength as well as thankfulness for the good coming our way. I chastised myself for abandoning a career in youth ministry. And even though I never quit praying, I felt God had me on a long leash, impatiently waiting for me to "find my way back."

I was ashamed that traumatic events stole me away, not bringing me closer like so many of the 'born again' stories I heard. On the occasional trip to church, I sat near loyal followers whose beliefs allowed them to express themselves outwardly with raised hands. I hoped some of their faith might rub off on me. But I never could quite regain the soulful rhythm. I felt robbed. I figured my long-gone faith had just been a naïve and gullible following.

As I repeated my therapist's question in my mind about my relationship with God, I shuddered at the thought of how I'd let the last 19 years evaporate.

We prayed. Well, Dr. James did. I leaned my head back like a passenger in a car that just bolted forward. *What's he doing? Therapists can't do this. I know I need to, but I'm not ready yet.* He invited me to participate. I cowered, and instead listened to each word, wanting to memorize his phrases so I'd know how to address God later, on my own, in private. I picked at a fingernail, pretending not to listen.

Dr. James told God I was mad at Him. That I was let down. I kept my head bowed down, sad that this was my reality and ashamed someone had to speak these words on my behalf.

With my strained memory repeating each word he uttered like a lifeline, I grasped for a personal meaning. Being angry at God was a natural response to my series of traumatic events. I no longer had to feel guilty for being disappointed in Him. All along I thought that my unwavering faith bought me a ticket to idealistic happiness and when that didn't happen, it was all His fault. Dr. James tiptoed into the idea of free will. And like a child who knew her parent was right, I sulked at the realization that God didn't do these things to me and He didn't allow them to happen.

That night I heard Gino Vannelli's song "Living Inside Myself." *Divine intervention? Hmmm...* I wasn't sure, but I knew that every time I listened to this song since abandoning church, it tugged at me to rediscover my spiritual path. "'Cause I am lost. Living inside myself. Afraid of what life really means. Living without your love." The clock ticked in my head. *I'm overdue. I've gotta straighten things out.*

Within a couple of weeks, I quit playing church on occasional Sundays and welcomed Him back, with the first full-time commitment since my early 20s. I dropped my guard and cautiously trusted again. I felt like I was silently daring Him to fail me once more in the near future so I could shout, "See? I knew I couldn't trust you!"

I realized that the stroke or neurological issues were the last in the series of reasons to be angry at God. So while I tried forgiving Him for shutting down parts of my brain, I found a new ability not to feel dismissed when loved ones said, "You seem just fine to me."

I learned that people always want to find the best in others. Even when it's not there. They accepted my less-than-perfect state, complete with newfound disabilities. It was human nature to overlook my shortcomings.

I realized that to most people, I was functioning at 100 percent. They didn't see the amount of effort required for me to recall the last thing they said. They didn't see me bounce from task to task like an ADHD child, unable to finish anything in a timely manner. They didn't realize that some projects never began because I was too scared of failing at something that was once easy for me. They didn't notice that sometimes I tapped the desk when the phone rang, instead of answering it, confused by a simple procedure.

It took a year for me to reveal that I made an error with my photography passion in fear of not being a "real photographer." On a trip, my memory card no longer fit in the camera. In a desperate move, I disclosed the issue to a camera shop. The problem? The memory card was being inserted the wrong way. Humiliating. I couldn't figure out basic issues. But even more important, no one could feel the weight of my past bearing down on me, pleading with my senses to just let me cry.

I refused to subscribe to the theory that "everything happens for a reason." This would shake my faith once more because there is no God who allows children to prematurely die or adults to survive the series of struggles I endured. But I strongly believe that what we do with those circumstances shape us, for better or worse. I decided to choose the better path.

Chapter 27: Hold On

March 17, 2010

With butterflies dancing in my belly, I dialed the number to Massachusetts General Hospital in Boston. *I'm not sure why I'm nervous. It's not like the doctor is going to answer.*

A friendly voice answered.

"MGH appointment line. May I help you?"

"Yesh," I replied.

Ugh. Not the slurring.

An awkward silence fell while the lady on the other line waited for my next response.

"I'd like to make an appointment with a neurologisht."

"Can you please provide a brief description of your visit? This will help us decide if a neurologist is the most appropriate specialist."

Please don't get in my way. No gatekeepers now. I just want help.

"I've been in touch with Dr. Jill Bolte-Taylor. You know, the Harvard brain shcientist who ..."

Deep breath.

"... tellsss her story of a major stroke in her best-shelling book, *My Ssstroke of Insssight*? ..."

No response. Not impressed with name dropping.

"... She suggested I ... ssseee a neurologist there at MGH due to what ... sounds like a ... sssstroke."

Could there be any more Ss in one statement??

I provided a few symptoms and a brief description of the onset.

"Please hold while I check availability for a neurologist."

My foot tapped. I squeezed a stress ball.

"Ma'am, are you able to come to the Boston area in mid-May?"

"Is that the earliest you have?"

"I'm afraid so with the type of doctor you need to see. This is a vascular neurologist."

Sounds impressive. Yes. It's worth the wait. Gives me time to collect medical records and get copies of MRIs.

"I'll take it."

The date stared back at me. I quickly looked up the doctor's profile, subconsciously deciding if I'd like him or if he'd frustrate me like so many of the others. His photo looked like he was waiting for the punch line to a joke. Thinning hair: experience. Thin face: he practices what he preaches. Eyes: caring and insightful. He resembled my favorite college professor, so I decided I liked him. I willed enough hope into his eyes that I thought the photo might diagnose me on the spot.

Dr. Hope smiled back, still waiting for the punch line. I rocked back and forth, singing Wilson Phillips' *Hold On.*

Don't you know. Things can change. Things'll go your way. If you hold on for one more day.

Even though Dr. Bolte-Taylor thought I should push for answers until I got the one that made sense, I closed the laptop, deciding that if I traveled all the way to Boston to meet with an expert, this would be my last big effort. I couldn't afford letting another doctor make me feel like a head case. This was it.

May 5, 2010

Dr. [Hope],

I have an appointment with you at 9 a.m. on 17 May at MGH West. The purpose of my visit is to seek more answers to a neurological episode I experienced on 6 February 2008, which has resulted in both short- and long-term impairments. To date, I've not had a definitive diagnosis and I'm seeking another opinion from a reputable hospital such as MGH for some potential closure on this experience and its chances of repeating itself.

I was referred to MGH by Dr. Jill Bolte-Taylor, the Harvard brain scientist who suffered a major stroke and has since taken her story public to help others. I saw her at an SMU lecture in Dallas and we've since exchanged several emails. She speaks very highly of your institution. I've attached the initial letter to her, which explains my episode in full detail. The subsequent attachments are my doctors' records and MRIs since this episode. All are attached with one exception: a TEE was performed in July 2008 and I don't have those records, although I can say that the heart appeared in good condition with no sign of a hole.

I look forward to meeting you in a week or so and am anxious to get your professional opinion.

Kind regards,

Rebecca (Becky) Dennis

May 9, 2010

Since the frank discussion on faith with Dr. James, I eased back into the thought of finding a new church home. I set aside my anger, coaxing myself to "let go and let God." My guilt tormented me during my church-going absence, regardless of my fury or reasons. My learned belief system fought my internal spirit. Good parents take their kids to church. Good parents overcome their own obstacles or dismiss them in order to serve the family.

I decided to take Cole to church after an off-and-on sabbatical. The 'on' part: when I wasn't worn out from travel, using a Sunday to catch up on sleep. Or when I dug my heels into the validity of my theological dispute. The 'off' part: when I created spiritual opportunities outside the organized church. Cole and I spent Sunday mornings in a park reading devotionals, dissecting verse meanings. And the occasional trip to church to check that box.

My childhood guilt strings lacked bungee elasticity. They held tight. I struggled with how to blend Cole's more rigid religious beliefs outside our home with my perspective: someone who believed in God, but begrudged the loose definition of Christianity. I resented the all-too-familiar "Christians" who used God as a weapon. Ones whose church attendance justified pitting them against well-meaning people. Ones who represented "what's right" verbally, but whose actions failed to match. Ones who created separation or tension within a family.

The week before heading to Boston, I got even with my guilt. I decided to attend a new church. A friend suggested we try a Lutheran congregation. So there Cole and I sat, in metal folding chairs that lacked the formality of the ritualistic Methodist church I knew so well. We didn't stand up and sit down, guided by creeds that we proclaimed. No booming organ that generated chills. A simple piano, worn by use. No large sanctuary with stained glass windows. The church consisted of a large room with tiled floor that might double as a Friday night dance floor. Crosses didn't hang in every line of sight.

With my head bowed and eyes closed during the prayer, I felt Cole wrap his hand around my arm. I wonder what he needs. He's so reverent. I'm surprised he'd ask for something at this time. I opened my eyes to help him. Except his hand wasn't on my arm. No one's hand was on my arm.

Chills tickled my spine, prompting an inner peace that seized me like a spiritual cocoon. At that moment, I knew God and I were good with each other and He would be with me in Boston.

Chapter 28: I'm Not Crazy

May 16, 2010 (2 years, 3 months after onset)

On the long-awaited morning trip to Boston, I felt like I should have been sent off with banners, balloons and streamers for good luck. I fantasized about the emotional satisfaction and relief of a definitive diagnosis, whatever that might be. My eyes stung in hopes of a brief cry. I wanted to unleash the constant time bomb feeling.

I absentmindedly rehearsed my story, afraid of leaving out details. I felt like a lone witness in court whose testimony determined an acquittal or a life sentence. *This is it. I have to get it right.* I feared a non-answer or that he might be influenced by all the non-conclusions.

May 17, 2010

8 a.m.

I gave up on sleep at my hotel after only three hours. I also rejected work, reading and anything else that required concentration. So I jumped in the car an hour before the appointment to ensure I didn't get lost.

On the way, I eased up to a green light, pressing the brakes while sitting in the right lane. The car behind me honked while I sat there. *Jerk. Sorry I stopped in the right lane, which I rarely do, but you'll have to wait your turn until the light changes to turn right.* More honking. And a gesture I couldn't ignore. *Give it up, buddy.* Cars on my left gracefully passed through the green light. As the light turned yellow, I realized my mistake, speeding through, feeling damaged.

I pulled into the parking lot 50 minutes early, contemplating how to kill time.

8:40 a.m.

I entered a waiting room, the only patient there. The waiting room felt more like a living room than a medical office. I perched on a blue chair, too eager to sit back. I studied Dr. Hope's bio one more time, unsure why. *What am I going to do? Cross-examine his qualifications?*

He entered the lobby casually, almost as if he were a patient. He sipped his coffee, greeting the office staff as if they were peers.

At 9 a.m. on the dot, a medical assistant with soothing eyes the green of aloe vera called me back to an examination room. She seemed relaxed, not pressured by a clock. She chatted while conducting the typical blood pressure and temperature checks, her voice a pitch suitable for a child. She didn't ask the purpose, which surprised me. Pleasantly. I never knew how much to tell the assistants who asked. I felt like they were going to screen whether I really needed the doctor's attention.

A few moments later, a tall Dr. Hope walked in with a big smile and firm handshake. *Just like his photo. I should tell a joke. Let him get that laugh out.* I felt optimistic, yet guarded. After traveling nearly 2,000 miles, I yearned for a conclusive answer.

Dr. Hope sat down, immediately crossing his legs and accepting that I sat in a regular chair, not on the exam table. His dark hair thinned on top despite his being probably only 10 years older than I am.

"I apologize for drinking coffee in front of you. Do you mind?" he asked.

I don't care if you smoke a joint as long as you listen.

"Not at all," I answered.

"So how can I help you, Miss Dennis?" he asked cordially in a strong accent that hinted Swiss, French and/or German. His head tilted, taking an immediate interest in me like we were on a first date, not a patient visit.

"I'm here to hopefully get some closure on a neurological event I suffered in India two years ago," I told him, accidentally adopting his accent.

Oh gosh. My band director, Mr. Kunkel, would be saying, "Paint your face red, hon'!"

He smiled, "Are you the one who sent the large packet?"

"Yes," I answered, careful not to repeat my lame European accent.

"I've been looking forward to meeting you," he said, taking a big sip of his coffee as if it might be awhile before he got to pick it up again. "Do let me step out and fetch your papers."

Within a minute he was back with my large pile of medical records. I felt like they should have been stamped with big red letters that said, "Wrong!"

"You have an interesting case, Miss Dennis."

"I guess you can call it interesting," I smiled back nervously. "But I suppose my words would be more like 'frightening' and 'hard to diagnose'."

"Why don't you start from the beginning and tell me the scenario in your own words," he prompted, sitting back in his chair and shifting to just one crossed leg, as if story time had begun.

Dimples formed on both of his cheeks even though he no longer smiled. His face looked perpetually pleasant. He bit his bottom lip ever so slightly. I thought about Cole telling me, "You can't say the word 'bubble' and be mad."

I started with the initial pain I experienced in my left leg. He nodded, glancing at my large packet of information as if he recalled this from reviewing my medical records. I continued ... how I felt great the morning of the event--mentally strong enough to make a presentation to my company's top leaders.

I paused, checking in for a response. Dr. Hope's boyish smile and long eyelashes blinked back, prompting me to continue.

I unfolded the neurological episode, starting with the disorientation and inability to form words. I talked about the brightness and feeling of being distant from everything.

"Then everything escalated nearly at once. Tingling, followed by numbness, followed by inability to grasp anything, then periods of blackout," I told him. I explained the impact to my day-to-day life since this inexplicable event. I felt more at ease to open up, perhaps because I knew I'd never see him again. Never judged on a return visit of "oh, here comes the crazy lady."

"That's quite a remarkable story, Miss Dennis," he offered.

Please, God, let him have answers.

"I have some theories in mind, so what I would like you to do is start over from the beginning and leave nothing out, even if you don't think it's relevant ... " he instructed.

Now he sat on the edge of his chair, seeming taller than when he stood. His hands clasped. His thumbs tapped as if counting.

"... Oh, and I will stop you occasionally with questions for clarification," he said.

This time, I went into painstaking detail, including everything I could recall from that day. I mentioned the inability to swallow. How I was freezing when they took me into the ER.

"Did you have fever?" he asked.

"I don't know. I don't remember them taking my temperature and it's not recorded on the medical records."

I continued and he stopped me many times, asking about the duration of a symptom or having me rate its intensity on a scale from one to 10. I'd answer and he'd jot down notes. Then I'd continue.

"Did you have rush?" he interrupted.

I could tell this was an important question from his change in demeanor, but I wasn't sure what "rush" was.

"I'm sorry, can you please repeat the question?" I asked.

"Yes. Did you have rush?" he stated with more clarity in his mind than certainly in mine.

I still didn't get it. *I've had lots of medical problems, but I have no clue what 'rush' is.*

Cued by my lack of response while I repeated "rush" in my head, Dr. Hope gestured as he touched all over his body, "You know, rush. Breakout all over the body?"

I laughed at the brief language barrier when I blurted out in East Texan, "Raaash! I get it now. No, I didn't have a rash. Nor a rush."

He laughed heartily, his dimples creating a canyon in his cheeks.

I explained I was from East Texas and that we exaggerated our vowels, sometimes adding more syllables to a word because of it. And he laughed again, making me feel more comfortable about being there.

I glanced at my watch. I'd already been there for 45 minutes.

After peppering me with more questions, he paused and took a deep breath. I tried not to read anything into it, but if I'd given myself another moment I would have guessed either futile exasperation or the calm before a storm.

"Miss Dennis," he began, straightening his posture. "I reviewed all of your records and I believe you have been misdiagnosed altogether. Let me help you understand why."

Please don't tell me this is just stress.

Dr. Hope dissected the complex migraine diagnosis, explaining that it would be impossible to have a migraine that lasted two years or for it to have developed a chronic condition like numbness, fatigue or memory issues. Then he attacked the TIA diagnosis, dismissing it simply on the fact that I had ongoing issues and a mini-stroke doesn't produce lingering symptoms after the episode.

"What about stroke?" I asked cautiously.

"While your MRIs show abnormalities, they are inconsistent with a stroke. The symptoms you experienced affected all areas of the brain, not just one hemisphere. Strokes are not bilateral like in your case."

I remembered Dr. Magnum, our family friend, saying this very thing.

"A stroke would have been readily visible on the MRI, too." He went into more detail about how my situation compared to a stroke occurrence. My concentration level dissipated, making it hard to keep up with him anymore. I pleaded for my brain to hang on a little longer.

"With what you have described, I believe that you were presented with encephalitis," he concluded, a tinge of worry in his eyes.

"Ensaphis?"

"Encephalitis ... is swelling in the brain and can be caused by a variety of sources. It can create long-term damage based on the intensity of swelling and the duration."

He squinted as if getting a read on my internal emotional reaction.

"So you don't think there was a clot in my leg?"

"I believe the pain in your leg was coincidental and not consistent with deep vein thrombosis ..."

My thoughts yelled louder than his voice. *Swelling in the brain? Yahoo! I feel vindicated. I'm not crazy!*

His worrisome look remained, as if he genuinely cared about my reaction to absorbing this new information. I scanned my brain for questions. I didn't know what to ask. My thoughts swarmed. None stuck long enough for me to remember.

Dr. Hope seemed to detect my state of bewilderment. He cleared his throat.

"One question you might ask is my degree of certainty of this diagnosis," he offered.

Such a mixture of feelings collided inside that I was certain I had uncovered a new emotion.

"Uh. Yeah."

"All of your symptoms are consistent with encephalitis. Many patients experience diarrhea or rush and with their absence in your case, did not trigger doctors to consider this diagnosis. I give this a 99 percent confidence rate. A spinal tap would make it 100 percent, but with all you've been through, I just don't feel like it's necessary or worth the risk. And the source may no longer be detected by testing."

I stared at him, uncertain what to do next. I marveled at his ability to reach a diagnosis through process of elimination.

He asked, "Do you have any questions? I can take as long as you'd like."

I felt guilty for taking up too much of his time.

"I've never heard of encephalitis, so I don't have a lot of questions."

"Ask what you want now and then I'll give you my business card with my personal contact information. You clearly aren't going to come all the way up here when you have questions, so I'm happy to help you as you need."

"Will this ever come back?"

My fingernails dug into my palms, fearful of his answer. I wished I hadn't asked it.

"Most likely, no. You've been through the worst and what you are experiencing now are sequela from the encephalitis."

Sequela?

"What caused this to happen?"

His legs crossed. The right one bounced up and down.

"A mosquito bite in India is the most likely cause. It would be uncommon for this to be contracted any other way based on the region of the world you were in at the time it unfolded and your current condition."

"Am I contagious?"

"No. You are not infectious anymore, and encephalitis is not contagious."

"Do the MRIs reveal anything related to encephalitis?"

"Yes. The abnormalities represent scarring from the infection in your brain."

"Will exercise, stress or anything else exacerbate the ... sequelae?"

I wasn't sure I used the term in the right way.

"Yes. Stress and exercise exacerbate them, but will not cause permanent damage. When the stress is over, the symptoms will return to be what they were before the trigger."

"Is there any particular diet you recommend to help on my way to a full recovery?"

"No. Try to live a normal lifestyle and allow for extra rest."

My head throbbed. I paused, wishing that my GP or therapist were there to step in. I learned that herpes was a common cause of encephalitis, but my MRI didn't fit the telling pattern of herpes. And another cause of encephalitis other than the mosquito-borne nature was an auto-immune disorder. That didn't fit either, or my symptoms would have been even more severe.

"You look tired, Ms. Dennis. I suggest you go back to your hotel to rest. Then study about encephalitis and email me directly with your additional questions. Unless, of course, there's anything else at the moment."

I paused, not wanting the appointment to end. I reveled in the moment of being in the presence of someone who understood me. Who believed me. Who had answers.

"Gosh ... I don't know how to thank you ..."

My right hand rested on my right temple, glued until my thoughts cleared.

" ... I got exactly what I came for: an accurate diagnosis. One that makes sense and doesn't cop out on stress as the answer."

He laughed, revealing the canyons again.

"There is no way stress caused any of this. You've been through a lot. It's amazing you've kept working through all of this. It's a real testament to your strength and fight for life," he said.

You can't even imagine. If only I had witnesses here to hear this first hand. I wanted to laugh and cry all at once.

Dr. Hope broke the silence, "Let me give you my card. It was a distinct pleasure meeting you, Ms. Dennis."

With my hand out, I accepted his card, resisting the urge to just give an all-out bear hug. I thanked him profusely, shaking his hand as if he were sent from Heaven.

Chapter 29: I Will Not Go Quietly

May 16, 2010
10:15 a.m.

Walking out of MGH, pride filled my spirits as if I'd just earned an esteemed award. My steps flowed with confidence. Birds and rustling leaves drowned out the traffic. Sunbeams shone down on me. And only me. This was my day.

With this revelation, I wanted to contact all my doctors and family to share the news right away. To tell them I wasn't a lunatic. I imagined a plane pulling a banner behind it with just one word: Encephalitis! The radio played light and fun music, an unfamiliar tune that made me feel like I was Mario in a video game. Nothing could destroy this high.

"So it wasn't a stroke," I told Gary on the phone as I walked to my rental car.

"What was it? Were they able to tell you anything definitive?"

"Encephalitis. Swelling of the brain."

I lobbed as much of my conversation with Dr. Hope as possible at Gary. He listened without interruption, an art I'd yet to master. I admired that trait in him.

"I told you it was all in your head."

I rolled my eyes, but noted how our flippant comments brought us closer together, not creating division.

"Yep."

"So how did you get it?"

"Most likely a mosquito bite in India, he thinks."

"I knew it," Gary said.

"You called it. I went back more times because I was certain it had nothing to do with where I was."

"You saying you were wrong?" he asked, laughing with caution.

"I'm saying you were right."

"Wait. Say that again. I was right?"

"You were right."

"Yes! Just made my day."

"So listen to this."

"Anything you want. Today I was right," he quipped.

"Shut up ... "

I thought of all the people I wanted to call.

"But it was your brain, for sure? Sounds like you're lucky to be alive. You're still my little be-otch."

I paused, distracted by which direction to go even though the hotel was only two blocks away. I couldn't remember how I got there.

"So do the symptoms ever go away?" Gary asked.

"Some already have. Appears the ones I still have may or may not. After this much time, it looks like they'll always be here and stress makes them worse."

"So quit your job," he said, as if that was an option.

"Right ... So I'm gonna go. Gonna make some calls."

"I'm proud of my little wifette. You're awesome. It took guts to go up there, uncertain if you'd get an answer."

"Thanks, Hubinator. I was scared of being stuck with nothing that made sense."

"I know you were scared. I know you better than you know you."

"Why did I know you'd say that?"

"I'm just sorry you're gonna be there the rest of the week on business. Wish I could hug you right now."

"Call ya later."

After reaching my hotel room, I pulled the long brown drapes open. Sun flooded into the room, magnifying the dust dancing in the air. My fingers rushed to Google, typing in "encephalitis" with excitement. You'd think I was researching the fine print of a free trip I just won. My foot tapped in time with my heart.

The first link, PubMed Health[4], offered a basic definition, so I clicked on it and read it out loud, a trick to help with my comprehension.

"Encephalitis is irritation and swelling (inflammation) of the brain, most often due to infections. Encephalitis is a rare condition. Mild symptoms are low fever, mild headache and low energy. Patients might also have clumsiness, disorientation or light sensitivity."

"Severe or emergency cases cause more serious symptoms such as poor responsiveness, muscle weakness, lack of emotion, withdrawal from social interaction, or memory loss," I read aloud again, remembering how I hated doing this in school. Afraid I might mispronounce something.

This is describing me! It's as if someone secretly followed me around, documenting my experience.

I leaned back in my chair, then got up to pace the room for a moment. I took a deep breath, then resumed the Web search, browsing a few more sites, trying to understand it better.

The Encephalitis Society[5], an organization committed to research and recovery of encephalitis, provided interesting facts. The stats alarmed me.

"The incidence is reported as 7.4/100,000 (based on U.S. statistics). Anyone can become ill with encephalitis, at any age. The inflammation can damage nerve cells resulting in 'acquired brain injury.'

Compared to other infectious diseases, encephalitis has a high mortality rate.

Recovery is a long and slow process. An initial period of convalescence with plenty of rest is recommended. This should be followed by a program of graded activity and rest over 3 - 6 months to give the brain the opportunity to restore function."

The last one cut deep. No wonder Dr. Hope looked concerned. I leaned back in my chair as my heart pumped as if in a tight race.

---

[4] PubMed Health www.ncbi.nlm.nih.gov/pubmedhealth/PMH0002388/
[5] The Encephalitis Society http://www.encephalitis.info/Info/TheIllness/TheIllnessPortal.aspx

I stared at the star patterns on the curtains. Hotel doors slammed in the distance. The smell of stale coffee lingered in from the hallway. I grew angry, thinking how hard I pushed myself.

"The illness can be very quickly fatal, causing extreme trauma for all the family. It is difficult to understand why a virus infection in the modern world can have such devastating consequences."

I felt robotic, able to take in the information intellectually, but not able to fully feel it yet.

I grabbed my iPod, searching for a tune to relax me and get me back in the moment. Don Henley's *I Will Not Go Quietly* grabbed me. The lyrics rattled in my head: "Woke up with a heavy head. I could've died if I wanted to. Slipped over the edge and drowned. I won't give up that easily."

My finger skimmed across the tabs along the left side of the site. With so much information, I couldn't decide where to start. My eyes stung from so much reading, blurring my vision. I spoke loudly in my room as if trying to crowd out other noises that distracted me.

"Diagnosis/Treatment

Types of Encephalitis

FAQs

Information for Family/Friends

Bereavement/Death"

Crap! The mortality rate is high enough that death is a tab? I gasped, as if suffocating from my own emotions. I felt the need to surface for air. Sadness. Anger. Confusion. Exasperation. Frustration. All mixed with a strange sense of relief from knowing I didn't have to feel like I was about to explode anymore.

My anger escalated as I reflected on how hard I had pushed myself to appear "normal" despite the constant distractions. The more I learned about the long recovery and mortality rates, the more I wanted my "stroke" diagnosis back. I sat there dumbfounded for a while until it registered that the worst was over: I was a survivor. An encephalitis survivor. A "cephivor."

A text message beeped, breaking my research trance. I looked at the clock, realizing several hours had ticked away during my fact-finding mission. *Time for a break.*

2:15 p.m.

"What will you have to drink?" the waitress asked. The lunch crowd had long disappeared.

"You know?" I paused. "I think I'll have a celebratory glass of wine."

The day was mine. I deserved to toast my perseverance despite it being a little early for some pleasurable imbibing.

"Sounds great," she agreed. "What are we celebrating?"

Her short blond hair bounced slightly. She smiled. Almost too quickly. *Fake? I don't know.*

Without a warning, I felt tears run down my face as I choked on the overwhelming emotions that absorbed me. I struggled to smile, finally registering I had an answer. A right answer. She squatted next to me.

I made it. If I'd been diagnosed correctly, I could have taken off months to recover. And maybe with better results.

"Sorry," I apologized at my unexpected release of emotions. "I just got good news from a doctor that I'm on the path to wellness." I couldn't think of how else to explain it.

"Oh, don't apologize," she fussed, patting me again, and then, like an angel, took my hand and looked me in my eyes. "I'm so happy for you. I can tell you deserve the good news. Let me get you that glass right away. First one's on me. I'm Lisa."

Visions of both of my grandmothers came to me when she left. I could picture Momo, my dad's mom, smiling and winking, telling me "I love you bigger than the moon." I could sense what she'd say at any moment with amazing clarity even though she'd been gone for three years.

I also pictured Mammo, my mom's mom. But instead of imagining her strapped to her wheelchair like a helpless elder, she appeared young as she strolled toward me with open arms, saying, "There now. You're gonna be just fine." My heart ached for both of them. Yet I knew they were present with me.

Fresh oysters jiggled and shined as Lisa ushered the tray to my table. Clam chowder steamed, as if freshly made just for me. Between serving other tables, Lisa checked in with me. A smile that felt like a long-time friend. Happy, yet concerned. She eyed my wine glass, then my eyes.

"Where are you from?" Lisa asked, topping off my water glass.

"Uh ... the Dallas area."

"Texas? Really? You came all the way up here for a doctor visit?"

"Long story, but yes."

I wondered if I should explain, but I didn't know where to begin. I didn't want to burden her with my crazy health journey. But inside, I craved letting it all out.

As I polished off the chowder, I tried constructing the recipe in my head. I realized how I had abandoned following recipes since the onset of encephalitis. How anything process-oriented proved too taxing. Especially getting online at a hotel. Or submitting a claim.

My second glass of pinot grigio temporarily warded off any discomfort from my earlier research. I sat among the handful of patrons, growing lonely despite Lisa's warmth. I sat there like a child who just made straight A's, eager to show off the report card but her parents weren't home.

I made a silent toast to my grandmothers and gulped down the last drop of wine.

"You heading out?" Lisa asked.

"Yeah. I guess I'd better get on my way."

"It was a pleasure serving you on this occasion of victory."

Her eyes misted. Her compassion revealed all my emotions bubbling beneath the surface. I felt bizarre. Even though I felt happy enough to break into air guitar and so vindicated that I fought the urge to yell like Tarzan, my sadness and frustration grounded me. *It shouldn't have been this way. It shouldn't have been such a struggle.*

As the check came, my fingers tapped away at text messages to my faithful doctors.

"Becky here. Just left my appointment at MGH. Would love to share his diagnosis if you have time to talk today or tmrw."

I wonder how they'll respond to the diagnosis. Will they concur or disagree? I hope I can remember enough to convey Dr. Hope's answer. I can't wait to talk to them.

Dr. Welby called right away. I filled him in, feeling like I'd earned somewhat of a medical degree through experience.

"I'm so relieved for you. Hearing this diagnosis makes me feel relieved, too. It makes perfect sense given your symptoms. I'm so glad you pressed on until you heard something that truly fit your situation. We all look at things through a different lens and none of us have all the answers."

"In my reading, I've discovered so many struggles I deal with daily that I didn't know to mention. I had no idea they were related."

"Like what? Give me an example or two. This is intriguing."

"Noisy environments are difficult. Like a loud restaurant. I give up. I just quit listening because it's too hard. Another one is missing words. I'm constantly editing in my mind before I speak because so many words 'go missing.'"

This research is so reassuring to me. Everything makes so much sense now.

"Becky, from now on, when you leave the country, you are required to be inside a giant bubble," he said, maybe just half jokingly. He'd helped me in other out-of-country instances, including my allergic reaction to the neoprene wetsuit during my recent trip to Australia.

My other doctors were just as supportive, commenting on how this diagnosis fit perfectly. They all expressed humility for not having had the right answer. I felt bad, having called out of excitement, not for an apology or an "I told you so." I didn't want them to feel bad about it. I just wanted to celebrate. For the first time since the onset, I knew the worst was behind me.

3:45 p.m.

After reaching my room, I resumed my research. Several sites mentioned the different strains of encephalitis based on the geography where it was contracted. Again, I read aloud to help comprehension, as if I had a classroom in front of me.

"In Southeast Asia, the most prevalent cause of encephalitis is known as Japanese Encephalitis (JE), caused by a mosquito." *That's what Dr. Hope said. Probably a freaking mosquito.*

I reread it again silently, as if embarrassed that my class might realize my difficulty in learning new information.

" ... JE is one of several mosquito-borne viruses that can affect the central nervous system and cause severe complications and death.[6]"

I looked up for a moment. *Death. My gosh.*

" ... There is no specific treatment for JE. Antibiotics are not effective against viruses, and no effective anti-viral drugs have been discovered. Care of patients centers on treatment of symptoms and complications."

God, thanks for giving me the courage to take one more journey. For taking the risk to search for the truth. For giving me the resources to push this hard. For loving me even when I've been so angry at You. I knew nothing would shake my faith again.

---

[6] Directors of Health Promotion and Education https://dhpe.site-ym.com/

I rolled my head from shoulder to shoulder to release the tightness gripping me.

" ... Confusion and agitation can also occur in the early stage.

The illness can progress to a serious infection of the brain (encephalitis) and can be fatal in 30% of cases. Among the survivors, another 30% will have serious brain damage."

My feet propelled me backward in my roller chair. I stood up and paced the room. My thumbs tapped together at a pace that only Looney Tunes could keep up with.

"... The chance that a traveler to Asia will get JE is very small: among persons who are infected by a mosquito bite, only 1 in 50 to 1 in 1,000 will develop an illness. As a result, less than 1 case per year is reported in U.S. civilians and military personnel traveling to and living in Asia. Only 5 cases among Americans traveling or working in Asia have been reported since 1981."

I stared in the mirror beside the desk, afraid of the anger in my own eyes.

"You're kidding me! If this was the cause, I'm the sixth unlucky schmuck in the U.S. in **30 years** to contract this deadly virus! Give me a freakin' break!" I yelled to no one.

I couldn't tear myself away from learning more. The more I read about lingering symptoms, the more I felt like someone had secretly conducted a case study on me and then documented it on this Web site. Easily distracted. Yep. Short-term memory loss. Yep. I thought about the exploded boiled eggs, and suddenly it made more sense. I pictured fun dinners with family or friends. Laughing, sharing, clearly enjoying myself. And the next day not being able to recall any of it other than where we ate, if lucky. The entire conversation melted like snow.

The Encephalitis Society[7] described how the inflammation damaged and destroyed nerve cells, referring to the resulting damage as acquired

---

[7] Encephalitis Society www.encephalitis.info/Info/TheIllness/TheIllnessPortal.aspx

brain injury (ABI). My jaw dropped, finally absorbing the realization that my remaining symptoms were 'brain damage.'

I felt like someone inflated with so much energy I might detonate. I wanted to run away from the facts. I grabbed my phone, scrolling with vengeance.

"Yo," I told Angela when she answered.

"Sup?"

"Got a freakin' diagnosis."

"Whoa. Hang on. Let me hang up on this call. Right back witcha."

She returned. Enthusiastic. Inquisitive.

"I freakin' have drain bamage!" I exclaimed when Angela came back.

"We always knew it, Beck. Guess you're the last one to know."

I pounded out the facts at her. Wishing she had made the trip with me. Wishing I'd asked in the first place. I need a tape recorder. I'm going to have to do this over and over. Each family member. Each doctor. Each close friend.

"I'm reading all this crap and it's like reading my own notes. Not all of it fits, but they say no two cases are alike. When I read this, I feel vindicated. Understood. Credible!"

"I'm sorry, Beck," Angela said softly. "None of us had any idea what you were really going through. We just know it's been tough and that this trip meant a lot to you ..."

I sniffled in response. No tears, but acknowledging this was what I wanted to hear. I needed this.

"So tell me more about it. Was there something they could have done for you?" Angela asked.

"I've read a ton so far ..."

"No surprise there."

"... and what's disturbingly comforting is that even if I'd been diagnosed accurately right away, there wasn't a damn thing they could have done for me."

"Dang, Beck."

My voice cracked, muting my reply. *Brain needs to rest. No treatment. Six cases in 30 years. Extreme fatigue. Bereavement. Memory loss. Mosquito bite. Fatal for one in three.*

" ... You okay? What is it? Do you want me to fly up there? Are they keeping you for treatment?"

"It's ... "

My thoughts disintegrated.

I felt my frustration rip through my veins. Dr. James would have been proud. Far from my "I don't know's" every time he asked what I felt.

"Take your time, Becky."

My hotel note pad looked like a medical roadmap. Facts and figures zigzagged in every white space possible. I turned the pages like a steering wheel to ensure I covered everything I knew.

"So there's absolutely no treatment for JE. It's preventable with a vaccination but not treatable," I said.

"JE?"

"Oh. Sorry. Japanese Encephalitis was the strain I evidently had."

"But you weren't in Japan."

"No, but if you look at a map of how widespread this strain of encephalitis is, it's amazing. JE is like the Southeast Asian version of West Nile. They're actually related."

"Ah. Got it."

My mind wandered as she spoke. I pictured myself in the backseat of the car on the way to the ER while I seemed to cling to life with each breath. *Thank God I didn't die alone half a globe away.*

"The stats basically said that if you, me and Gary had contracted this strain, one of us wouldn't be coming back. One would have brain damage. The other would be counting blessings, or perhaps not even be aware they'd ever contracted it. Amazing odds. Not in the thousands or even hundreds. Just 'one in three die.'"

"I hate to say you're lucky, cuz I know you're not. You deal with stuff every day or you wouldn't have pursued this trip. But Becky. My gosh. You made it. You're still functioning, and it sounds like it could have been devastating."

"I know it could have, but the silent nature in which it has attacked me is cruel in itself. The daily struggles on top of a lack of diagnosis are like a brain wreck."

" ... I'm so glad you have answers. Try not to read too much so you don't worry yourself with new stuff. You've made it through the roughest parts, I'm sure. Does it say anything about it coming back?"

"I haven't found anything that would suggest that. Based on what the MGH doctor told me, I think I'm just dealing with the infection leftovers or whatever it was he called them. But what those 'leftovers' are is brain damage. That's hard to swallow. What if the rest of my life is this much of a struggle?"

"Most people wouldn't notice because you work so hard at it," she said.

"But I'm tired. I don't want to have to work this hard to appear 'normal.'"

I paced the room, then sat on the edge of the bed, then stood and paced.

"Believe me, there's never been anything normal about you, Beck. As far as I'm concerned, you're the same inside."

"Well, I know the difference and that's enough for me," I shot back. "It's like flying first class your whole life and then going back to coach. You know what you're missing."

"Well, you still make good analogies ... "

I stretched and bit my tongue.

" ... Take a break. Go have a drink and chill out for a while. You're up there by yourself, Beck. If you keep reading, none of us can be there for you when you uncover the more emotional aspects."

My mind flipped back to when I was 8 and a redheaded kid shot me the finger. Thinking it was a secret hand code, I returned the gesture with a big smile on my face, happy to have made a new buddy. Angela had a word with the kid. She enjoyed the role of looking out for me.

"You're right," I admitted. "I'll save the rest for when I get home. I've got a list of questions going for the doctor."

"Promise me you'll stop for a while."

"Promise. I'm headed to get a drink right now. I'll get in my bubble before I leave the room."

4:15 p.m.

"Hang on while I get your dad on the line," Mom said.

I took a deep breath, debating on how much detail to go into.

"So whatdja find out?" Dad asked.

Most of my symptoms only remained noticeable to me at this stage. So much that my parents questioned the expense of the MGH trip the week prior.

"Encephalitis," I replied, flatly.

I twirled in the hotel chair, my feet up in the air, seeing how many times I could make a full circle. Silence stretched through the lines between us. My feet slammed on the brakes.

"Are you still there?" I asked, confused.

"We are very familiar with encephalitis, Pumpkin," Dad said, clearing his throat. " ... A church friend who worked with your mother got this many years back."

He paused, a brief hum that indicated a wish for words, but they didn't come. Mom's silence saddened me. I pictured her sitting down, her eyes locked in a gaze as she digested the facts. Her hands wringing, but every hair in place and her lipstick perfect. I wanted to rub her back to soothe her like she did for me when I was little.

"Oh my gosh ... Oh my gosh. Beck ... her case was terrible. She's a whole different person now. It was severe," Mom said.

My point exactly.

"You have dodged two bullets," Mom continued. "No stroke. And you didn't die from this horrible illness. Oh, Sweetie, we are counting our blessings ..."

Chapter 30: Push to Be "Normal"

May 20, 2010
9:35 p.m.

I returned from Boston, buoyed, feeling that our home no longer represented the most likely place where I might suffer another episode. I felt light for a change. I twirled, singing into my hairbrush, my faux microphone.

"Times have changed and times are strange. Here I come but I ain't the same," I crooned, afraid to admit to Gary it was Ozzy.

"You really shouldn't dance," Gary said.

I wrinkled my nose. My smile brightened. I danced harder.

"You have no natural rhythm. Never do this in public."

I raised my arms in the air, wiggling my butt at Gary, looking for rhythm. Not finding it. Even though the cats wanted to walk figure-eights around my feet to welcome me, they stood their distance. Afraid of my jerky toe-stepping.

My methodical packing and unpacking habits annoyed Gary. I returned toiletries, dirty clothes and shoes to their proper places, abandoning him despite finally being home. He retreated to our bedroom.

10:15 p.m.

"Gary!" I yelled from the office to the bedroom, hoping he'd come find me.

I felt guilty for not coming to bed. For staying up to read an old journal instead of snuggling up to him. For having to investigate something that could wait until the next day. Another change since contracting encephalitis.

"Is something wrong?" Gary asked, darkening the office doorway.

"Listen to this!" I shouted, even though he was standing next to me. I pointed to my journal from the day after my hospital visit in India.

My fingers traced the words as I read him a journal entry:

I'm feeling that my head does not fit in its skull. I'm exhausted, but I move on knowing there's lots to do and observing that my older colleagues who have endured the same late nights and long flights are totally fine.

"Wow!" Gary remarked.

"It's as if I knew what was wrong with me. Why didn't I say it like that to the doctor in India? To [Dr. Welby?] To [Dr. Complacent?]"

Gary rubbed my shoulder, pulling me in toward him.

"Don't beat yourself up. You did the best you could."

"I don't mean it that way. I just mean how in the world did I know that my head didn't feel like it fit in its skull? That's very specific. I remember it was more than feeling stuffy like when you're sick with the flu. And it was different than a migraine. I nailed it back then without even knowing it!"

I shook my head in disbelief.

"Sounds like your condition is so rare that it may not have made a difference."

11:59 p.m.

From my journal:

Got home from Boston tonight. Tired. Absolutely whipped from the week. Monday's news about encephalitis was mentally draining. And then I met 15 clients Monday through Thursday afternoon. I get home and am so happy to be here in my place of comfort. It's now midnight and I feel myself begin to rapidly soften like butter in a microwave. Now that I'm home, I melt emotionally as I absorb the news of the week.

I grieve for myself ... the uncertainty of not trusting the diagnoses received for the last two years. Trusting my gut that something wasn't adding up. Regretful of how I felt I had to conceal so many of my symptoms in fear of sounding like a "head case." Pushing myself so hard to be "normal" so I wouldn't miss work or appear damaged.

I feel lucky to be alive and to have survived when I consider the stats. I feel relieved to have closure.

Chapter 31: Coming Out Party

May 24, 2010

"Becky! Oh my gosh. I've been thinking so much about you," Dr. Welby said, giving me a hug.

I grinned, thinking of a time in the past when he asked about how I found one of my doctors and I told him "at a strip joint." I recalled the look on his face, shocked until he realized I meant "strip mall."

"Pretty big change of diagnosis, huh?"

It felt good to feel like a normal patient. I felt almost giddy in my newfound medical verdict, like I was throwing an encephalitis "coming out" party.

He smiled while backing up -- a teary smile -- maintaining eye contact while maneuvering his butt to locate his chair.

"It really makes perfect sense and I'm so sorry you had such a long journey to figure this out. Like I said before, I admire your tenacity."

Despite resolution, I still felt angry about the stress diagnosis. Even though Dr. Welby cheered me on in my fight for diagnosis, I felt compelled to explain my stance. The year leading up to contracting encephalitis included many stress-reducing actions. Quitting a stressful work environment. Drawing boundaries for work hours. I shuddered at the humiliation caused by the suggestion of this being a psychosomatic issue.

"I'm so sorry you felt that way. I certainly hope I didn't make you feel embarrassed or think that I didn't believe you."

I tried to assure him that, without an accurate diagnosis, some moments I thought I <u>was</u> crazy.

"You offered to send me to MGH two months after it happened and I didn't do it," I said.

Dr. Welby inhaled a big breath and slowly let it out.

"Okay, so tell me what's still bothering you."

I blushed, feeling like the nerdy kid who loves science so much she creates extra credit projects just for fun. I whipped out a chart I created that categorized all of the symptoms I detected. Along the top row, I detailed a series of time lapses, starting with the first day, then the first three months, then the first year, then all ongoing symptoms. The columns listed 36 ailments and disorders I could recall experiencing, including confusing the letter "m" for "4," difficulty concentrating, and a change in smell and taste.

Dr. Welby let out another deep sigh as he studied the long list, going to the far right column where it noted which ones still bothered me.

"Talk to me about your memory loss," he said, as he leaned in to listen.

Ninth grade. Forgot my music folder at the school. Played the entire musical by memory because I was afraid to tell my orchestra director that I left it in the band hall.

"I can't remember conversations. I remember that I had a good time talking with someone, but I can't recall what we discussed. I have to jot down notes constantly."

I tried ignoring my sad and helpless feeling as I looked at the list. I thought of Dr. Bolte-Taylor. *How you react is a choice.* I silently praised her for being the catalyst that led to answers. I might have otherwise still been in the dark.

"Give me other examples if you can."

I leaned my head back and studied the ceiling, as if looking for answers.

"Okay. We have cats and they have their own cat room for their food and litter boxes. I never can remember if I've fed them and scooped litter. I check multiple times because I can't remember what I saw when I last checked. So, we came up with a system. After I take care of their needs, I turn off the light for that room. The switch is on the outside of their room, so now when I wonder if I've actually taken care of them, I look at the switch and know that I have. I don't remember that I have. I just trust that the light switch is in the correct position. And sometimes the only way I know to feed them or check the light switch in the first place is if the cats are dancing across my keyboard to tell me their tummies need feeding."

"Any other examples?" he pressed.

"Gary often has to tell me the same thing as many as 10 times before it's committed to memory. I ask Cole to remind me of things when I don't have a pen and paper available. He's accepted this as a new job: Becky's substitute memory. I never can remember if I've taken my medications. I have a day-of-the-week container but I look at Tuesday's empty container and wonder, 'Did I take those today? Or did I take them last Tuesday and it's time to refill it?'"

"Those are good examples and enough to indicate your memory was definitely compromised. I'm going to recommend that you get a neuropsychological examination so you can work with a specialist who has experience with encephalitis and can give you therapies to help with the recovery process."

He glanced back through my symptom chart tracker and we discussed some of the other struggles. Most I had already come up with strategies as 'work arounds.' But the two that were more physical in nature concerned the constant tingling across my face, exacerbated by stress, and my clumsy right hand.

"Tell me exactly what you mean when you say your hand just doesn't feel right."

"It's hard to describe. It's functional, but I never got all the feeling back. And these two fingers ... it's like they're married."

Using my left hand, I manually pulled the two fingers apart on my right hand. They fused again, like magnets.

"This slows me down in typing. I constantly have to hit backspace to fix errors."

"Uncanny. Only you," he said.

He shook his head and smirked slightly. He seemed to look through me, as if reading a textbook behind my head. I broke the silence, yielding to the family rule.

"I read that some patients experience symptoms for as many as eight years after the swelling and infection," I said. "Some are permanent."

I braced, hoping he'd tell me that mine wouldn't last near as long.

"The brain is an amazing organ, Becky. All I can tell you is that it's great at healing itself and finding new paths where old ones are broken."

I know he can't give me a definitive time frame. I'm not sure why I brought it up.

"You're going to your neurologist, too, right? He may have other tests to recommend."

"Yep. Headed there two days from now."

Water returned to his eyes. *I wonder if he's this gentle with every patient. Or maybe I'm just special. Or maybe my situation hits home with him because someone close had similar issues. Whatever the reason, I appreciate his graciousness.*

May 27, 2010
10:40 a.m.

"So what did your Boston trip reveal? Anything different or interesting?" Dr. Candor asked.

"Encephalitis. Or most likely Japanese Encephalitis based on the region where I was," I replied.

Confidence filled my voice. I smiled, studying his expression.

"What in the world?"

He crinkled up his face like a kid being forced to eat green peas, while scanning the MGH doctor's notes. I fought the urge to break the silence.

"In 29 years of practicing medicine, I've never run across anyone with encephalitis."

He paused, looking me directly in the eyes.

"How in the world did you get ... what did you call it? Japanese encephalitis?"

I laughed, "Supposedly a mosquito bite."

"When you were traveling overseas?"

"Well, I remember mosquitoes on the plane, so it may have been during flight. But I also remember getting bitten on my hand as soon as I left the airport. Hadn't even pulled out of the parking lot yet. I never thought anything of it again."

My body shook as I visualized all the disgusting mosquito images during my Internet research. I felt dirty.

"Huh. Did you have vomiting or fever?" he asked, scrunching up his face again.

"No. And the MGH doctor said that's probably what threw everyone off."

I worked that statement in on purpose, careful not to offend him.

"If I had any stomach issues, I didn't factor them into the equation. I probably just chalked it up to travel tummy, but I really don't recall having a problem of that sort ..."

I paused. His eyes darted between the chart and me.

" ... I do remember shivering uncontrollably at the hospital, though. But they didn't take my temperature, so I don't know if I had a fever. I could hardly talk at the time. They kept covering me with blankets."

"Amazing."

His head swayed like a pendulum keeping time. His eyes widened in unabashed surprise.

"Well, thanks for coming back to tell me. I learned something new."

5:45 p.m.

"Happy anniversary, Wifette!" said Gary, greeting me with a surprise glass of champagne as I walked in the door.

"I heard it was your anniversary today, too, so cheers to you as well," I countered, rolling my eyes at my own lame joke.

He toasted our ninth wedding anniversary and led me to sit in our new screened-in porch. This haven served as a respite for me and the kitties to breathe fresh air while listening to the birds and rain. It created conflict for Gary and me, though. We sat side by side, often sharing more intimate thoughts. I loved that. Yet our eyes focused on our surroundings, and not each other. *It's like a phone date. I'm safe to say stuff without his looking me in the eye.*

"Wanna play golf this weekend?" Gary asked.

"I'd love to be outside."

"Come out to the practice greens and I'll help take a couple of strokes off your game."

Gary's patience, sense of humor and God-given talent for golf made him the perfect teaching pro. But the image of an afternoon on the links with him began to float away. I felt an anxiety attack and looked down to see my foot twitching. *Why am I nervous all of a sudden?*

Silence.

"What? What just happened?" Gary asked.

My mind scanned the previous moment, trying to grasp the details. *Don't drift away. Wait. I need those words.*

"Aha!"

"What?"

"Oh my gosh. I'm going to have to recondition myself."

"What do you mean?"

"You said something along the lines of 'take a stroke off your game,' right?"

"Yeah."

"The word 'stroke,' regardless of its context, has haunted me for the last two years. Every time I hear it, I freeze and a feeling of loss overwhelms me. I just realized I don't have to react to that word anymore."

Gary grabbed my hand and squeezed it. A few tears broke loose, escaping my emotional prison, dripping to my shirt.

"You all right? I'm sorry."

"No, no. These are tears of happiness. They don't last long, but I feel like the drought is over. I don't know how to cry, but it's happening with more frequency at the appropriate times now."

"The worst is over, Dollface."

He pulled my arm in the direction of the kitchen, smirking all the while.

"Now go fix me some dinner!" he barked, before breaking into laughter.

May 28, 2010 Journal Entry

Thank God, the worst is behind me. However, I feel like I've missed out on so much. Present, but vacant. Like someone forgot to put a quarter in me so I'd operate.

I miss the taste of a juicy steak. And the smell of garlic. I fix meals like I used to, but I don't know if they're truly any good.

Chapter 32: Flashes of Unintelligence

June 4, 2010

I beefed up my bucket list despite knowing that death no longer hid around the corner. Previous snorkeling trips had fascinated me. I wanted Gary and Cole to experience the underwater world with its amazing colors and unique fish. We planned a Caribbean cruise.

"Hey there. Me again," I greeted Dr. Welby on the phone.

"Oh no. I hope nothing's wrong."

"Nothing new here, I promise. Just a question."

He probably cringes when he sees me on the schedule or returns my calls.

"How can I help?"

"Gary, Cole and I are headed to Mexico soon and I just wanted to find out if there's some inoculation I should get before we leave."

He laughed. *At least I always make him laugh.*

"I'm scouring through your medical records and it appears you've had every vaccination known to man other than JE, and it's not a risk in Mexico. Becky ... regardless, please put the bubble on anyway before you leave. We don't want anything happening to you. Have a fun ... *safe* trip."

I grabbed a pen and started a list of things to pack. Prescription goggles. Sunscreen. Photo gear. Swimsuits.

"So what'd he say? Don't go to Mexico?" Gary asked, peering over the rims of his thumb print-stained reading glasses.

"No. He said not to leave the bubble."

"That's a given. What else?"

"For you to give me a back rub every night. Top priority."

"That's why you have a massage therapist."

"Hey. Know what I've been thinking?"

"That it's your turn on Words with Friends?"

"You know how we get all these graduation and baby announcements this time of year?"

"Yeah."

"We should send diagnosis announcements! Maybe people will send in gifts to go toward medical expenses."

June 30, 2010

A receptionist greeted me at the neuropsychologist's waiting room. She handed me a stack of paperwork that looked like I was buying a house.

A short, smiling Hispanic man approached me. His jovial expression made it easy to picture him as a four-year-old ripping the paper off a birthday gift. His chubby cheeks reminded me of Cole's marshmallow game, the chubby bunny contest. I wondered how many marshmallows this man could fit in his mouth.

"Becky?" the guy asked, revealing teeth. No marshmallows.

"Yes?"

"I'm the doctor," he said, extending his hand. I shook it. *Wow. He looks too young to be a doctor. A Doogie Howser neuropsychologist.* I followed him to a small conference room with bare walls, a table and six chairs.

"This is going to be a very long day. I hope you got some restful sleep," Dr. Howser said.

He studied me like high school girls check out each other's clothing, makeup and hair.

"I need you to try your hardest at everything today. Even if you think something is hard, just try and do the best you can."

The doctor straightened his jacket and leaned back. The chair dwarfed him, making him look like a little kid who got to eat at the adult table without a seat booster. He tapped his pen on the table, then began to pour a bucket of questions over me, drenching my brain before the tests even began.

"Have you had any major surgeries?"

"How much time do we have?"

"Why?"

"Eight so far."

"And you're 40?"

"Yes. Ridiculous, isn't it? My medical history looks like a professional criminal's rap sheet."

"What about grades in high school and college?"

"A's and B's. Graduated in the top 10 percent of my high school class and cum laude in college."

"And your current profession?"

"Bullshit artist."

His eyes widened, emphasizing his puffy cheeks. I remained deadpan.

"I'm sorry. Could you please elaborate?"

"Did [Dr. James] warn you about my humor?"

I snickered before covering my mouth. He looked nervous.

"No. But feel free to use your humor throughout the day if that helps you. Just remember to try your hardest."

Oh brother. I'm gonna need a better audience than this. How can he not be jovial with cheeks like that?

"Could you please go ahead and answer the question about your profession?"

I'd love to have fun with this guy. How about a circus stuntman? A professional bowler. A wedding singer.

"I'm the Senior VP of Influencer Relations for an outsourcing company."

"Could you please elaborate on what that means?"

"I have hundreds of relationships across the industry. My company uses my relationships to help position us for new business. I built and lead a program to influence my contacts, who serve as brokers between buyers and providers."

His pen raced across the page. *Can he really write that fast and read it?*

"Uh huh. OK. Got it."

Liar.

He studied me for another moment, tapping his pen again.

"Have you ever been diagnosed with a psychological disorder?"

"Yes."

His chair snapped forward as he leaned in.

"You have?"

"PTSD. Never quite got over a rape in college."

"Oh... Sorry."

His voice softened, though his brown eyes and smooth skin tensed up. He sucked in his cheeks. *This topic always makes men squirm.*

"I just needed to get some basic information. This helps serve as a baseline for the tests you'll be taking, along with the MRIs and other records you provided."

He checked his watch. The door opened, as if on cue. Two young women stepped in, circling to his side of the table.

"Laura and Stephanie will be administering the majority of the tests over the next 10 hours."

Did he say 10 hours?

"Remember ..."

"I know. Try hard."

He shot a fake smile back at me. His cheeks drooped.

For the next 10 hours, the clinical assistants administered test after test. Their second most important rule: no writing things down. *That's not fair. Don't they know how hard this is for me?*

First test: they rattled off 20 or so words, pausing a second between each. The words melted like snow as they landed in my ears. They asked me to list as many back to them as possible. I got two.

I leaned back, titling my head all the way, staring at the ceiling. My lungs filled from a deep inhale. I lounged while exhaling, my shoulders dropping like a tire losing air from a deep puncture.

They repeated the test five times. I got more each time. In total, I ended up with eight words on the list.

Test two: They told a short story. They instructed me to tell the story using their words and in the same order. I failed to organize the details properly. *The guy went to the store, right? Or was it to the post office? Crap. I don't know. And he came home and the dog needed out. Wait. Was there a dog in the story?*

Test three: An elaborate design looking like a geometry project gone bad.

"Study this for a minute, then we want you to draw it from memory."

Despite their pleasantry, their voices reminded me of an annoying little girl. As I drew, I imagined games of Pictionary with my mom. Her word might be "smile," yet she created a perfect image of a little girl. I would yell, "Girl! Child! Hair! Eyebrows! Eyelashes! Nose! Ears!" She proceeded drawing while my eyes bounced back and forth between the sand timer and her design. Just before the last bits of sand gushed through the tiny hole, she drew a smiling mouth with perfect lips. "Smile!!" I'd scream. She'd jump up smiling, "Yes! You got it! It was 'smile'!" As I fussed about just using a circle, two dots and a swish for a smile, she shrugged and stuck her tongue out.

I'd had my fill of long days throughout my career. This neuropsych test challenged even my most grueling, non-stop work period of nearly three days straight. I stood and stretched, then sank back down into the chair. *In a typical workday, colleagues take turns being in the hot seat. I'm the only one now. No deflecting. Just like therapy.*

Test four: They listed a string of numbers, then asked me to repeat them, starting in groupings of three, then four, then up to six or seven numbers at a time. The groups of three proved far less daunting than the long strings of numbers.

"Repeat these back to me, Becky."

"K."

"Seven. Four. Three. Six. Two. Seven."

Seven. Seven. Don't forget the seven. Wait. Slow down. What else did she say? Wait! Come back, numbers!

Her smile faded. I loathed someone feeling sorry for me.

"Can you repeat any back?"

"Seven. Six. And I'm pretty sure there was a nine in there."

"Any others?"

"I don't know."

Reverse order suffocated my memory. Sometimes I got none. The numbers floated away like a helium balloon on a windy day. *This feels like a cruel joke. I'm a lab rat.*

Flash cards with colored shapes tested my problem-solving skills the most. Each card featured varying numbers of colored shapes. The clinical assistant displayed four cards: one blue circle, two red squares, three yellow triangles, and four green stars. Then she drew one at a time out of a stack of 100 cards, asking me to determine where to place each card.

"Where does this one belong?"

I looked at the new card with two yellow triangles and pointed to the triangle card already displayed.

"Wrong."

"Huh?"

"Wrong."

"Why?"

"I can't tell you. I'm just supposed to give immediate feedback so you can change your strategy."

"Fine."

Her next card exhibited four blue circles. *Remember, it's not about matching the shape. Must be about the number of objects per flash card.*

I pointed to the card with the four green stars and looked to her for approval. She frowned.

"Wrong."

"What?"

"I'm sorry. It's wrong."

For the next 20 minutes, she repeated "wrong" about 85 out of 100 times. When my selection was correct, I didn't know why, so I never figured out the pattern. I felt defeated. Stupid. I felt more damaged in that moment than the whole previous two-and-a-half years. I regretted taking the test at all. *You couldn't just stop with finding out the diagnosis, Becky, could you? Had to go find out how dumb you are now.* The tests forced all the issues that plagued me to surface at once.

As the day concluded after another 10 or so tests, Dr. Howser revisited the words, short stories and pictures from the morning.

"Was 'apple' one of the words you heard?"

"I don't know."

"What about banana?"

"I'm pretty sure."

"What about this picture? Did you see this picture today?"

"Yes. I'm certain of it."

"Can you tell me about your strategy on the flash card test?"

My eyes welled up with tears. *I'm damaged. I used to love brain-teasers.*

"I don't know. I got frustrated hearing her say 'wrong' time after time."

"There's sufficient evidence that the encephalitis caused multiple areas of impairment. You're doing well, though, Ms. Dennis. You're gainfully employed and seem to have strong coping skills."

Don't mock me. I want outta here. You didn't know me at my best. You don't know what it's like to be firing on all cylinders and then have two little 20-somethings list a few numbers, only not to be able to recollect any of them. This isn't me! This is who I've become because of an injury ... maybe just a damn mosquito.

I stared ahead, blankly. There was no one to blame. No one to shake a finger at, to be mad at. Chalking my struggles and brain damage up to a mosquito bite seemed unfair. Just bad luck.

July 8, 2010

Dr. Howser called, confirming impairment in multiple areas, including auditory memory, concentration, verbally mediated tasks and problem solving.

"Becky, I think one key aspect to this is how much your problem-solving skills were negatively impacted."

I didn't comment. I just waited for him to continue, pissed off at the world. Although he stated his findings -- facts to him -- I hated everything I heard. Therefore, I hated him.

"Your deficits are consistent with individuals who have contracted Japanese Encephalitis ...," he said.

Goggles. I need to remember to pack goggles for our trip.

"They're also similar to victims of dominant hemisphere middle cerebral artery stroke ..."

Of course. Please elaborate with more technical terms.

"It makes a lot of sense that you weren't able to report symptoms like loss of taste, inability to emote or why it took so long to realize why you felt uncomfortable driving. We can attribute that to your challenged problem-solving abilities. You experienced difficulty learning about your own changes in faculties."

I didn't share his enthusiasm about my deficits.

"Another interesting discovery is that although your expressive vocabulary falls in the superior range, your confrontation naming is impaired."

"What does that mean?"

"It means you have a strong vocabulary and are able to articulate well. But do you recall when we held up pictures of common objects like a wheelbarrow, hammer and feather that you couldn't name them even though you knew what they were?"

"Yes." *Thanks for the reminder.*

"That's confrontation naming. Aphasia. Lacking the ability to call up a word on demand. You seemed to really struggle with that."

"I remember."

I paused, biting my lip, dreading the next question I wanted to ask. Deep breath.

"So ... "

Another pause.

"Is this as good as it gets? Will I ever get better?"

I regretted asking as soon as the words left my mouth. Like sending an email during an angry moment and then wanting to dive into the computer wires to grab it back.

"Encephalitis is a rare disease. Every case is so different. You seem to have developed good work-arounds to accommodate your impairments. I'm including some suggestions in my report."

For the love of God. Please choose another word when you're talking about my freakin' brain. And by the way, just tell me you don't know.

"Do you mind sending the report to [Dr. James]? I'd like him to have a copy."

I'd heard enough. I needed to hear this from someone who knew me. Well. Someone I trusted, someone who could soften the hard parts and explain the jargon. Someone who could read my emotions and know when I'd had enough.

July 9, 2010

"You're angry, aren't you?" Dr. James asked, watching my toe bounce up and down.

"Yep," I snapped. My anger level could drive a nail into a wall with just my fist.

Silence. He waited me out.

"It's just so damn unfair. Even though I've known there were deficits in my performance and I knew the difference between me before and after, it's different when you're told you're impaired. Hearing it out loud or seeing it on paper makes it too real. Now there's no denying it."

I fumed. And he waited. His eyes studied me, just like our friend James would have. Even though he didn't know me outside of his office, he knew me to the core. Probably better than anyone. I sensed that this was hard on him, too. My pulse slowed. I prepared myself to listen, knowing he'd choose words carefully.

"Can you help me understand the scores? What all of this means?" I finally asked.

"Sure, Becky. Let's take a look."

His deep and gentle voice punctured my rage, deflating it to a manageable size. He rolled his chair toward me, holding his marked-up copy of my test results. I felt touched that he'd already printed it and made his own notes.

We talked through the biggest deficits -- short-term memory, problem solving and absorbing information. I got caught up on IQ scores that graded my intellect.

"You're disappointed in the numbers, aren't you?" he asked.

"How could I not be?"

"Let me tell you that I don't judge you based on these scores. An IQ test is so limited in what it measures. They've only come up with 15 subscales of assessing performance. The test itself is limited because there are many other aspects of intelligence that they haven't yet developed testing for. So this is just a fraction of your potential."

He paused, a reverent check-in for the data I tried to consume. Especially now that he knew that auditory learning proved laborious to me.

"From what I see between the baseline you provided from 19 years ago and these results, your IQ was compromised about 20 points. I know that this probably sounds devastating to you, but you overcome it so well that most don't find it apparent ..."

I remained speechless. *A mosquito. Potentially one simple mosquito caused all of this.* I stared at the floor, then glanced his direction.

"... You know, you had a perfect score on speed of thought," he offered.

"Yeah? So what does that mean? How does that help?"

Dr. Bolte-Taylor, where are you? Make me find the adventure in all of this!

"It's what helps you compensate so well. It's what fools the rest of us into thinking that you're just as good as you always were."

"Or that I was good in the first place."

He laughed heartily, breaking my state of frustration.

"It's what enables you to pop off witty one-liners that interrupt our sessions with laughter. That's what it's good for."

Chapter 33: I Can See Clearly Now

July 2010 (Two and a half years after onset)

"We have to hurry," said Cole, running ahead of Gary and me on the Carnival cruise ship bound for Cozumel.

A photo scavenger hunt challenged our creativity between ports. Each competing group received a list of obscure items, such as a man dressed like a woman, an animal-shaped towel and a strawberry dressed in a tuxedo. We had 20 minutes to find the dozen items. The grand prize: a plastic replica of our cruise line. We just had to have it. I could picture it already, its golden steam pipes collecting dust on our mantle.

Cole clutched the list. His nails needed a trim. I didn't dare say so given his entry into teenage-hood.

"Hear no, see no, speak no evil! It's 10 points. One of the highest," Cole screamed.

"Let's just grab three random people to pose!" I yelled back, caught up in the excitement.

Gary rolled his eyes at me, yet plunged ahead, his competitive nature besting the silly nature of the hunt. And as much as Gary would like to deny it, Cole inherited his enthusiasm for competition. He expressed it in ways other than sports.

Several groups of people passed us in the wide corridors connecting art galleries, arcades, libraries and ice cream shops. Cole rushed to them, wanting to ask them to pose for the "no evil" shot. He took a deep breath and pointed his finger in an attempt to stop them. I could see the words forming in his mouth. Then he froze.

"Do you want me to ask them?" I asked. *I don't understand how he's so shy one-on-one when he's so animated and comfortable on stage.*

"Yes," he replied.

"Would y'all mind posing for us? We're in a photo scavenger hunt and we need a shot of 'see no, hear no, speak no evil,'" I asked the next group.

All four family members covered their mouths, as if rehearsed. They looked at each other, realizing their cloned reactions, and began to laugh. The lean dad adopted our sense of urgency and organized the family. Petite, busty mom kept her mouth covered. The teenage daughter in braces placed her hands over her ears. *This looks too natural. Must be a common gesture given her age.* And the son, who appeared as if he camped out at the ice cream shop for the trip's duration, squeezed his eyes shut and forced his fingers against his face. *Good grief. It's 'see no evil,' not 'poke your eyes out.'*

I imagined the dad as some type of instructor by profession. His direction was natural yet a bit stuffy. As the family finalized their poses, Cole grabbed the camera to snap the shot. I glanced back at the dad, who covered his crotch for 'do no evil.' *Now there's a surprise. Not so stuffy after all.*

We thanked the family, relieving them from their 'evil' duty. They lingered, as if now part of the game.

"Good day. At ease. Y'all are dismissed now," Gary said, tipping his hat.

My hubby. He can get away with saying anything. Kills me.

Cole and I darted ahead, embarrassed.

"What's next? What has the most points?" I asked Cole.

Gary shuffled along behind, pretending not to care.

"A poorly dressed person for a cruise," Cole slowly read, seeming to ponder the image while he read it aloud.

"Points?" I asked.

"Fifteen. The biggest."

"You looking?"

"Yep."

"That guy has so much hair he looks like a bear. He should have a shirt on," I said.

"That's disgusting, Becky. I'm not taking his picture."

"What about the lady over there in the pink swimsuit?"

Where does an adult find a Barbie bathing suit?

"You can stop looking. I'll find this one," Cole said, sounding like an annoyed teen.

We followed Cole along the upper deck past sunbathers, ping-pong players and putt-putt contestants. I felt a group tension creeping into our quest to win as our time limit slipped away.

"Dad, stop!" Cole yelled at Gary, holding his hand up like a traffic cop.

"What?" Gary asked.

As Gary scanned the scene to discover what caught Cole's attention, Cole snapped a photo of Gary's denim jeans that clung to him in the 90-degree heat.

"Did you just take a picture of my jeans, you little twerp?"

Cole's face lit up. *That kid of ours is hilarious. I love seeing his creative juices flow when he's so determined to win. Makes me wish I was a kid again. Makes me proud. I want those weekends back when I was too fatigued to be with him.*

We rushed to the deck below to check in. Other families matched our pace, as if trying to run for a train before the doors closed. *Isn't today Sunday?* A twinge of guilt tugged at me for missing church. *Wow. I'm back in the saddle.* Chills spiraled down my neck.

One by one, the contest judge reviewed each item from each group to determine if the photos met the criteria. When we reached the most poorly dressed person for a cruise, the judge studied each group's photos.

"Speedos really should be outlawed," the female judge commented. We all nodded in agreement, but she declined points. Too common a mistake among cruise goers, she explained.

She looked at the next photo entry.

"Oooh. Poor taste. Poor schmuck needs a shirt on."

Cole's head snapped my direction.

"Same guy," he mouthed. Yet, the photo of the hairy guy photo fell short of points as well.

I winked back at Cole.

"Dennis family. Let's see what you've got," the judge asked.

Cole shoved the camera at her as fast as a soldier might snap to attention.

"Oh goodness. I think we might have a winner," she said.

Everyone moved in closer to see what photo persuaded her to award points.

"Who in the world wears jeans on a cruise?" a kid remarked, scrunching up his face.

"Wow, that guy must be miserable. I can't imagine wearing jeans in this heat," said a large man.

"This definitely wins," declared the judge.

Her eyes stopped at Gary's denims, everyone following her sight path. Then the laughter exploded. Gary pulled his cap over his face, simulating shame.

Cole high-fived me, celebrating our victory, even at Gary's expense.

"Y'all suck," Gary said.

"Sorry, Dad."

"No you're not."

"You're right. I'm not."

"Shut up," Gary said to me after I failed to conceal my schoolgirl giggles. "I'm not the only person in jeans on this ship."

"Yeah, but you're the only one consistently wearing them, even during the hottest part of the day," I jabbed back.

"You don't see me making fun of your spray tan," Gary quipped.

"Hey. I see that as a service to everyone on this ship. If I didn't use tan-in-a-can, the sun might bounce off my white legs and blind everyone." I glanced over at Cole to see him grinning ear to ear.

We claimed our plastic trophy ship as the prize. I imagined the futile effort to get it home without snapping the lifeboats or lido deck. I vowed to put it in a prominent place to give us a daily reminder of Gary's fashion faux pas.

"Watch the sunset?" Gary asked.

His shift in demeanor amused me. *That's one of the things I admire about Gary. He might actually get his feelings hurt, but he seems to process it so differently than I do. He snaps out of it. He doesn't force me to adopt his mood. And even if he's annoyed with me, he wants me to be happy. He notices the little things.*

"Of course. Sunset has been mentioned," I said, copying one of Gary's common quips.

Cole's excitement level drained from his "chore" of having to carry the trophy.

At the top deck, a mom and young son snapped photos of themselves with their backs to the sunset. The mom's long dark hair shimmered in the falling sun. Hollywood lips outlined her smile. Her son, with curly blond hair and brown eyes, stood there with her, proud – not because of her beauty, but because she was his mom.

The extended-arm-with-the-camera-facing-yourself shot topped my pet peeve list of bad photos. *How do they not know the picture will result in big noses?* I couldn't bear to watch any more.

"Ma'am, I'm a photographer. Would you care for me to take a picture of you and your son?" I asked.

"Oh, I'd love that."

I glanced back at Gary and Cole, who assumed the "this will take a while" stance. She handed me her camera and backed up to the railing with her son. She appeared thankful.

I took the photo. *This would be so much better if they were facing the sun with their backs to me. What an awesome silhouette. They'll always treasure it.*

"Mind if I get you in a different pose?"

"Sure. I'd love it," the woman answered.

Gary and Cole sat down, careful not to sigh out loud.

With the mom's arm around her son and their heads leaned toward each other, I snapped away as if it was a paid photo shoot. *I love the implied intimacy.*

"Why don't I get one of you and Cole of that same pose?" Gary suggested.

I nearly stumbled.

"What?"

"You and Cole. Let me shoot that same pose of you and Cole that you just did of them."

"You like it?"

"It's brilliant, Wifette."

"I thought you were annoyed by my photography addiction."

"No. Just fascinated with the shots you see."

"Thanks, your dudeness."

Cole and I stepped up to the same spot against the railing. *He is such a good sport when it comes to all our photo taking. I'm certain I was not this good as a child. Cole is so patient. I remember praying for patience when I was a kid. And I'm just now getting some of it, but only because my life was in limbo.*

I put my arm around Cole and leaned my head in, just like the mom and son. I anticipated Gary telling us he was done. Instead, Cole piped up.

"Becky, you're looking the opposite direction of the camera."

"Right," I agreed.

Where is this going? The objective is a backside silhouette of us.

"Then why are you smiling so big?"

He cracked up. I stood there confused.

"Away from the camera?" he added after my silence.

I love my crazy family. How we can jab each other. How we can be real. How I can have "encephalitis moments" and not feel embarrassed. I might be looking away from the camera, but my smile reveals my heart. I can't be any happier knowing I'm here on a trip with my boys. The ones who have stuck by me and overlooked the fatigue, the confusion and the frustration I sensed for so long. I'm so thankful they love me back the same way I love them.

Johnny Nash's '70s hit played loudly in my head as I looked across at the sunset, Cole still at my side. *"I think I can make it now, the pain is gone. All of the bad feelings have disappeared. Here is the rainbow I've been praying for ..."*

"Snorkeling is the coolest thing ever," Cole remarked, his eyes as big as his smile. "Did you see the stingray and the huge school of fish?"

"I sure did. It's a whole other world underwater. Fascinating."

I felt proud. *Those burdensome business trips are paying off by giving us the opportunity to go on vacations like this. I never pictured myself as the business executive, but here I am. My career chose me. It just happened. I had things to prove, but didn't realize it. But this trip means more to me than anything I've accomplished. I'm so thankful to be with Gary and Cole to experience these amazing sights.*

The boat sauntered to another location, where, one by one, the snorkeling enthusiasts plopped into the ocean. We swam close to the instructor, who casually pointed out a barracuda.

I surfaced, pulling off my snorkel. Gary followed.

"Did he say barracuda?" I asked.

"Yes."

"Do you have Cole in your line of sight?"

"He's with the instructor. We're falling behind."

"Well, I don't want him too close to the barracuda."

"Then keep up."

Gary swam ahead, with me pedaling in my flippers to keep up.

My leg brushed across a jellyfish, almost invisible to the eye. I felt a surge of pain and cursed through my snorkel. I surfaced.

Though 15 feet ahead of me, Gary stopped in reaction to my outburst. He surfaced, pulling off his mask and snorkel.

"What's up? What happened?"

"Jellyfish sting! Ouch!" I said. I rubbed my leg, done with our underwater journey.

A school of fish wove their way through the snorkelers, creating a yellow cloud. Cole reached out, testing if they'd change course. *I just love the innocence of a child. They do whatever comes to mind, and without feeling self-conscious.*

The instructor guided us all back to the boat.

"How's the leg?" Gary asked.

I pointed to the wiggly red blemish.

"Still stings," I replied.

I grabbed my cell phone, giggling as I texted Dr. Welby.

"Becky here in Mexico. Stung by jellyfish. No worries. Crew thinks it's Tourette's syndrome. 8-)"

Dr. Welby's response popped up on my phone moments later.

"Becky, you should have stayed in the bubble."

Afterword: A Different Journey

My journey taught me far more than perseverance. After my diagnosis, I scoured the Web daily, trying to make sense of my supposed viral aftermath. These searches prompted three big epiphanies about encephalitis: 1) the lack of information available, 2) the frequency of misdiagnosis and 3) the comfort of being connected with other survivors of this cruel illness.

The U.S. sees 20,000 cases of all forms of encephalitis annually, 1,400 resulting in death. In contrast, in the U.S. each year roughly 6,000 babies are born with Down Syndrome[8] and only 1,000 people are diagnosed with cystic fibrosis[9]. "High fives" to the hard-working folks who made these rare illnesses more widely recognized. But why not encephalitis if it's more common?

Encephalitis causes brain injury that often means the patient is changed forever ... unable to work, unable to take care of themselves. Even though I struggle, I'm one of the lucky ones. I've seen firsthand the spouse grieve the "loss" of her husband, who can no longer be by himself for fear he'll catch the house on fire or walk into traffic. That doesn't even factor in the emotional impact of the love not being returned because essentially that person is gone. No longer the husband, dad or brother he used to be.

The Burden of Encephalitis

More than 50 percent of encephalitis survivors suffer from cognitive dysfunctions that prevent them from returning to work, according to a 2012 survey[10] of encephalitis survivors.

In 1997, the National Center for Infectious Diseases reported that the annual cost for encephalitis hospitalizations in the U.S. alone was

---

[8] CDC, *Facts About Down Syndrome*, http://www.cdc.gov/ncbddd/birthdefects/DownSyndrome.html (June 2011)

[9] Cystic Fibrosis Foundation, *About Cystic Fibrosis: What You Need to Know*, http://www.cff.org/AboutCF/ (Sept. 2012)

[10] Encephalitis Global and Inspire.com, "I'm Not the Me I Remember: Fighting Encephalitis" (February 2012): 15

$650 million[11]. This doesn't count the cost of endless trips to find medical professionals familiar enough with encephalitis to recommend treatments or therapies. Nor does it include the treatments, medications and therapies. Nor the lost wages of those who couldn't return to work. Nor the cost of care for those left unable to care for themselves.

In a French study of the long-term outcomes of encephalitis patients, the most frequent symptoms reported by the general practitioners of survivors were difficulty concentrating, behavioral disorders, speech disorders and memory impairment.[12] The authors underscore the need for long-term evaluation and neuropsychological rehabilitation, "even [in] those whose acute symptoms are apparently resolved at hospital discharge."

A Call to Action

Over a third of the causes for encephalitis are viral[13], most commonly from mosquitoes. In the U.S., that includes Eastern Equine Encephalitis Virus and West Nile Virus, among others. Yet there are no vaccines available for these viruses in the United States.

Unless you're a horse.

Our equestrian friends have been protected from the West Nile and Eastern Equine viruses by vaccine for several years. In Dallas this year, I'm sitting in the middle of a West Nile epidemic, feeling personally assaulted each time another death or neuro-invasive case is reported. Like Japanese Encephalitis, there is no treatment. Many of these innocent victims will undergo life-changing experiences, like I did.

---

[11] Nino Khetsuriani, Robert C. Holman, and Larry J. Anderson, National Center for Infectious Diseases, *Oxford Journals*, "Burden of Encephalitis-Associated Hospitalizations in the United States, 1988–1997" (July 1998): 175

[12] Alexandra Mailles, DVM, Institut de Veille Sanitaire, *Oxford University Press*, "Long-Term Outcome of Patients Presenting With Acute Infectious Encephalitis of Various Causes in France" (March 28, 2012)

[13] Nino Khetsuriani, Robert C. Holman, and Larry J. Anderson, National Center for Infectious Diseases, *Oxford Journals*, "Burden of Encephalitis-Associated Hospitalizations in the United States, 1988–1997" (July 1998): 175

Also, roughly a quarter of patients are misdiagnosed with flu, MS, complex migraine, psychological disorders and stroke. Sound familiar? After getting my diagnosis, I began sharing my story with a childhood friend, Dr. David Witt, now a general practitioner in our hometown. Excited about mentioning a rare illness he may not have seen, I started with the symptoms, about to build up to all the diagnoses I received. But half-way through my symptoms, he stopped me.

"Encephalitis. Yeah ... so what happened next?"

I sat there baffled.

"How in the world did you know? I was about to take you down a 27-month journey. I could have just used a life line and called you?!"

"I saw it at an ER in Houston. The parents were hysterical. Thought their daughter was on drugs," David told me. "I had to tell the parents their daughter was gravely ill."

So it almost seems to me that unless you've seen it in practice, the text book detailing encephalitis is long forgotten, too rare to be on physicians' radars.

Dr. Gordon Deen of the Mayo Clinic notes that many patients are often misdiagnosed since the symptoms "may be attributed to another diagnosis, such as the flu or even a psychiatric disorder."

For those who develop encephalitis from the herpes simplex virus (yes, the cold sore virus can cause encephalitis), treatment is available. Quick diagnosis is key. In untreated cases of herpes encephalitis, 50 percent to 75 percent of people die within 18 months. Treatment with acyclovir (Zovirax) can increase survival up to 90 percent[14].

Consider the stark differences in outcome in these two patients.

Patient A: The Rev. Bob Morris

Always in good health and full of energy, Bob Morris enjoyed putting others first. An Episcopal priest in his early 60s, he practiced

---

[14] Charles Patrick Davis, MD, PhD, Encephalitis, http://www.emedicinehealth.com/encephalitis_ (2012)

what he preached, looking for opportunities to serve others. His congregation enjoyed his leadership, charismatic persona and an unconventional sense of humor.

In April 2010, Bob and his wife, Cathleen, left their Florida home for South America and their first-ever sabbatical. During the trip, Bob suffered a sudden onset of severe diarrhea and vomiting. A headache nearly incapacitated him. Ailments seemed foreign to Bob, especially given his exercise regimen and resistance to getting sick.

For 24 hours Cathleen nursed his symptoms, assuming food poisoning. But when this accomplished clergyman began hallucinating as he chewed handfuls of antibiotics, claiming they were "his M&Ms and you can't have them," Cathleen sought medical help, fearful of something much more severe. Bob sank into a child-like state, trembling uncontrollably, with visions of flying fish in his hair and blood dripping from his limbs. He poured with sweat from a high fever.

Twelve hours later, in the hospital, Bob slipped into a coma. With scant resources on a holiday weekend, the available staff administered IV antibiotics and oxygen. Four days later, a neurologist discovered a shadow on Bob's CAT scan, indicative of head injury from a fall. A spinal tap and MRI revealed viral meningoencephalitis (meningitis and encephalitis), showing significant damage to the frontal and temporal lobes. The presumed cause was the herpes simplex virus. Doctors immediately put him on Acyclovir.

Bob regained consciousness six days later. Sensitivity to light forced him to wear sunglasses. Vertigo nauseated him with any slight movement. Food and water terrified him after such severe abdominal issues, accelerating a weight loss of 25 pounds in only 10 days.

Inflammation of his brain slowly dissipated. After two weeks of bed rest the hospital released him but didn't clear him for travel back to the U.S. His first journey out of bed was an assisted walk of just a few yards. He collapsed, completely drained from fatigue.

A full month later, Bob returned to his Florida home, where he underwent comprehensive rehabilitation including cognitive therapy, physical therapy, biofeedback and psychological counseling. Most encephalitis patients never have access to such optimal medical care or insurance coverage.

With a relatively quick diagnosis and extensive rehabilitation efforts, Bob returned to work part-time nearly five months later. After almost two years, Bob went back to work full-time, traveling again to see his daughters in Pittsburgh, PA, and Washington, D.C., and enjoying walks on the beach with Cathleen. Not even his lingering fatigue, short-term memory loss or aphasia can extinguish his passion for serving others. He is immensely grateful to Cathleen, his advocate throughout this ordeal. He knows she saved his life by getting swift medical attention for him.

Patient B: Jesseca Morey

While in her late teens, Jesseca Morey's life focused on collecting food for the homeless, earning 50-plus community service Girl Scout patches, and working at a nursing home to earn money to pay for her own car. Since she was 10, Jesseca dreamed of being in healthcare to help others, a desire that was amplified by her father losing a leg in a car accident six years earlier.

Within months after college graduation, Jesseca started her new career as an occupational therapy assistant at a rehabilitation center near her Tacoma, WA, home. At 21, she enjoyed a healthy life, dashing through the house with excitement each time snow blanketed her neighborhood.

Jesseca's first week on the job excited her. She was so happy about having her first patients, and providing them the skills they needed to return to a productive life.

But just days after starting her job, on Wednesday, Nov. 15, 2006, headaches and stomachaches riddled her body. She told her mother,

Cheri, "Must be related to pressures of being in a new job. If I'm not feeling better by the end of the week, I'll see a doctor."

Two days after talking to her mother, Jesseca came home from work and said she wanted to see a doctor. She lay down on the couch, comforted by her mom. A few hours later, Cheri awoke to the sounds of Jesseca having a seizure. Cheri called 911. An ambulance whisked Jesseca away, and she suffered another seizure en route to the hospital. Blurred vision, confusion, numbness, hallucinations, fever and vomiting ensued.

Doctors ran a CT scan, chest X-ray and blood work. They decided Jesseca suffered from a seizure disorder and the flu. They recommended she see a neurologist in two months. They sent her home, but her headaches intensified.

On Saturday, Nov. 18, Jesseca's family drove her to a clinic, which retrieved her records from the hospital. They ran blood work, reinforcing a flu diagnosis. The clinic administered a shot for her headache, then released her.

That evening, Jesseca's fever increased. Her headaches became unbearable. An ambulance rushed her to a different ER where they performed a lumbar puncture. The results confirmed that she had contracted herpes simplex encephalitis and meningitis. An infectious disease doctor and neurologist were assigned, and they administered Acyclovir to treat her herpes-induced symptoms.

On Nov. 22, however, a week after her first headache, doctors put Jesseca on life support. The next day Jesseca lost her battle. Snow sprinkled her grave. Her first paycheck arrived two days later.

The Psychological Impact

A great book for any patient or doctor is "How Doctors Think" by Jerome Groopman, M.D. He discusses a cognitive error called the "satisfaction of search[15]" or "search satisficing," which is the tendency to

---

[15] Jerome Groopman, M.D., *How Doctors Think* (First Mariner Books, 2007), 169

stop searching for a diagnosis when the doctor finds something that seemingly fits. Looking back at my experience, I believe Dr. Complacent immediately threw me into the bucket of "stress" when he hit a diagnosis brick wall, and that his dismissal of my neurological reality damaged my own "self think."

Dr. Groopman's book also addresses how he's learned to replace the phrase, "Nothing is wrong with you[16]," with "I believe [you] when you say something is wrong, but I haven't figured it out." I can't imagine how those words would have helped me during my course of searching for a diagnosis.

"Dealing with this sudden and dramatically life-altering illness is overwhelming enough, but when a healthcare provider or family member dismisses the patient's experience, it can be traumatic and lead to painfully isolating and shaming conclusions for the patient," said psychologist Steven W. Sliwinski, Ph.D.

No one should have to suffer in silence. I found that journaling significantly helped my outlook when no one else understood what I was going through. I could at least write to acknowledge my own struggles, which helped me understand myself better so I could confide in those closer to me after I had adjusted to my "new identity."

Surround Yourself with Support

Until I met other survivors, I felt isolated in my experience. Dismissed unknowingly by loved ones. With my hidden struggles, I felt trapped in my condition. No longer "me." I spent many days mad at the world, grieving that I lost the ability to do what used to be easy for me. Phrases like: "You seem fine to me." or "I forget all the time, too." are two of the most dismissive phrases that people unintentionally use. The patient, in almost every case, suffered these changes overnight, not gradually as in the normal course of aging. Some patients grow tired of

---

[16] Jerome Groopman, M.D., *How Doctors Think* (First Mariner Books, 2007), 264

explaining the difference between "me before" and "me after," so they choose to suffer in silence.

This frustration silenced me until I found Encephalitis Global (E Global), an organization formed to help connect encephalitis survivors and caregivers. Many survivors get a huge dose of validation in interacting with others who have similar issues.

Initially, I spent mornings and evenings reviewing all the posts on E Global's discussion forum. Some posts offered suggestions for coping mechanisms. Some mourned loved ones. Others wanted to vent - to just be heard. And some were recently diagnosed, desperately looking for answers. The postings amazed me in the striking similarities to the answers we all sought and the expressions of helplessness we felt by not receiving sufficient information.

E Global hosted a conference that featured experts on encephalitis from The Mayo Clinic and Brooks Rehabilitation. I jumped at the opportunity to attend.

Within 30 minutes at the conference, I compared notes with another survivor. I found that she too suffered a host of issues, including two fingers that clung together. *Oh my gosh. I've met my new family. These people totally get me.* The experience of meeting other survivors is healing. Motivating. Less isolating. This connection created a healthy new extension of my weekly therapy sessions with Dr. James.

One month later, I joined the board of E Global, fortunate to be in a position to help others deal with their encephalitis aftermath issues.

20 Lessons I Learned the Hard Way

1. *Trust your gut*: You're the only one who knows how you really feel. Even if you can't put a finger on it. Honor yourself by listening to what your body tells you.

2. *Be your own advocate*: You are the only one managing your healthcare. Even when you run across the medical professionals who have a strong interest in helping you find answers, it's still up to you

to take the next steps or to seek additional answers until one fits. You are not their responsibility. You are *your* responsibility. Never stop pursuing options toward better health.

3. *Find your higher power*: If my faith hadn't been broken from the pains of my past, I often wonder whether my coping mechanisms might have been stronger. Since piecing it all back together, I gaze at the moon longer. I marvel at vivid colors of blossoms and sea life. And I've quit asking, "Why me?" My church is a life line and God is my ally.

4. *No one knows everything - not even doctors*: Consider your own job. Do you know everything there is to know about finance, law, marketing, or whatever it is you do? No. You continue learning as your career expands. Doctors are the same. They are people first. Doctors second. The good ones are the ones who shepherd you through the process, like some of them I am grateful for today. They listen. Are willing to learn. They took an oath to uphold ethical standards, not to know every illness imaginable.

5. *Get psychotherapy*: This isn't the '70s or '80s where psychotherapy means you're crazy. If you don't have a therapist, you're in denial. Find a good therapist in whom you can confide. Be willing to listen. And be willing to be honest with yourself. The results will work wonders. Did I sound irritable at the beginning of my journey? Yes. But could I recognize it on my own? No. Get a therapist.

6. *Join an online support group*: I can't emphasize enough the healing aspect of interacting with others with similar health issues as you. Check out Inspire.com. It has a support group for illnesses I've never even heard of.

7. *Create memory strategies:* Instead of standing in a room across the house with no idea why I was there, I began singing the reason for

urgently needing to leave my office to go to the garage ... or kitchen ... or bedroom while I was en route. Sticky notes litter our house and cars. Resting or taking breaks help restore memory. I record important calls and carry notebooks in my purse. Go down the alphabet as a means of triggering thoughts.

8. *Establish rituals to relax:* Let's face it. Health issues cause an abundance of stress. Find the rituals that work for you to comfort yourself. For me, it's a variety of activities, including exercise, hot baths, prayer, massages, journaling and photography. Find yours.

9. *Track symptoms*: The list I created of onset symptoms versus those that lingered for various durations proved very helpful for the doctors. The lists helped them determine what symptoms resolved over time and where we needed to get to work.

10. *Send info in advance*: In multiple situations, I've sent a cover letter before my appointment so the doctor is expecting me. This helps the doctor understand my expectations for the visit and gives them relevant information that might get them thinking before I arrive. It shows that I "mean business" and am ready to get answers.

11. *Prepare questions in advance*: Organize questions in order of importance. Tick them off the list as you and your doctor talk through your condition. Don't be afraid to speak up if they aren't all answered.

12. *Learn about neuropsychological options for treatment*: It's true that some forms of encephalitis, such as West Nile and Japanese Encephalitis, are not "treatable." That mostly means drugs aren't available to stop the swelling or damage in the acute phase. Yet any form of brain injury has some level of responsiveness to occupational, speech, physical, psychological and cognitive

therapies. A neuropsychologist can assess the damage to determine what types of therapies are most effective.

13. *Keep a sense of humor*: I frequently get a dose of humility when I have an "E" moment. But I've learned to enjoy sharing them. Just two weeks ago, I pulled the door handle to enter a restaurant, but the door didn't open. I peered through the window, looking at the diners. I decided the door was perhaps locked because there was a private event. It never dawned on me to *push* the door handle until a group of men approached, easily going inside. Laugh. And laugh hard.

14. *Learn to say "no"*: The fatigue after encephalitis can be crippling. Odds are you won't be able to do everything you used to do. Listen to your body and say "no" to prevent further compromising your health.

15. *Take notes*: It's your medical appointment. You are paying for it. And you deserve the benefit of having notes to refer to later to better absorb the information once your emotional distress has declined. If you can't listen and write, take someone with you to help with the note taking.

16. *Four ears are better than two:* Take someone with you if you don't think you can comprehend all the data. Also, a family member or friend may think of questions that don't occur to you. They aren't as close to the issues and often can be more objective. And for most suffering from encephalitis, their short-term memory is compromised, so extra ears are a necessity. Draw boundaries for those who accompany you, distinguishing your expectations of taking notes versus speaking on your behalf.

17. *Dress for success*: I found that if I dressed professionally for a doctor's appointment, especially a first-time visit, I was treated

better. Dress nicely and drop the jeans and T-shirt. I find that the practitioner tends to take me more seriously.

18. *Make lemonade out of your lemon*: I had several options in my situation. My creativity blossomed while my analytical thinking tanked. Writing and photography are lemonade for my soul. But even more important, there are options to help others who are recovering and to raise awareness for an overlooked illness. Life isn't over after a brain injury. You're just on a different journey.

19. *Travelers: subscribe to a medical travel assistance program:* I joined one of these programs that accommodates you in any part of the world should you become ill. With an annual subscription, I am entitled to free medical care from anywhere in the world--from a hospital visit to a private jet with medical staff on board. Worth it if I ever need it again. Hopefully not.

20. I'm certain there was one more, but I forgot it. Happens.

Acknowledgements

My family, most notably my husband Gary and son Cole, cheered me on during every aspect of this journey. They patiently waited throughout my necessary napping as my brain recovered. And once I decided to document this chase for diagnosis, they patiently waited again while I wrote ... and wrote some more ... until I finally closed the top of my Mac each night. Their love and support motivated me to finish.

My sister Angela's compassionate ear has been the most reliable source of encouragement, regardless of life's challenges. Her support fueled me when I felt like giving in to the "crazy talk." I thank her for pushing me when I didn't think I had anything left in me. She's been my most consistent source of positive energy; and I thank God she's always been my best friend, and most recently, my "check it off the bucket list" companion.

My parents, the ultimate optimists and yet the biggest of worriers, praised me for seeking answers, rooting me on until solving the medical mystery. They encouraged rest, offered support, shuddered after more bad news, but always kept the faith. Their love was evident in each question they had for the next doctor, each extra-firm embrace, and each near-concealed tear in their eyes.

I'm so thankful for my India-based colleagues and Deborah Kops for helping me during my scariest moment of life. For being so accommodating and supportive. And for allowing me to recover at my own pace despite our demanding industry.

I've been so blessed to have found such great doctors before and during my journey. Dr. Doug Stafford, D.O., my trusted medical advisor and friend, treated my bizarre medical needs regardless of where I was on the globe or how far-fetched the symptoms. I appreciate his guiding me to answers and his regarding me as a person first, and as a patient second.

Dr. Steve Sliwinski, Ph.D., gave me the courage to find God again and conquer my life's biggest struggles. His non-judgmental life coaching inspired me to be a better person, and to believe in myself enough to put my story into writing. I'm grateful for his believing in me ... and laughing with me when humor was my only defense against the chaos in my life.

When explanations were scarce, Dr. Danny Malone, O.D., pulled out medical textbooks to help me understand the brain's inner-workings. His gentle approach comforted me, making me feel less "crazy." Dr. Jill Bolte-Taylor, Ph.D., despite a hectic global travel schedule for her lecture series, took the time to correspond with me on many occasions. I'm appreciative of her encouragement to fight my fear and to press for answers. With her guidance, I found Dr. Guy Rordorf, M.D., who ultimately ended my chase for answers by recognizing my illness and providing a firm diagnosis, relieving me finally from the dreadful time-bomb feeling that had interfered with my enjoyment of life.

When I wrapped up my writing journey, I sent my manuscript to Franz Wisner, best-selling author of *Honeymoon with My Brother* and *How the World Makes Love*. His coaching and discerning insight helped me transform a historically accurate documentation of my career and medical issues into a story. One with characters and emotion. One that made me appreciate what matters most. Cheers to Franz for challenging me in my writing to recognize and express my perspective of the events that make life worth living and the nuances that make life fun.

Several loved ones and friends contributed to finalizing this manuscript into a word-filled newborn: Tony Martin, Albert Rodriguez (author of *White Bread and Coconuts*), the Rev. Bob Morris, Cathleen Morris, Carolyn Moore, Kym Webster, Polly Dunlap, Rosemary Snider, Dawn Hoverson, Cheri Morey and Les Roka, Ph.D.

And lastly, there are countless friends and colleagues who helped me, supported me, covered for me and laughed at my stupid jokes at the peak of the encephalitis and my recovery. You are not nameless and faceless. There are simply too many of you to mention, but your contribution to my survival from the toughest trial of my life is well noted. You know who you are.